THE

ILLUSION

OF PRESIDENTIAL

POWER

How America's Focus on Leadership is
Undermining its Empire

A.J. Kennedy

DEDICATION

Raise a glass to the lads and lasses at the local who, after a couple of rounds, have more coherent foreign policy strategies than any current world leader with a press briefing that I can think of.

DISCLAIMER

This book is a work of commentary and analysis based on publicly available information and my own interpretations. It represents my personal views and opinions on the political system of the United States, particularly the evolving role of presidential power. It is not intended as an attack on any individual politician, past or present, but rather as a critique of the broader structures and dynamics at play.

The content in this book should not be interpreted as having any political motive or agenda beyond examining the impact of leadership styles and governance approaches on the American political landscape. Any references to specific politicians or administrations are made solely to illustrate systemic patterns, not to target individuals.

While every effort has been made to ensure the accuracy of information presented, this book is not a definitive or exhaustive account of the subjects discussed. Readers are encouraged to engage critically with the material and recognize that the views expressed are meant to provoke thought and dialogue rather than assert absolute truths.

The purpose of this book is to foster a greater understanding of political systems and encourage informed, constructive conversations about the complexities of governance.

ACKNOWLEDGMENTS

Thank you to my friends and colleagues for the lively debates and endless inspiration, my family for their unwavering support, my dog for listening intently without criticism, my editor for not losing their sanity (yet), and to the presidents: past, present, and future, who have inspired this book.

CONTENTS

CHAPTER 1

INTRODUCTION TO POLITICAL THEATRE

What began as a republic built on the balance of powers has morphed into a stage for spectacle, where policy substance is sidelined in favor of personality, and long-term vision is sacrificed for short-term applause. Presidential tweets replace diplomacy, charisma overshadows competence, and celebrity status trumps statesmanship. This shift, from leadership to showmanship, has not just reshaped American politics; it's weakening the very foundations of America's global influence, turning a once steady empire into a series of fleeting performances.

This transformation didn't happen overnight. It is the product of decades of increasingly media-driven politics, where each administration builds upon the theatrics of the last. Presidents have become more than mere officeholders; they are the protagonists in a 24-hour news cycle, their every move, speech, and misstep dissected and amplified.

The American people are no longer just citizens, they are an audience, and the world watches on as this spectacle unfolds. The emphasis on personality and performance has led to a system where image takes precedence over impact, and where policy decisions are made not for their strategic value, but for their optics. As allies struggle to predict America's next move and adversaries exploit the chaos, the nation's ability to project a stable and coherent global presence wanes, undermining the empire from within.

In 1787, when the delegates of the Constitutional Convention convened in Philadelphia, they embarked on a task both monumental and delicate: creating a system of government that would stand in stark contrast to the monarchies of Europe. They sought to establish a republic, a state where power would not be vested in the hands of a king or emperor but distributed among branches of government and ultimately, in the hands of the people. The presidency, as it was conceived, was meant to be, can you believe, a ***modest office***, one of balance, not of dominance. It would be a position of responsibility, not a pedestal of unchecked power.

Today, more than two centuries later, the vision of the Founders seems both prophetic and distant. The United States, once a symbol of democratic restraint and balance, finds itself gripped by a paradox: its identity and global power have become increasingly tethered to the office of the president, an office that now resembles the very kind of centralized authority its creators feared.

The Presidential Performance

The world watches every move made by the American president. In an age of instantaneous information and digital connectivity, the spectacle of the presidency has become a central feature of the global stage. Presidents don't just govern; they perform. They tweet. They appear on television, not only to make policy announcements but to craft narratives, to tell stories that reach millions. The American president is not just a leader; he (or she) is a character, a persona with followers, fans, groupies, disciples and critics all over the globe. In the words of political scientist Richard Neustadt, "Presidential power is the power to persuade," yet I argue it has increasingly become the power to entertain, to incite, and to polarize.

This phenomenon is not entirely new. One could argue that it began with Franklin Delano Roosevelt, who mastered the art of radio communication through his "fireside chats" and used them to present himself as a comforting, paternal figure during the Great Depression. John F. Kennedy, with his sharp wit and Hollywood-esque charisma, transformed the presidency into a media event. Ronald Reagan, once a film star, perfected the act, turning the White House into a stage. Barack Obama used social media to engage with younger audiences and fostered a global image of cool-headed intelligence. Then came Donald Trump, who took the performance to its extreme, tweeting policies and insults in real-time, turning the Oval Office into the epicenter of a global spectacle.

But it's not just about who occupies the office; it's about how the office is perceived, used, and misused. The American public, and indeed the world, has been drawn into this performance, so much so that the image of the president has overshadowed the office's original intent. We have moved from the symbolic power of Roosevelt's fireside reassurance to the volatile tweets of modern leaders. The focus has shifted from the structure of governance to the personality of the one governing. **Herein lies the illusion of power.**

The Illusion of Control

On the surface, the American president appears to wield immense power. This is the figure who speaks for the nation, who represents its military might, who signs laws into action with the stroke of a pen. But this perception is deceptive. Beneath the grandeur of the office lies a tangled web of limitations, constraints, and dependencies. The president may set the agenda, but Congress, the courts, and various federal agencies hold the reins of actual implementation. Executive orders, for instance, may seem like declarations of power, but they are often tied up in judicial challenges or blocked by legislative gridlock.

Moreover, the global economy, once firmly under American influence, has become a realm where even the most ambitious presidential policies can falter. Take, for instance, the U.S.-China trade war under the Trump administration. While tariffs were levied with the intent to bring manufacturing back to American shores, the complexities of global supply chains and the influence of multinational corporations meant that these policies often had unintended and diluted effects. Despite the rhetoric of a strong, assertive leadership, the real power to control economic forces often eludes the grasp of the president.

The illusion of control is particularly evident in the military realm. While the president of the United States holds the title of Commander-in-Chief, the reality of military engagement is far more complicated. Decisions regarding military actions are influenced by a host of factors, including intelligence assessments, advice from military leaders, international alliances, and congressional approval. The fiasco in Afghanistan, culminating in a chaotic withdrawal in 2021, is a stark example of how presidential decisions, even those rooted in years of policy-making, are subject to forces beyond a single leader's command. It revealed the gaps between the image of a powerful commander and the reality of geopolitical complexities and logistical challenges that can derail even the most carefully laid plans.

The Global Perception

From an external vantage point, the fixation on presidential power in America is both captivating and concerning. The world looks to the United States as a bellwether of democracy, an empire built not on colonies but on ideals. Yet, this fixation on the American president, viewing him as the primary driver of policy, obscures the deeper, structural issues that threaten the country's stability and global influence. When every issue, whether domestic or international, is framed as the responsibility or fault of the sitting president, the narrative simplifies complex realities and distorts the perceptions of American governance.

Internationally, this focus on the persona of the president rather than the system of governance has shifted alliances and altered perceptions. European leaders, once confident in the stability of American foreign policy, found themselves unsettled during Trump's presidency, with its erratic statements and sudden policy reversals. The trust in American leadership, a trust built over decades of consistent, if sometimes controversial, international engagement, began to waver. The Paris Climate Agreement, the Iran Nuclear Deal, NATO contributions, each became battlegrounds for a presidency more concerned with projecting strength and winning points at home than with maintaining consistent diplomatic ties.

It is not just allies who are watching; rivals and adversaries are, too. Countries like China and Russia have long understood that American politics is as much about spectacle as it is about substance. They have taken advantage of the focus on the presidency, investing in disinformation campaigns designed to exploit the divisions heightened by American political theatre. The more polarized and personality-driven American politics becomes, the more vulnerable it is to external manipulation.

Have we learnt anything from history?

History tells us that empires often collapse under the weight of their own contradictions. The British Empire, at its zenith, spanned over a quarter of the globe, ruling territories on every continent and controlling vast oceans, making it the largest empire in world history and the most influential global power of its time. When you're in the middle of it the mere thought of an empire crumbling seems ludicrous, but fall they always do. For the British Empire its downfall was hastened by overreach and the refusal to adapt to changing global realities. The Roman Empire, whose leaders were often seen as god-like figures, succumbed to internal corruption, economic decay, and military overstretch. America, it seems, is not immune to these historical patterns. The illusion of presidential power, where every president is expected to be a saviour, a unifier, or a conqueror, distracts from the deeper, systemic challenges that no single leader, however charismatic or competent, can resolve alone.

The British Empire, thrived during the 19th century, when its prime ministers operated behind the scenes while parliament and other institutions managed the complexities of imperial governance. It was only in the twilight of the empire that figures like Winston Churchill emerged, embodying the "great man" model of leadership. Even then, it was clear that Churchill's success was not due to individual brilliance alone but was supported by an intricate network of institutions, policies, and international alliances. America's current emphasis on the president risks repeating the mistake of equating empire with individual leadership rather than the strength of institutions.

The illusion is not just an internal affair; it influences how America is perceived abroad. While the United States once presented itself as a beacon of democracy, today's fixation on presidential identity politics, where each leader's personality and actions are seen as defining the nation, has led to global scepticism. Foreign leaders now view the U.S. as unpredictable, and allies seriously question whether American commitments will last beyond a single administration.

The Impact on Domestic Policy

Internally, the illusion of presidential power also creates its own set of problems. When a single office is seen as the focal point for all policy and national direction, it places an impossible burden on the individual who occupies it. The recent trend of executive overreach is not merely a grab for power; it is a desperate attempt to fill the void left by a paralyzed Congress and a fragmented political system. Executive orders become the tools of governance when legislative consensus is unattainable, but they are temporary solutions at best, often challenged in courts or reversed by subsequent administrations.

This cycle creates instability. One administration signs executive orders promoting climate action, the next dismantles them. One president signs healthcare reform, another undercuts it. The image of power persists, but the substance is fleeting, dependent on electoral cycles and the whims of political actors rather than a sustainable, systemic approach to governance.

A Way Forward?

As an external observer, the United States' future as a global power seems contingent on its ability to move beyond this illusion. The presidency, while powerful, should not be the focal point of an empire as vast, complex and beautiful as America's. For the U.S. to navigate its decline or sustain its influence, it must return to the fundamentals laid out by its founders; balance, restraint, and an emphasis on institutions over individuals. The true power of the United States has always been in its people and its system, its capacity for self-correction, and its ability to adapt. But to do so, it must shift focus away from the spectacle of the presidency and back toward the shared responsibility of governance.

The illusion of presidential power is not just a political problem; it is a cultural one. It is tied to the narratives Americans tell themselves about who they are and what their country represents. Reclaiming the vision of shared leadership, robust institutions and an engaged citizenry, is the challenge ahead. This book, *The Illusion of Power: How America's Focus on Leadership is Undermining Its Empire*, is an exploration of that very challenge. It seeks to unravel the reasons behind the concentration of power and focus on the presidency, to understand how this phenomenon emerged, and to examine the consequences, both domestically and globally.

Each chapter will take you through different dimensions of this illusion, from the media's role in shaping narratives to the economic constraints that limit presidential influence.

We will also explore the historical parallels, the echoes of past empires that also believed in their own invincibility, only to crumble under the weight of their contradictions. The illusion of power is truly seductive, and America's fixation on its leaders is part of a much larger story about the challenges of maintaining influence in a rapidly changing world. In understanding this dynamic, perhaps the United States can find a way to reclaim not just its power but its purpose, one that goes beyond the spectacle of the moment and towards a future built on lasting foundations. Let's hope so.

This isn't a criticism, it is a challenge.

The Illusion of Presidential Power

CHAPTER 2

THE CULT OF PRESIDENCY

Origins and Evolution
The presidency of the United States was never meant to be a throne. When the Founding Fathers gathered in Philadelphia in 1787, they were haunted by the spectre of monarchy, a memory still fresh in the minds of the new republic. George Washington, the war hero and unifier, stood as the obvious choice for the first president, but even his ascension was shadowed by the cautionary tales of unchecked power. The Constitution was crafted with an eye toward balance, ensuring the executive branch would not dominate. The role of the president, as conceived by the founders, was that of an impartial executor, a figurehead who acted within the constraints set by Congress and the courts. The American president was to be a servant of the people, not their ruler.

But the story of the American presidency didn't unfold exactly as the framers of the Constitution envisioned. The evolution from a modest, limited role to a global powerhouse was not instantaneous. It happened in stages, each marked by a shift in the country's needs, the pressures of historical crises, and, increasingly, the personalities of the men who held the office. Over time, the presidency transformed into something far beyond the modest office intended, into a near-mythical institution, the central figure in the American imagination. Today, we live in a world where the president is expected to embody the nation's aspirations, defend its moral compass, and steer its economy, all while commanding the world's most formidable military force. The reality of this shift is both fascinating and troubling, and it brings us to the question: how did we get here?

The Founders' Intentions: A Limited Role

The American Revolution was a revolt against tyranny, and the architects of the American government were determined not to replace one form of autocracy with another. The debates at the Constitutional Convention revealed a fierce commitment to preventing any single branch of government from becoming too powerful. The presidency, they decided, would have enough authority to enforce laws but would be balanced by the powers of Congress and the judiciary. The Electoral College, a system designed to prevent the direct election of presidents, was a reflection of this desire for moderation, an attempt to shield the office from the passions of the mob.

George Washington himself, the nation's first president, embodied this vision of restraint. Refusing to be called "Your Excellency" or any other regal title, he insisted on being addressed simply as "Mr. President." Washington was acutely aware of the fragile balance the new nation needed to maintain. His decision to step down after two terms set a precedent for peaceful transitions of power and reinforced the idea that the presidency was a duty, not a reign.

But even from the start, the seeds of expansion were there. The flexibility of the Constitution, while designed to adapt to changing circumstances, also allowed for the gradual expansion of executive power. The question of what the president could do, especially in times of crisis, would continue to test the boundaries of this role.

Expansion Over Time: Crisis and the Growth of Power

The Civil War marked a pivotal moment in the evolution of the presidency. Abraham Lincoln, faced with the greatest existential threat the nation had ever known, assumed powers that would have been unthinkable in peacetime. He suspended habeas corpus, expanded the military without congressional approval, and issued the Emancipation Proclamation, an act that, while morally revolutionary, was legally ambiguous. Lincoln's presidency demonstrated that in times of national emergency, the office could stretch its constitutional limits. His actions set a precedent that future presidents would invoke, often with far less justification.

Fast forward to the 20th century, and the presidency continued to expand, particularly under Franklin Delano Roosevelt (FDR). The Great Depression and World War II demanded decisive action, and FDR's New Deal programs fundamentally reshaped the role of government in American life. To many, FDR became the saviour of the nation, wielding executive power to alleviate economic hardship and mobilize the country for war. His unprecedented four terms in office further solidified the idea that the president was not just a leader but a guardian of the nation's welfare.

Similarly, Lyndon B. Johnson (LBJ), during the tumultuous 1960s, pushed the boundaries of presidential authority with his Great Society programs and the escalation of the Vietnam War. Like Lincoln and FDR, LBJ faced crises that, in his view, justified an expansion of presidential power. The rationale was simple: when the nation was under threat, be it economic, military, or social, the president needed the flexibility to act swiftly and decisively. But each instance of executive overreach, whether for noble or questionable purposes, paved the way for an office that increasingly viewed itself as the answer to the nation's problems.

The Modern Presidency: From Policy to Performance

Today, the American presidency bears little resemblance to the modest office envisioned by the Founders. It has evolved into a complex amalgam of leadership, spectacle, and performance. Modern presidents are not just policymakers; they are public figures whose personas often eclipse their policies. This transition began in earnest with the advent of radio and television. As technology advanced, so did the platform from which presidents could project themselves directly into American homes. FDR's fireside chats, designed to comfort a nation in distress, were among the first steps in this transformation. But it was John F. Kennedy who truly mastered the visual medium. With his charisma and telegenic appeal, he demonstrated how presidents could captivate the public, creating an image that could transcend politics.

From that point on, presidents increasingly relied on their image as much as their policies. Ronald Reagan, dubbed "The Great Communicator," used his background as an actor to present a carefully crafted narrative of American optimism and strength. Bill Clinton, with his charm and empathy, connected with voters on an emotional level. Barack Obama leveraged social media to create a sense of direct, personal engagement with millions of Americans. And then, there was Donald Trump, whose presidency was a masterclass in using social media and spectacle to maintain attention, creating an illusion of action and power even as the complexities of governance went unaddressed.

The Role of Media: Amplifying the Presidency

Media has always played a role in the evolution of the presidency, but its influence has grown exponentially. In the 19th century, newspapers often aligned themselves with political parties, shaping public opinion in favour of or against a particular administration. By the time radio and television arrived, presidents had the power to bypass traditional media gatekeepers and speak directly to the public. Today, with the advent of social media and the 24-hour news cycle, the president's visibility is greater than ever before.

This constant exposure creates a double-edged sword. On one hand, it allows presidents to rally support and communicate policies with unprecedented immediacy. On the other, it transforms the office into a source of continuous entertainment. Every tweet, every appearance, every word spoken becomes a headline, and the lines between governing and performing blur. The result is an office that is both omnipresent and paradoxically distant from the realities of governance. The media's focus on the president as a singular figure distracts from the broader system of government and its many players, creating the illusion that all power and responsibility lie with the president alone.

Expectations vs. Reality: The Burden of Perception

The American public's perception of the presidency has also evolved. The expectation that the president can solve every problem, from economic downturns to international crises, has become a deeply ingrained part of American culture. When things go wrong, the president is blamed; when things go right, he is praised, often regardless of his actual influence on the outcome. This focus on the presidency as a one-stop solution for the nation's challenges is not only unrealistic; it is detrimental.

The truth is, no president, no matter how skilled or charismatic, can singlehandedly navigate the complexities of American governance. The framers of the Constitution knew this, which is why they designed a system of checks and balances. But as the public increasingly expects more from the presidency, the office is forced to project an image of power it cannot always deliver. This expectation feeds the cycle of illusion: the more the public demands, the more the office strains under the weight of those demands, and the further it diverges from its intended purpose.

The Illusion of Power: A Distraction from Systemic Issues

The cult of the presidency is, in many ways, a distraction. By focusing so intensely on the individual in the Oval Office, the nation overlooks the deeper, systemic issues that lie at the heart of American governance. Legislative gridlock, the influence of lobbying, economic inequality, these are challenges that no single president can solve. Yet, by placing so much emphasis on the individual, the public and media create an illusion of power that obscures the need for broader systemic reform.

The evolution of the presidency into a larger-than-life institution is a story of both expansion and illusion. As the chapters ahead will explore, the consequences of this transformation are far-reaching, affecting everything from domestic policy to America's standing on the global stage. The cult of the presidency is a powerful force, but it is also a fragile one, built on the perception of power rather than its reality. To understand America's current political landscape, we must first understand how the presidency became what it is today, a role that, despite its grandeur, may be as much a burden as it is a symbol of authority.

The Founders Intentions

When the Constitutional Convention convened in Philadelphia in the summer of 1787, the air was heavy with the sense of purpose and ambition. The American Revolution had been won, and the task now was to create a nation, an entirely new experiment in governance, free from the tyranny of monarchy that had plagued Europe for centuries. The men who gathered, figures like James Madison, Alexander Hamilton, and George Washington, were acutely aware of the weight of history and the gravity of their mission. For them, designing a republic meant avoiding the pitfalls of both tyranny and anarchy, and the presidency was the linchpin in this delicate balance.

The Fear of Tyranny

The American Revolution had been, above all, a rebellion against centralized and unchecked power. King George III and the British Parliament had ruled the colonies from afar, imposing taxes and laws without representation, and this was the spark that ignited the call for independence. The bitterness towards a distant, overbearing ruler ran deep, and as the Founding Fathers set about creating a new government, they were determined not to repeat the mistakes of the Old World.

The Articles of Confederation, the country's first attempt at governance after independence, had granted the states substantial autonomy, but it quickly became clear that this decentralized approach led to chaos. States quarrelled over boundaries, trade policies clashed, and the fledgling nation's economy floundered. There was no single leader to unify the country, no figure with the authority to enforce laws or provide stability in times of crisis. This realization, that anarchy was as much a threat as tyranny, set the stage for the Constitutional Convention.

James Madison, often called the "Father of the Constitution," was instrumental in shaping the debate. A small, slight man with a keen intellect, Madison was deeply influenced by his studies of ancient republics and confederations. He understood the need for a stronger central government but was also wary of concentrating too much power in any one place. His Virginia Plan proposed a framework where the federal government would have significant authority, but with checks and balances to prevent any one branch from dominating.

Madison's vision for the presidency was cautious. The executive should be powerful enough to enforce the laws and respond to emergencies but not so powerful that it could become a threat to liberty. He had seen what happened when unchecked power was granted to a single individual, the abuses and overreach that characterized monarchies, and he was determined that America would be different.

14

Washington: The Reluctant Leader

As the delegates debated the structure of the new government, one figure loomed large in their minds: George Washington. Though not an outspoken participant in the debates, Washington's presence alone lent gravity to the proceedings. His reputation as the hero of the Revolution and a man of unimpeachable character made him the obvious choice for the nation's first leader. But Washington's virtues were also a bittersweet dilema. His integrity made the idea of a strong executive palatable, yet there was also the fear that not every president would be a Washington.

Washington's reluctance to seek power was crucial in shaping the office. He had retired from public life after the war, returning to his estate at Mount Vernon, and he only agreed to preside over the Convention out of a sense of duty. His humility reassured the delegates that a strong presidency did not necessarily mean a descent into tyranny. Washington's example showed that power could be wielded responsibly, but the challenge was to design an office that would not depend solely on the character of the person occupying it.

John Adams, who would later become the second president, was another voice advocating for a balanced executive. Adams, an intellectual and diplomat, had seen the tumultuous politics of Europe up close. He believed that the presidency should be strong enough to provide stability but limited enough to prevent autocracy. Adams feared the rise of demagogues and populists who could manipulate public sentiment to seize control, an apprehension that continues to resonate in American politics today. I wonder what Adams would make of the presidential election in modern times.

The Balance of Power: Crafting the Constitution

The central challenge for the framers was finding the right balance. They wanted a government strong enough to maintain order and enforce laws, but they feared giving any one branch, especially the executive, too much authority. The separation of powers became the cornerstone of the Constitution, with the presidency as a crucial but constrained role within this framework.

Alexander Hamilton, perhaps the most vocal advocate for a strong executive, argued that the presidency needed sufficient power to act decisively, especially in times of national emergency. Hamilton's vision was shaped by his own experiences during the Revolutionary War, where he had served as Washington's aide-de-camp. He saw firsthand the limitations of a weak executive and believed that, for the republic to survive, the president must have the authority to protect and govern effectively.

Hamilton's influence can be seen in the Constitution's provisions for the presidency. The president was granted the power to enforce laws, command the military, and conduct foreign policy. However, the framers also built in significant checks to ensure that this power could not become absolute. The requirement that the Senate approve treaties and presidential appointments was one such measure. Similarly, the power to declare war was reserved for Congress, ensuring that the president could not unilaterally lead the nation into conflict.

Madison and others argued for term limits and regular elections to prevent the emergence of a permanent ruling class. The president would serve a four-year term, with the possibility of re-election, but the framers stopped short of imposing a term limit in the Constitution itself, a decision that would later lead to Franklin D. Roosevelt's four terms and eventually, the 22nd Amendment.

The Electoral College was another attempt to strike a balance. The framers were wary of direct democracy, fearing that a populist leader could exploit the passions of the people. Instead, they created a system where electors, individuals presumed to have the nation's best interests at heart, would choose the president. While this system was meant to insulate the presidency from direct manipulation, it also revealed the framers' scepticism about the masses and their desire to place a buffer between popular sentiment and executive power.

The Federalist Papers: Justifying the Balance

In the months leading up to the ratification of the Constitution, a series of essays known as *The Federalist Papers* were published to argue in favour of the new government structure. Among the most influential of these were written by Alexander Hamilton and James Madison, who defended the proposed presidency against accusations that it would be too powerful.

Hamilton's essays, particularly *Federalist No. 70*, articulated the need for "energy in the executive" while also reassuring sceptics that the

Constitution contained enough safeguards to prevent tyranny. Hamilton argued that a single executive would provide clarity and decisiveness, qualities necessary for effective leadership, especially in emergencies. He believed that a council or group of leaders, as some delegates had suggested, would lead to indecision and conflict, weakening the executive branch.

Madison, writing in *Federalist No. 51*, emphasized the importance of checks and balances to prevent any one branch of government from becoming too dominant. He famously wrote, "Ambition must be made to counteract ambition." For Madison, the very structure of the government, its division into three branches, was a way to control the natural human tendency to seek power. The system was designed so that the executive, legislative, and judicial branches would compete with and limit one another, ensuring that no single individual or group could gain unchecked control.

Early Tests: Washington and Adams in Practice
When the Constitution was ratified, and George Washington was elected as the first president, the nation had its first chance to see the new system in action. Washington's presidency became the template for all others, and his choices in office set critical precedents that would shape the nature of the executive branch.

Washington was deeply conscious of the need to embody the spirit of the new republic. He understood that every decision he made would set an example for future presidents. When faced with domestic challenges like the Whiskey Rebellion, Washington exercised his authority to call up the militia, demonstrating that the federal government had the power to maintain order. But he did so with restraint, ensuring that the action was seen as a defence of constitutional law rather than a show of force.

Washington also established the precedent of consulting his cabinet, a group of advisors that included figures like Hamilton and Jefferson, before making major decisions. This practice was not mandated by the Constitution but reflected Washington's belief in collaborative governance. It was an early attempt to balance the power of the presidency with input from other leading figures in the government.

John Adams, Washington's successor, faced his own set of challenges as the second president. Adams was a man of principle and intellect but also one who struggled with the realities of politics. His presidency was marked by the passage of the Alien and Sedition Acts, laws that allowed the government to prosecute those who criticized it. These acts were widely viewed as an overreach of executive power, highlighting the tension between maintaining authority and protecting liberty.

Adams' actions revealed the fragility of the balance the founders had tried to create. While he justified the laws as necessary for national security, they were seen by many as a betrayal of the revolutionary ideals. This episode demonstrated that even within the framework designed to limit power, the presidency could still overstep its bounds. It underscored the ongoing challenge of maintaining the equilibrium the framers had envisioned.

The Founders' Legacy: A System of Trust and Caution

The Founders left behind a blueprint for a balanced presidency, but they also left behind a warning: the strength of American democracy would depend on the character of those who occupied its highest office. They knew that no system was foolproof and that the Constitution, as Madison put it, was designed for a virtuous people. Without citizens and leaders committed to its principles, even the most carefully crafted government could falter.

As the presidency evolved over the centuries, the tension between power and restraint has remained a central theme. From the expansionist impulses of Andrew Jackson to the unprecedented scope of executive action under Franklin D. Roosevelt, every generation has tested the limits of what the founders intended. The framers' caution against tyranny has, at times, clashed with the demands of a growing nation, and the role of the president has often shifted to meet those needs.

But the initial intentions of the founders, those men who sat in the heat of Philadelphia, debating the future of their new republic, still resonate. The fear of unchecked power, the emphasis on balance, and the desire for a government that serves rather than rules are principles that continue to guide American governance. The presidency, in its ideal form, remains a reflection of those values, a role that, while powerful, is always checked by the people, the Constitution, and the system of government designed to prevent tyranny.

Expansion Over Time: How Presidents Expanded Executive Power During Crises

When the Founding Fathers set forth the blueprint for the American presidency, they envisioned an office of measured power, a check against tyranny. But they also understood that in moments of great peril, extraordinary measures might be necessary. The Constitution, with its vague language regarding executive power, was designed to be flexible, and it is precisely this flexibility that later presidents would exploit and expand upon. Over time, the evolution of the American presidency has often been shaped by crises, periods when the nation's survival seemed to hang in the balance, and bold action was required. The stories of Abraham Lincoln, Franklin Delano Roosevelt (FDR), and Lyndon B. Johnson (LBJ) illustrate how the American presidency, once modest in scope, became an office of expansive, sometimes unchecked, authority.

Abraham Lincoln: The Weight of the Union

Abraham Lincoln entered the White House in 1861 at a moment when the nation seemed irreparably fractured. The Southern states, having seceded from the Union over the issue of slavery, formed the Confederate States of America. With civil war imminent, Lincoln faced a crisis of unprecedented scale, one that demanded swift and decisive action. The Constitution, however, did not offer a clear roadmap for how to handle such a crisis. It left the question of secession, rebellion, and executive authority deliberately vague.

Lincoln, a deeply introspective yet resolute man, understood that the survival of the Union depended on his ability to act decisively, even if that meant stretching, or outright breaking, the boundaries of his constitutional power. He famously suspended the writ of habeas corpus, allowing the military to detain suspected Confederate sympathizers and saboteurs without trial. Critics argued that this violated the Constitution, but Lincoln justified his actions by citing the necessity of preserving the Union. "Are all the laws but one to go unexecuted, and the government itself go to pieces, lest that one be violated?" he asked.

In addition to suspending habeas corpus, Lincoln authorized the expansion of the military and the blockade of Southern ports, both actions that, according to the Constitution, required congressional approval. Yet, Congress was not in session when the Civil War erupted, and Lincoln acted unilaterally. When Congress finally reconvened, it retroactively approved Lincoln's measures, setting a precedent that executive power could expand dramatically during emergencies, even without initial legislative consent.

One of Lincoln's most controversial acts was the Emancipation Proclamation. By framing it as a military measure to weaken the Confederacy's war effort, Lincoln bypassed Congress entirely. The Proclamation, which freed slaves in the rebelling states, was not just a moral decree; it was an assertion of executive authority on a scale previously unimaginable. Lincoln's justification was that in times of rebellion, extraordinary measures were needed to preserve the nation. His decisions shaped the trajectory of the war and fundamentally redefined the power of the presidency, but they also raised profound questions about the limits of executive authority.

Lincoln's legacy, therefore, is a paradox. While he is celebrated as the saviour of the Union and the Great Emancipator, his use of power foreshadowed the expansion of the presidency into an office that could act with near-autonomy in times of crisis. His actions set the stage for future leaders to claim similar powers when facing their own national emergencies, marking a departure from the presidency's original, limited intent.

Franklin Delano Roosevelt: The New Deal and Wartime Leadership

Fast forward to the 1930s, and the United States was again on the brink of collapse, this time due to economic, rather than military, crisis. When Franklin Delano Roosevelt took office in 1933, the Great Depression had already ravaged the country for several years. Unemployment was soaring, banks were failing, and millions of Americans faced poverty and despair. Roosevelt, an ambitious and charismatic leader, saw an opportunity not only to address the immediate crisis but to transform the American economy and society through sweeping reforms.

Roosevelt's New Deal, a series of government programs designed to provide relief, recovery, and reform, required an unprecedented expansion of executive power. He declared a "bank holiday" just days after his inauguration, closing all banks to prevent further runs and restore confidence. Using the authority granted by the Emergency Banking Act, Roosevelt acted swiftly, exerting control over the financial system in a way no president had before. His fireside chats, radio addresses that bypassed traditional media and spoke directly to the

American people, helped solidify his image as a man of action, someone who could steer the country through its darkest hours.

The New Deal programs that followed, including the Works Progress Administration (WPA) and the Civilian Conservation Corps (CCC), fundamentally changed the role of the federal government in American life. These programs were massive in scope, employing millions of Americans and providing direct government intervention in the economy. They were also controversial. Opponents accused Roosevelt of overstepping his authority and likened his programs to socialism. The Supreme Court, in several cases, ruled against key New Deal measures, asserting that they exceeded the powers granted to the federal government.

But Roosevelt, undeterred, took on the judiciary itself. Frustrated by the Court's decisions, he proposed the Judicial Procedures Reform Bill of 1937, often called the "court-packing plan", which aimed to add more justices to the Supreme Court, effectively allowing him to appoint judges who would support his policies. Though the plan ultimately failed, it showcased the lengths Roosevelt was willing to go to consolidate executive power. He framed his push for judicial reform as necessary to protect the country's future, demonstrating how crises could be used as justifications for expanding the reach of the presidency.

World War II provided another opportunity for Roosevelt to exert and expand his authority. As the global conflict loomed, he initiated the Lend-Lease program, providing military aid to allies without direct involvement in the war, despite significant isolationist sentiment in Congress and the public. Roosevelt argued that aiding allies was necessary for national security and positioned himself as the ultimate arbiter of America's foreign policy. Once the United States entered the war, he assumed even greater powers, overseeing the wartime economy, commanding the armed forces, and shaping global strategy.

Roosevelt's legacy is twofold. On the one hand, he is celebrated as the leader who guided the country through the Depression and World War II, using his powers to protect and rebuild the nation. On the other hand, his presidency expanded the office's scope so dramatically that it permanently shifted the expectations of what a president could and should do. Future leaders would look to Roosevelt's example as a justification for using executive power to enact broad, sweeping change.

Lyndon B. Johnson: The Great Society and Vietnam

Lyndon B. Johnson's presidency offers yet another example of how crises, both domestic and foreign, can lead to an expansion of executive power. Johnson inherited the presidency under tragic circumstances, following the assassination of John F. Kennedy in 1963. His early days in office were marked by a determination to honour Kennedy's legacy and push through an ambitious legislative agenda. However, Johnson's vision went far beyond what Kennedy had proposed. Driven by a personal commitment to eradicate poverty and racial injustice, Johnson launched the Great Society, a set of programs aimed at transforming American society.

The Great Society initiatives, which included Medicare, Medicaid, and the Civil Rights Act, required extensive use of federal power. Johnson's "War on Poverty" involved large-scale government intervention in healthcare, education, and social services, areas traditionally managed by states or private entities. Like Roosevelt before him, Johnson justified this expansion as necessary to combat a national crisis. The poverty and inequality that plagued the country, he argued, were as significant a threat as any foreign adversary. But while the domestic reforms of the Great Society were groundbreaking, they also stretched the limits of executive authority and raised questions about federal overreach.

Internationally, Johnson's presidency was defined by the Vietnam War, a conflict that, much like Lincoln's Civil War, tested the boundaries of presidential power. Determined to prevent the spread of communism in Southeast Asia, Johnson dramatically escalated U.S. involvement in Vietnam. The Gulf of Tonkin Resolution, passed by Congress in 1964 after reports (later disputed) that North Vietnamese forces had attacked American ships, gave Johnson broad powers to conduct military operations without a formal declaration of war. This resolution effectively handed Johnson a blank check, allowing him to deploy hundreds of thousands of troops and oversee a full-scale war effort.

Johnson's handling of Vietnam illustrates the dangers of unchecked executive power. While he used the conflict to justify an expansion of presidential authority, his decisions ultimately led to a quagmire that cost tens of thousands of American lives and divided the nation. As public opinion turned against the war, the limitations of executive power became painfully clear. Despite his extensive use of authority, Johnson was unable to control the course of the war or the backlash it provoked. His presidency, once ambitious and hopeful, ended in disillusionment and withdrawal.

The Legacy of Expansion
The stories of Lincoln, FDR, and LBJ show that crises have consistently been catalysts for the expansion of presidential power. In moments of great urgency, these leaders believed that extraordinary times called for extraordinary measures. They acted in ways that were often controversial, sometimes bending or outright breaking the boundaries set by the Constitution. Their motivations, however, were complex and varied.

For Lincoln, it was the preservation of the Union that drove him to assert his authority. For Roosevelt, it was the twin crises of economic collapse and global war that justified his use of power. For Johnson, it was a vision of a transformed American society and the fear of communism's spread. In each case, these presidents framed their actions as necessary for the greater good, and in many ways, they succeeded. Lincoln preserved the Union and ended slavery; Roosevelt led the country through depression and war; Johnson passed landmark civil rights legislation. But their legacies are also marked by the precedents they set, precedents that allowed for the expansion of executive power beyond the limits the Founders had imagined.

Crisis ~ Catch 22
The expansion of executive power during crises reveals a fundamental paradox in American governance. The presidency is often at its most powerful during times of upheaval, when decisive action is needed to address existential threats. Yet, this concentration of power can be both a necessity and a danger. While Lincoln's suspension of habeas corpus or FDR's wartime measures may seem justified in hindsight, they opened the door for future presidents to claim similar authority, sometimes without the same level of justification.

The stories of Lincoln, FDR, and LBJ illustrate that the power of the presidency is not static but fluid, expanding and contracting based on the needs of the moment. As each of these leaders showed, crisis provides an opportunity for bold action. But with each expansion of power comes the risk that future presidents will push the boundaries even further, relying on the precedents set by their predecessors. The evolution of the presidency is thus a story of necessity and ambition, of crisis and consequence. It is a reminder that the power of the office, once expanded, is rarely constrained again, and that every crisis leaves a lasting imprint on the American political landscape.

The Modern Presidency: Transition from policy-oriented leadership to image-based public figures.

The modern American presidency is a far cry from the office envisioned by the framers of the Constitution. In its earliest form, the presidency was meant to be a dignified, if somewhat subdued, position, anchored in policy and focused on governance rather than spectacle. Over time, however, the role has evolved, indeed, one might say it has mutated, into something quite different: a platform for image-making, performance, and media manipulation. This transformation did not happen overnight, nor was it the product of a single administration. Instead, it is the result of a century-long evolution that saw the American president shift from being primarily a policy-oriented leader to an image-based figure, a shift that has profound implications for American democracy.

The Early Seeds of Image-Making: Theodore Roosevelt

The shift towards an image-based presidency can be traced back to Theodore Roosevelt, the first president who understood and harnessed the power of media and public perception. Often referred to as a "man of action," Roosevelt was a larger-than-life figure who relished the spotlight. His energetic, cowboy persona was no accident; it was carefully crafted to present an image of strength, masculinity, and decisiveness. Roosevelt was acutely aware of the power of photographs and press coverage, and he used both to his advantage. Whether he was leading a cavalry charge up San Juan Hill or inviting photographers to capture him chopping wood, every image was designed to project an ideal of rugged individualism that resonated with the American public.

Roosevelt's "bully pulpit" approach, as he called it, was groundbreaking. For the first time, a president actively engaged the press and used the power of his personality to rally public support for his policies. Roosevelt's style was policy-oriented, but it was also deeply performative. He understood that by creating a powerful image of himself, he could sell his ideas more effectively. He was not just leading; he was embodying leadership. This was a subtle but important shift: policy was still at the core, but the way it was communicated became just as important.

Franklin D. Roosevelt: Master of the Media

If Theodore Roosevelt planted the seeds of an image-driven presidency, it was Franklin Delano Roosevelt (FDR) who cultivated and grew it into an essential tool of modern governance. FDR, faced with the dual crises of the Great Depression and World War II, recognized that in order to maintain public trust and push through sweeping policy changes, he needed to communicate directly with the American people. His fireside chats were revolutionary, not just in their content but in their format. Sitting by the radio, millions of Americans heard the soothing, confident voice of their president, who made them feel as if he was speaking to them personally. FDR's brilliance was not only in the policies he enacted but in how he presented those policies. He knew that his image, as a calm, paternal figure guiding the nation through turbulent times, was as crucial as the content of his New Deal programs.

FDR's presidency marked a turning point. It was no longer enough for presidents to develop and implement policies; they had to become the face of those policies. The image of the president became inseparable from the message itself. While FDR's fireside chats were an authentic attempt to reassure a desperate nation, they also set a precedent. Future presidents would increasingly rely on their personal appeal and media presence to sell their policies.

John F. Kennedy: The Telegenic Leader

If Roosevelt's fireside chats marked the beginning of the modern presidency's marriage to media, John F. Kennedy's (JFK) presidency was its consummation. Kennedy was the first president to fully embrace television as a tool for shaping public perception. His telegenic looks, sharp wit, and ease in front of the camera made him a natural star in an era when television was becoming the primary source of information for millions of Americans.

Kennedy's understanding of the medium was not incidental; it was integral to his success. The 1960 presidential debate between Kennedy and Richard Nixon was a pivotal moment in American political history. Those who listened to the debate on the radio believed Nixon had won; he was experienced, knowledgeable, and articulate. But those who watched on television saw a different story. Kennedy appeared poised, youthful, and confident, while Nixon, pale and sweating under the studio lights, seemed uneasy.

The power of television transformed the debate into a victory for Kennedy, underscoring the importance of image in the modern presidency. It was no longer just about what was said, but how it was presented.

Once in office, Kennedy continued to cultivate his image. His press conferences were not just opportunities to disseminate information but to showcase his charm and wit. He used these moments to reinforce his brand as a young, dynamic leader, capable of navigating the complexities of the Cold War with grace and intelligence. His image of "Camelot," filled with glamorous parties, artistic performances, and moments of family togetherness, was meticulously crafted. But behind the scenes, Kennedy's administration struggled with serious challenges, from the Bay of Pigs fiasco to the Cuban Missile Crisis. Yet, because of his image management, he maintained public approval. The focus was on the man and the myth he represented, not always the policies he enacted.

Ronald Reagan: The Great Communicator

While Kennedy was the first television president, it was Ronald Reagan who mastered the art. A former actor, Reagan had a natural advantage in front of the camera, and he used it to great effect. Dubbed "The Great Communicator," Reagan's ability to connect with the American people was central to his presidency. Whether delivering a rousing speech at the Brandenburg Gate in Berlin or addressing the nation from the Oval Office, Reagan's charm and calm, reassuring presence allowed him to project an image of strength and optimism.

Reagan's presidency was a carefully managed production. His team understood that every image, every word, every scene had to reinforce the narrative of America as a "shining city on a hill." During his presidency, the White House communications team perfected the art of media management, ensuring that Reagan was always presented in the most favourable light. This wasn't just about appearances; it was a strategic effort to align Reagan's image with his policies. Tax cuts, the Strategic Defence Initiative (popularly known as "Star Wars"), and his approach to the Cold War were all underscored by the image of a strong, capable leader who embodied American values.

But the focus on image sometimes obscured the complexities of governance. Reagan's genial demeanour masked serious issues, including a growing national debt and the Iran-Contra scandal. Yet, his image as a friendly, avuncular leader remained intact. Reagan's presidency was a triumph of media management, a demonstration of how the modern presidency had become as much about performance as policy.

Barack Obama: The Social Media President

The 21st century brought new challenges and opportunities for the presidency, particularly with the rise of social media. Barack Obama's campaign in 2008 was the first to fully harness the power of platforms like Facebook and Twitter, transforming the way political messages were disseminated and creating a sense of direct engagement with voters. Obama's team understood that the modern electorate was not only consuming information through traditional media but was increasingly turning to social networks for news and connection.

Obama's image as a cool, collected intellectual was central to his brand. His speeches, often eloquent and filled with references to American history and ideals, were designed to appeal to a broad audience. But his mastery went beyond the podium; it extended into the digital realm. His campaign's use of data analytics to target voters, his presence on social media, and his engagement with younger demographics all reinforced the image of a modern, tech-savvy leader.

Once in office, Obama continued to use these tools. His administration frequently released videos and statements directly through social media, bypassing traditional news outlets and creating a sense of accessibility. Whether it was a humorous interview on *Between Two Ferns* or his annual "dad jokes" at the White House Correspondents' Dinner, Obama knew how to use new media to maintain his image as a relatable, down-to-earth leader. However, this focus on image and digital engagement sometimes overshadowed policy complexities. For instance, the rollout of the Affordable Care Act (ACA), or "Obamacare," was plagued with issues that exposed the limits of the image-oriented presidency. Despite his charismatic digital presence, Obama faced significant challenges translating his message into legislative success.

Donald Trump: The Presidency as Spectacle

If Obama's presidency demonstrated the power of social media, Donald Trump's took it to its extreme. Trump's use of Twitter was not a supplement to traditional communication; it was his primary mode of engagement. His tweets, often impulsive and provocative, dominated news cycles and created a constant state of media frenzy. Trump's presidency was a spectacle, and he was its star. Unlike his predecessors, who sought to create an image of unity or strength, Trump's brand was chaos and conflict. He positioned himself as a disruptor, a leader who would "drain the swamp" and shake up the establishment.

Trump's presidency was built on image and narrative rather than policy. His rallies, filled with chants, slogans, and fiery rhetoric, were less about policy proposals and more about maintaining the loyalty of his base. Trump's approach was to present himself as a champion of the "forgotten" Americans, using his unfiltered style to connect with voters who felt alienated by the traditional political system. This was not a presidency defined by a coherent policy platform but by the spectacle of Trump's persona.

His use of media was unparalleled. Traditional media outlets found themselves caught in a dilemma; they could not ignore his often-outrageous statements, but by covering them, they became complicit in amplifying his image. Trump's presidency showed how the modern media landscape, particularly cable news and social media, could be manipulated to create an unending stream of controversy and attention.

The Consequences of the Image-Based Presidency

The shift from policy-oriented leadership to an image-based presidency has had profound implications for American democracy. On the one hand, the ability of presidents to engage directly with the public has democratized access to information and allowed for more personal connections between leaders and citizens. On the other hand, it has created a superficial understanding of governance, where image often outweighs substance.

The focus on the president's persona, rather than the complexities of their policies, has led to a public discourse that is increasingly polarized and simplified. Presidents are judged not just by the success of their legislative agendas but by how effectively they project themselves on television or social media.

This emphasis on personality over policy has consequences; it creates unrealistic expectations that presidents can solve complex problems with the wave of a hand or a powerful speech. It also distracts from the realities of governance, which often involve compromise, nuance, and gradual change, elements that are far less glamorous than the spectacle of a charismatic leader.

This image-based presidency has allowed for the rise of populist figures who prioritize personal brand over coherent policy. When voters are more drawn to the charisma of a candidate than their experience or platform, the result is a political landscape where spectacle and controversy become more valuable than competence and consistency.

The modern presidency, as a media-driven institution, reflects both the strengths and vulnerabilities of American democracy. It has given presidents the tools to engage with the public in ways unimaginable to the framers of the Constitution. Yet, as the line between governance and performance blurs, it raises questions about the true nature of leadership. Are modern presidents leaders, or are they performers in a political theatre that prioritizes spectacle over substance?

As the digital age continues to evolve, so too will the nature of the presidency. Future presidents will undoubtedly find new ways to adapt and engage with the public. But as they do, they must grapple with the fundamental challenge of the modern era: balancing the demands of image-making with the realities of governance. The story of the American presidency is far from over, but its current chapter is one defined by a transformation that has both captivated and complicated the nation's democracy.

The Role of Media: How 24-Hour News Cycles and Social Media Have Amplified Presidential Visibility

Imagine it's the early 1930s, and the United States is struggling under the weight of the Great Depression. Breadlines stretch for blocks, banks are failing, and people's faith in the government is crumbling. It is in this context that Franklin D. Roosevelt, with his patrician accent and reassuring tone, speaks directly to the American people over the radio in a groundbreaking use of media, bridging the gap between the government and the public. For the first time, a president was not just a distant figure, he was a voice in people's living rooms, one they could connect with personally.

FDR understood the power of radio and how it could be harnessed to shape public perception, build trust, and amplify his presence. In doing so, he laid the foundation for a new kind of presidency, one that relied heavily on the media to maintain its power and influence.

Fast forward to today, and that same evolution has taken a path no one in FDR's time could have predicted. Presidents are not only voices in living rooms; they are omnipresent figures appearing on television, smartphones, and social media feeds 24 hours a day. The media landscape has shifted from the deliberate, scheduled programming of radio and television to a constantly flowing, instantaneously updated stream of information. In this new reality, the American president has become not just a leader but a permanent fixture in the daily lives of citizens and a focal point for global audiences. The consequences of this transformation are far-reaching and complex, reshaping not only how presidents are perceived but also how they govern.

The Birth of the 24-Hour News Cycle

The 24-hour news cycle as we know it today began in 1980 with the launch of CNN, founded by Ted Turner. Before this, television news was limited to scheduled programming, usually morning, evening, and nightly news segments. It was curated and edited for accuracy and relevance, and viewers had time between broadcasts to process the information presented. The introduction of CNN changed all that; it created a world where news was available at any moment, and coverage could adapt and evolve as stories unfolded. It meant that events like the Gulf War in 1991 were no longer just updates delivered at fixed times but became live, real-time spectacles.

The impact on the presidency was immediate and significant. The president's every action was now not only visible but also subject to continuous scrutiny and commentary. Bill Clinton's administration, for instance, was a turning point in the relationship between the presidency and the 24-hour news cycle. Clinton, with his charisma and telegenic appeal, understood that this new media environment could be both a powerful tool and a potential trap. He famously navigated the media during the 1992 election campaign by appearing on programs like *The Arsenio Hall Show*, where he played the saxophone. This appearance humanized him, making him seem relatable and down-to-earth, a stark contrast to the traditional, buttoned-up image of past presidents.

But Clinton also learned the hard way how relentless the 24-hour news cycle could be. During the Monica Lewinsky scandal, the constant media coverage turned his personal life into a public spectacle, and every detail was scrutinized, replayed, and analysed. The scandal dominated the news cycle for months, showing that while the media could elevate a president, it could also drag them down. The 24-hour news cycle turned the presidency into a reality show, where personal character and entertainment value became as significant as policy and governance.

The Rise of Social Media: Direct Access, Unfiltered Power

While the 24-hour news cycle revolutionized how the public consumed information, the advent of social media took things a step further. Social media platforms like Twitter, Facebook, and Instagram have fundamentally changed the relationship between presidents and the public by giving leaders the ability to bypass traditional media entirely. Suddenly, presidents had direct, unfiltered access to millions, no journalists, no editors, just a digital megaphone.

Barack Obama was the first to harness the potential of social media, particularly during his 2008 campaign. His team's use of platforms like Facebook and Twitter was innovative, mobilizing young voters and building a grassroots movement online. Obama's online presence presented him as modern, tech-savvy, and in touch with the digital age, a sharp contrast to his opponents. It was a powerful image, one that resonated deeply with voters and helped him build a loyal following. As president, he continued to use social media to communicate directly with the public, posting messages of hope, policy updates, and personal insights that created a sense of closeness and authenticity. This was a new way of doing politics, intimate and direct, but it also began to blur the lines between the public and private, between the leader and the celebrity.

But it was Donald Trump who truly transformed the way presidents use social media. Unlike Obama, whose posts were often crafted to project optimism and unity, Trump used Twitter as a weapon, a tool for both rallying his supporters and attacking his opponents. His unfiltered style, filled with insults, provocations, and policy declarations, captivated the media and the public alike. With each tweet, Trump generated headlines, dominated the news cycle, and often distracted from more substantive issues. The sheer frequency of his posts and the often controversial nature of his statements kept the media constantly on its toes, chasing after every tweet as if it were a breaking news event.

Trump's use of social media revealed both the power and the peril of this new digital landscape. On the one hand, it allowed him to speak directly to his base, mobilizing a loyal following without the need for traditional press conferences or official statements. On the other hand, it highlighted the dangers of a president who could set policy, attack individuals, and stir public sentiment in real-time, all with a few taps on a smartphone. The impact was immediate and profound, Trump's tweets could send the stock market into a tailspin, spark diplomatic incidents, and set the national agenda in ways that traditional media could never have anticipated. His presidency was a prime example of how the amplification provided by social media can make the president seem omnipotent, even as the underlying mechanisms of government remain complex and constrained.

The Amplification of Presidential Visibility

With the rise of the 24-hour news cycle and social media, the American presidency has transformed into an almost omnipresent force. This visibility is not just about politics; it's also about creating a personality, a brand. The media's focus on the president has shifted from policy to spectacle, from governance to entertainment. This change is evident when we look at the coverage of modern presidents and how their public personas are shaped.

Ronald Reagan, often called "The Great Communicator," was among the first to understand the power of the media in modern politics. As a former actor, he had the ability to craft an image that resonated with the public. His presidency was defined by a carefully controlled narrative of American strength, optimism, and resilience. Reagan's team orchestrated his appearances with precision, ensuring that he always looked presidential, whether standing against the backdrop of the Berlin Wall or meeting with world leaders. His skillful use of television created a visual brand for his administration, one that has become a template for subsequent presidents.

However, the challenge for contemporary presidents is that they cannot always control the narrative in the way Reagan could. The constant, unfiltered nature of social media and the round-the-clock news coverage make it nearly impossible to present a single, unified image.

Today's presidents are at the mercy of a media environment that demands drama, controversy, and spectacle. Even seemingly mundane actions are scrutinized and turned into major stories.

For example, consider the presidency of Joe Biden. Unlike his predecessors, Biden has largely shied away from the spotlight, preferring to focus on policy rather than personality. Yet, despite his efforts to downplay the performative aspects of the office, the media still fixates on every move he makes, analysing his stumbles, parsing his offhand remarks, and framing every decision within the broader narrative of his administration's competence. The 24-hour news cycle and social media mean that the president can never truly step out of the public eye; every action, no matter how small, is broadcast and dissected, often in real-time.

The Consequences: Perception vs. Reality

The amplification of presidential visibility through media has led to a fundamental shift in how Americans perceive the office. On one hand, this heightened visibility has the potential to bring the public closer to the government, making politics more accessible and engaging. On the other hand, it creates unrealistic expectations about what the president can achieve. When the president is always visible, always speaking, tweeting, or appearing on camera, it gives the impression that the office holds more power than it actually does.

This amplification can create the illusion that the president is omnipotent, responsible for every success and every failure in the country. The media's constant focus on the president as the central figure in every national crisis reinforces this perception, leading the public to believe that all issues, whether economic downturns, natural disasters, or international conflicts, can and should be solved by the individual in the Oval Office. It ignores the reality of American governance: that power is distributed among various branches and levels of government, each with its own responsibilities and limitations.

When Hurricane Katrina devastated New Orleans in 2005, for example, the media spotlight fell squarely on President George W. Bush. Images of him looking down at the wreckage from Air Force One were replayed endlessly, casting him as distant and indifferent. The failure of the federal response was laid at his feet, despite the fact that disaster management involves a complex web of local, state, and federal agencies. The media's portrayal of Bush as singularly responsible for the disaster response highlighted how the amplified visibility of the president can create a distorted understanding of governance, leading the public to conflate the office with all facets of power.

The Transformation of Governance: Policy as Performance

The evolution of media has not only changed the public's perception of the presidency; it has also transformed the way presidents govern. The constant need to appear engaged, decisive, and in control has forced presidents to think of their actions in terms of media optics. Policies are not just decisions made behind closed doors; they are performances staged for public consumption. Press conferences, photo-ops, and social media posts are all carefully crafted to convey the image of an active, responsive leader.

This transformation was evident during the Obama administration's response to the 2008 financial crisis. Beyond policy measures like the stimulus package and banking reforms, Obama's team understood the importance of narrative. His administration launched a media campaign that portrayed him as a calm, steady hand guiding the nation through turbulence. From televised town halls to carefully framed moments in the Oval Office, every action was designed to project confidence and reassurance. The optics were as important as the policies themselves because, in the age of media saturation, the image of the president working to solve the crisis was essential to maintaining public trust.

Donald Trump took this approach to new heights, treating policy announcements as opportunities for spectacle. Whether signing executive orders in dramatic fashion or holding rallies to galvanize support for his immigration policies, Trump's presidency was defined by the performance of governance. His reliance on social media to announce policy shifts often bypassed traditional government processes, turning governance into a series of staged events that blurred the line between showmanship and leadership.

The Media ~ blessing or curse?

In the end, the media's amplification of the presidency can be seen as a blessing or a curse. On one side, it offers presidents a powerful platform to communicate directly with the public, rally support, and shape their image. On the other, it subjects them to constant scrutiny and criticism, creating a political environment where every action is magnified, every misstep becomes a scandal, and every statement is dissected. For presidents who navigate this terrain skilfully, it can be an asset; for those who falter, it can be a liability that undermines their credibility and power.

The role of media in amplifying presidential visibility has reshaped the American presidency into something the Founders could never have anticipated, a role where the image and perception of power often overshadow its actual execution. As we move further into the 21st century, the relationship between the presidency and the media will continue to evolve, but the fundamental truth remains: the American president is as much a product of the media as of the ballot box, a figure defined as much by the spectacle of politics as by the realities of governance.

Expectations vs. Reality: The public's unrealistic expectation that presidents can solve pretty much everything

The presidency, a role forged with the noble intention of leading a fledgling republic, has transformed over centuries into something almost mythic. Today, the American public holds an image of the president not merely as a head of state, but as a saviour, a national figure capable of solving every conceivable problem. From the economy and healthcare to race relations and foreign policy, Americans expect their leader to manage an overwhelming array of issues. This expectation, however, is not only unrealistic; it is a burden that no individual, no matter how skilled or charismatic, could bear. It creates a narrative where the successes and failures of a nation rest solely on one person's shoulders, fostering an illusion of omnipotence that diverges significantly from the reality of presidential power.

The Origins of Presidential Expectations: Lincoln and the "Savior" President

To understand how this mythic perception of the presidency emerged, one must look back to Abraham Lincoln, a figure whose legacy set the tone for future expectations. Lincoln's presidency came at a time when the United States was teetering on the brink of collapse. The Civil War, the nation's greatest crisis, was not just a political and military struggle; it was a test of the very ideals that the nation was founded upon. Lincoln's leadership in preserving the Union, abolishing slavery, and guiding the country through a bloody and divisive war elevated him to an almost messianic status.

Lincoln's portrayal as the "Great Emancipator" and the saviour of the nation established a powerful precedent. Here was a president who did not merely execute policy; he represented the moral fibre of the nation and carried the weight of its future on his shoulders. In moments of crisis, he stepped beyond the boundaries of his office, assuming extraordinary powers to keep the Union intact. This sense of urgency and responsibility shaped the American psyche: in times of national crisis, the president was expected to be more than just a leader, he had to be a hero.

Yet, Lincoln himself was acutely aware of the limitations of his power. Despite the almost divine status granted to him by history, Lincoln faced intense opposition within his own party, an obstinate Congress, and the fierce reality of a divided nation. His struggles with the Radical Republicans, who often criticized him for moving too slowly on abolition, and the Copperheads, who called for peace with the Confederacy, demonstrated that even in his moment of greatest influence, he was far from all-powerful. Nevertheless, the image of Lincoln as a saviour has lingered, setting a template for the unrealistic expectations that would shape future presidencies.

Franklin D. Roosevelt: The New Deal and Presidential Responsibility

If Lincoln laid the groundwork, Franklin D. Roosevelt (FDR) solidified the modern expectation of the presidency as a force capable of tackling any crisis. When FDR took office in 1933, the United States was mired in the depths of the Great Depression. Unemployment rates were sky-high, banks were collapsing, and the American public was losing faith not only in the economy but in the government itself. Roosevelt's response was to take swift and bold action, launching the New Deal, a series of programs and policies aimed at revitalizing the economy and providing relief to millions of Americans.

FDR's approach marked a turning point in the public's relationship with the presidency. For the first time, Americans saw a president as not just a political figure but as a personal advocate for their well-being. When Roosevelt spoke directly to the American people in a calm and reassuring manner, he created an intimate connection between the president and the public. It wasn't just policy; it was performance, and it was deeply effective. The public believed that FDR, with his confident tone and ambitious plans, could fix the economy and restore the nation's prosperity.

36

But while Roosevelt's charisma and determination brought hope to many, the reality was more complex. Despite the successes of the New Deal, the Great Depression persisted for years, and the economy remained fragile. FDR's policies, though expansive, faced opposition in Congress and legal challenges in the Supreme Court, which struck down several New Deal programs. Additionally, some of his initiatives, such as the Agricultural Adjustment Act, had unintended consequences that harmed certain sectors of the economy, particularly small farmers. The limitations of presidential power were evident; even with a sweeping mandate and widespread public support, the president could not unilaterally solve every problem.

Nevertheless, the image of FDR as the president who "saved" America during its darkest hour has endured. This perception set the stage for future presidents to be viewed not just as policy makers but as personal guardians of the nation's well-being. The expectation that the president could, and should, solve everything from economic downturns to social inequalities became increasingly ingrained in the American consciousness.

The Modern Era: Clinton, Obama, and the Illusion of the Omnipotent President

As the presidency evolved into a more visible and immediate institution, expectations only grew. Bill Clinton's administration is a prime example of the growing disconnect between public perception and the reality of presidential power. Elected in the post-Cold War era, Clinton entered office with promises to revitalize the economy and tackle domestic issues such as healthcare reform. With his charisma and relatable persona, he seemed the perfect candidate to connect with Americans on a personal level and fulfil their expectations.

However, the reality of governance quickly complicated this image. Clinton's attempt to overhaul the healthcare system in the early 1990s met fierce resistance from Congress, resulting in failure. The initiative, which had been a central campaign promise, showcased how even a popular president could be thwarted by the complexities of legislative politics. Clinton's administration also faced scandal, most notably the Monica Lewinsky affair, which distracted from policy efforts and underscored the fragility of a president's image in the face of public scrutiny.

Despite these setbacks, the public continued to look to Clinton, and future presidents, as the central figure responsible for steering the nation. The expectation that the president should fix everything persisted, even as the reality of partisan gridlock and the limitations of executive power became increasingly apparent.

Barack Obama's presidency further illustrates the gap between public expectations and presidential capacity. Elected on a wave of hope and change, Obama's election represented a historic moment, one that promised to heal racial divisions and fundamentally transform America. His charisma, eloquence, and optimism made him a beacon for those seeking solutions to issues ranging from healthcare to the economic recession. When he entered the White House, the American public expected immediate and sweeping reforms.

The passage of the Affordable Care Act (ACA), often called "Obamacare," exemplifies both the promise and the reality of the modern presidency. While Obama succeeded in passing one of the most significant pieces of legislation in decades, the process was fraught with compromise, delays, and bitter partisan opposition. The ACA, intended as a comprehensive solution to America's healthcare woes, became a symbol of both success and limitation. It expanded healthcare access for millions, but it also faced numerous challenges, including court battles and implementation issues that complicated its impact.

Obama's presidency, like those before him, also faced external crises that underscored the limits of presidential power. The Deepwater Horizon oil spill in 2010, for example, revealed the expectation that the president should manage every disaster, even those involving private companies and natural phenomena beyond government control. Obama's efforts to manage the situation, while earnest, could not prevent the spill's damage, nor could they undo the environmental and economic impact overnight. Despite his role as the most powerful man in the world, he was ultimately constrained by circumstances and the nature of the problem.

The Trump Phenomenon: Performing Power
Donald Trump's presidency pushed the narrative of the omnipotent president to its extremes. A former reality television star, Trump's campaign and presidency were built on the promise of a powerful, decisive leader who would "drain the swamp" and "make America great

again". He presented himself not as a conventional politician but as an outsider who could fix everything that the Washington establishment had failed to address.

His use of social media, particularly Twitter, allowed him to create the illusion of immediate, unfiltered power. By tweeting about issues ranging from the economy to immigration, Trump gave the impression that he could, with a few characters on a screen, direct national policy and solve complex problems. His followers, drawn to his image as a strongman, believed that Trump alone could tackle the issues that had plagued America for decades.

Yet, like his predecessors, Trump found that the realities of governance were far more complicated than the image he projected. His administration's attempts to build a border wall, a central promise of his campaign, were mired in legal battles, funding disputes, and logistical challenges. His efforts to repeal and replace Obamacare, despite being a rallying cry for his supporters, ultimately failed in Congress. Even his tariff policies, intended to strengthen American industries, led to unintended consequences, such as retaliatory tariffs from other countries that hurt American farmers.

Trump's presidency was a vivid example of the gap between perception and reality. Despite his assertive and aggressive posture, many of his policy efforts either stalled or produced mixed results. The performance of power, projected through social media and the spectacle of his rallies, masked the constraints of his role. The public expectation that Trump, or any president, could singlehandedly transform the nation and fix its problems was once again shown to be an illusion.

The Burden of Unrealistic Expectations

The weight of public expectation creates a paradox for the presidency. On one hand, presidents are expected to solve all the nation's problems, yet they often lack the tools, authority, and support necessary to enact such sweeping change. This disconnect not only disillusions voters but also fuels polarization and frustration. When presidents inevitably fall short of these impossible expectations, they are vilified or dismissed as ineffective. This cycle of hope, disappointment, and blame contributes to the broader dysfunction in American politics, as it distracts from the systemic issues that no single individual can address.

Moreover, the expectation that the president must fix everything reduces the incentive for other branches of government to act. Congress, designed to be a powerful legislative body, often defers to the executive branch, waiting for the president to take the lead rather than exercising its own authority. This not only distorts the balance of power envisioned by the Founders but also creates a government where true reform is stymied by gridlock, as both the executive and legislative branches play a game of political brinkmanship.

Rethinking the Presidency

The expectation that the president of the United States can solve all of the nation's problems is a powerful and enduring myth. Rooted in historical moments of crisis, amplified by charismatic leaders, and sustained by a media ecosystem that thrives on drama, this perception has become a central feature of American political life. Yet, it is a myth that does more harm than good. It distracts from the systemic issues that require collective action and creates a political culture where the focus remains on individuals rather than institutions.

For the United States to move forward, there must be a reckoning with this reality. The presidency, while powerful, cannot bear the weight of every issue facing the nation. As long as the American public clings to the illusion of an omnipotent president, it will remain trapped in a cycle of unrealistic hope and inevitable disappointment. The challenge for the future is to redefine the expectations of presidential power, to recognize the office's limitations, and to re-engage other institutions and actors in the governance process. Only then can the myth be shattered, and the nation move towards a more realistic and effective understanding of leadership.

The Illusion of Power: A Distraction from Systemic Governance Problems

The American presidency is an office shrouded in mystique and power, a beacon of authority that stands as both a symbol and an enigma. The president, portrayed as the commander-in-chief, the economic architect, the diplomat, and the nation's conscience, is often regarded as the most powerful individual in the world. This perception, however, is more illusion than reality. In truth, the hyper-focus on the presidency distracts from the broader, systemic governance issues that shape the country's politics and policies. It creates a captivating narrative where the president seems to be the solution to every problem or the cause of every crisis, leaving the complex machinery of governance overshadowed, and often, ignored.

The illusion of presidential power is not just about the grandeur and spectacle of the office; it is a distortion that masks the reality of American governance, a reality in which the president is only one part of a vast network of institutions, actors, and influences. This singular focus has the effect of obscuring the deeper issues within the system: congressional gridlock, lobbying influence, judicial overreach, and the fragmentation of the political landscape. Let's explore how this illusion unfolds, the individuals who have shaped it, and the consequences it has had on the governance of the United States.

Congressional Gridlock: The Hidden Reality

One of the most significant systemic problems obscured by the illusion of presidential power is congressional gridlock. The founders designed the American government to be a system of checks and balances, where the legislative branch would hold considerable power. Over the years, however, as the presidency has taken centre stage, Congress's role has often been diminished in the public eye. The reality is that no matter how compelling or charismatic a president may be, their power is limited if Congress remains divided and unable to pass legislation.

The Obama administration provides a poignant example. After the 2010 midterm elections, Republicans gained control of the House of Representatives, creating a gridlock that stymied much of Obama's legislative agenda. Despite his efforts to push forward comprehensive immigration reform and gun control measures, Congress remained a formidable obstacle. The president's powers were not sufficient to overcome the deeply entrenched partisanship that had taken root in Congress. And yet, public and media attention remained focused on Obama himself, as if he alone could break the deadlock. The illusion of power not only placed an unrealistic burden on the president but also distracted from the dysfunction and paralysis within the legislative branch.

Even when presidents resort to executive orders to bypass congressional gridlock, these actions are often temporary and face legal challenges. For instance, Trump's executive orders on immigration faced immediate judicial pushback, and Biden's attempts to address student loan debt relief through executive action encountered similar obstacles. These examples illustrate that while the president may appear to wield sweeping power, the reality is that their actions are frequently subject to the checks of other branches of government. This ongoing tug-of-war is a feature of American democracy, but one that is often hidden behind the theatrics of the presidency.

Lobbying and Corporate Influence: The Unseen Power Brokers

While the spotlight remains on the president, another powerful force operates in the shadows, lobbyists and corporate interests. The American political system is heavily influenced by lobbying groups that pour billions of dollars into campaigns, policy initiatives, and legislative lobbying efforts. These entities wield significant power, often far beyond that of a single individual, even if that individual is the president.

Consider the pharmaceutical industry's influence on healthcare policy. Despite Barack Obama's efforts to introduce comprehensive healthcare reform, the final version of the Affordable Care Act was significantly shaped by pharmaceutical and insurance companies. These corporations lobbied aggressively to protect their interests, ensuring that certain provisions, like the public option, were excluded from the final bill. The media and public, however, focused largely on Obama himself, either praising or criticizing him for the outcome, while the systemic issue of corporate influence went largely unnoticed.

This pattern is not unique to healthcare. The energy sector, defence contractors, and technology giants all exert immense pressure on the political system. Presidents often find their hands tied by these influences, forced to negotiate and compromise. And yet, the illusion of presidential power persists, as if the president alone can stand against, or with, these powerful entities. The truth is that these corporations, with their vast resources and political leverage, frequently shape policies more profoundly than any single administration.

The Judicial Branch: The Quiet Arbiter of Power

Another systemic element overshadowed by the focus on the presidency is the judiciary. While the president appoints judges, including Supreme Court justices, the judicial branch operates independently, often acting as a check on presidential power. Many presidents, despite their ambitions, have found their actions curtailed by court rulings that highlight the limitations of executive authority.

Franklin D. Roosevelt's New Deal faced significant opposition from the Supreme Court, which struck down several of his key programs as unconstitutional. FDR's frustration led him to propose the infamous "court-packing" plan, aiming to add more justices to the bench in order to secure favourable rulings. This move was widely criticized and ultimately failed, demonstrating that even one of the most influential presidents in American history could not easily bend the judicial branch to his will. The illusion of power suggested FDR had unchecked authority, but the reality was far more complicated.

In more recent times, Donald Trump's attempts to implement a travel ban on several predominantly Muslim countries faced judicial scrutiny and multiple defeats in lower courts before a revised version was eventually upheld by the Supreme Court. The spectacle of the ban and the president's insistence on its necessity captured headlines, but the deeper story was one of judicial checks and balances. The courts' role in shaping policy and holding the executive accountable remains a crucial, though often underreported, aspect of American governance. The public's focus on the president as the architect of every action obscures the judiciary's influence and the systemic balance that was designed to prevent the concentration of power in a single office.

The Fragmentation of American Politics: A Divided System

The illusion of presidential power also diverts attention from another critical issue: the fragmentation of American politics. The rise of hyper-partisanship and the widening ideological gap between political parties have made it increasingly difficult for any president to govern effectively. Rather than focusing on the systemic issue of a divided nation and the polarization of Congress, the media and the public often fixate on the president, expecting them to bridge these divides. The result is a cycle of unrealistic expectations and inevitable disappointment.

This fragmentation has made bipartisan cooperation almost impossible, rendering the legislative process ineffective and turning the president into a lightning rod for criticism. For example, despite Biden's promises to unify the country, his administration has struggled to pass significant legislation without resorting to partisan tactics, as seen with his infrastructure bill. The public conversation, however, tends to centre around Biden's effectiveness as a leader, rather than the deeper issue of a fragmented political system that no single president could realistically repair.

The Danger of the Illusion: Ignoring the Real Problems

The most significant consequence of the illusion of presidential power is that it distracts from the systemic issues that truly impact governance. When all eyes are on the president, other actors and institutions operate with less scrutiny. Congress, the judiciary, lobbying groups, and corporate interests all play vital roles in shaping policy, yet they often escape the level of attention given to the president. This not only perpetuates the illusion but also reinforces a cycle where deeper reforms, those that target the structural imbalances of the system, remain unaddressed.

The American people, conditioned by the media and political culture to focus on the president as the hero or villain of every narrative, often ignore the importance of local elections, congressional races, and state-level politics. The fixation on the presidency creates a distorted picture of power that undermines the collective responsibility inherent in a functioning democracy.

The illusion of power, then, is not just a political problem, it's a cultural one. It's a narrative that Americans tell themselves about their system of governance, one that emphasizes the individual over the institution, the spectacle over the substance. As the focus remains on the persona of the president, the need for systemic reform goes unheeded. To confront the real challenges facing American governance, the nation must first break free from this illusion and shift its gaze back to the broader, interconnected system that truly shapes its politics.

CHAPTER 3

THE SHIFT FROM POLICY TO CHARISMA
& LEADERSHIP TO CELEBRITY

Introduction: Personality Politics:
In 1960, America watched as the first-ever televised presidential debate unfolded between John F. Kennedy and Richard Nixon. It was a defining moment, not just for that election but for the trajectory of American politics. Those who tuned in via radio felt Nixon's expertise and policy focus had won the day, but for the millions watching on television, Kennedy's charm, youthfulness, and composure won them over. It was the beginning of something new, a shift from substance to style, from policy to personality, from leadership to celebrity.

Today, the notion that charisma can propel a politician to power isn't just accepted; it's expected. The American public craves a leader who inspires, entertains, and personifies their ideals and aspirations.

The presidency has evolved from a role of governance and policymaking to a stage where performance matters as much, if not more, than policy. This chapter delves into how and why this transformation occurred, highlighting the individuals, media forces, and cultural shifts that have shaped what we now know as personality politics.

Charisma has long been a powerful force in politics, but in the modern era, its impact has intensified. Charisma in leadership is not new; historical figures like Julius Caesar, Napoleon Bonaparte, and Winston Churchill wielded personal magnetism as a tool of influence. However, the American presidency's relationship with charisma is distinct, evolving in tandem with technological advancements and changing societal expectations.

In the American political landscape, the presidency has always been about more than policies and legislation. It has been about symbolism, identity, and character, traits that the public, and indeed the world, have come to expect from those who occupy the highest office. But somewhere along the way, the emphasis on character evolved into something more pervasive: personality politics. Today, it seems that the persona of a president, his or her charisma, their relatability, age or stage presence, matters more than the policies championed or the governance implemented. We have entered an era where charisma often outshines competence, where the performance of leadership overshadows its substance.

This shift did not happen overnight, nor is it unique to any one figure or administration. It's a product of a society where media plays an increasingly dominant role in shaping perceptions, where the spectacle of politics often eclipses its practicalities. As a political observer from the outside looking in, one can't help but notice how the American political narrative has transformed into a kind of theatre, where presidents are not merely leaders but actors cast in the most important role of their lives. The focus on policy and expertise has, in many ways, been replaced by an obsession with image and celebrity. This chapter delves into how this change unfolded, the individuals who defined it, and the consequences for governance.

Ronald Reagan, the Hollywood actor turned politician, took Kennedy's example and perfected the art of charisma in the media age. Reagan's presidency marked the full emergence of the "star politician." His background as an actor gave him a unique advantage: he knew how to use the camera, deliver lines, and craft a narrative. Reagan's warmth, humour, and ability to present himself as a confident and optimistic leader helped create a sense of stability and strength during his administration. He portrayed himself as the embodiment of American values, resilient, hopeful, and strong.

Reagan's presidency illustrated the power of narrative over policy. The famous "Morning in America" campaign during his re-election bid in 1984 exemplified this. The ad painted a picture of national renewal, economic prosperity, and American optimism, all tied to Reagan's leadership. It wasn't about the specific policies he enacted; it was about the image he projected. Reagan's charisma was so potent that it often overshadowed the details of his administration's policies, some of which, like his handling of the AIDS crisis and foreign interventions, remain controversial.

One of Reagan's most iconic moments came when he addressed the nation after the Challenger space shuttle disaster in 1986. His empathetic and reassuring message, quoting poet John Gillespie Magee, was crafted for television and delivered with poise. The address showed his ability to connect with the public emotionally, providing comfort during a national tragedy. Reagan's presidency was a performance, and he was its leading actor, demonstrating how charisma could define and sustain political power in the modern era.

Barack Obama's rise to prominence was marked by his eloquence, optimism, and ability to connect with a new generation of voters. His campaigns were built on the promise of hope and change, a message that resonated across demographics. But what made Obama's charisma particularly effective was his ability to harness the power of new media— social media. Obama's use of platforms like Facebook, Twitter, and YouTube revolutionized political campaigning and communication, allowing him to craft a carefully curated persona that was accessible, modern, and forward-thinking.

Obama's charisma was not just about his speeches, although they were powerful and often stirring; it was also about his presence online, where he engaged directly with voters in a way that felt personal and authentic. His digital savvy made him seem more connected to the everyday American, and his campaign's use of social media to mobilize grassroots support was groundbreaking. Obama was not just a leader; he was an influencer, and this shift blurred the line between traditional political leadership and the celebrity culture of the digital age.

Yet, as with his predecessors, Obama's charisma often overshadowed the substance of his policies. His message of hope and unity resonated, but the complexities of governing were less emphasized. His administration faced significant challenges, such as the economic crisis, healthcare reform, and international conflicts. But the public's focus remained largely on his image, his family, his speeches, his calm demeanour, rather than the intricacies of policy-making. Obama's presidency further demonstrated how charisma, amplified by modern media, could become the defining feature of a president's legacy, sometimes at the expense of policy depth.

The culmination of this evolution arrived with Donald Trump, whose presidency was the ultimate expression of charisma as a political weapon. Trump's background as a reality TV star and businessman positioned him uniquely in the American political landscape. He understood that in an age dominated by social media and a 24-hour news cycle, the key was not necessarily to be right but to be entertaining. Trump's unfiltered, brash style was a sharp contrast to his predecessors, but it tapped into a public increasingly accustomed to, and perhaps craving, spectacle.

Trump's use of Twitter to bypass traditional media was not just a tactic; it was central to his strategy. By tweeting directly to millions of followers, he controlled the narrative, ensuring that he was always the centre of attention. His tweets, often inflammatory and controversial, dominated news cycles, creating an atmosphere where his persona was ever-present. This direct, unmediated connection with the public was unprecedented, and it reshaped the political landscape in ways that will have long-lasting effects.

Trump's charisma was not of the polished, statesman-like variety of Kennedy or Reagan. Instead, it was raw, aggressive, and designed to provoke. He positioned himself as the ultimate outsider, a champion for those who felt alienated by the political elite. His charisma was rooted in disruption, in challenging norms, and in presenting himself as a fighter against a corrupt system. For his supporters, this authenticity, however polarizing, was precisely what made him appealing.

But Trump's dominance on social media also highlighted the dangers of this shift. The platform rewarded drama and controversy, reinforcing the idea that the presidency was more about visibility and engagement than governance. His ability to dominate the media meant that his image, both to his supporters and detractors, overshadowed the reality of his policy failures and successes. The performance of leadership became the presidency itself, leaving the substance of governance as an afterthought.

The Media's Role: Shaping Public Personas

If charisma is the fuel of modern politics, the media is the engine that drives it forward. The media's role in shaping public perception has evolved dramatically, particularly with the rise of television and, later, the internet. Each technological shift has amplified the focus on personality and image, changing how presidents are perceived and evaluated.

The modern presidency cannot be separated from the media that covers it. It's a symbiotic relationship, one that has existed since the advent of radio but has been amplified by television, 24-hour news cycles, and social media. The media doesn't just report on presidents; it curates their personas, amplifies their messages, and, at times, even manufactures controversies to keep the public engaged. The line between reporting and entertainment has blurred, and in this blurred space, presidents have become more than policymakers—they have become celebrities.

When radio became a household staple in the 1930s, Franklin Delano Roosevelt was the first to harness its power fully. His fireside chats were more than just speeches; they were carefully crafted conversations designed to foster a sense of closeness and trust between the president and the American people. Understanding the power of radio, Roosevelt aimed to cut through the formalities and stiffness that often characterized presidential addresses. He wanted to create the persona of a calm, approachable leader, a neighbour or friend sitting by the fireplace, speaking plainly about the nation's challenges and instilling hope.

Roosevelt didn't always write the scripts himself, but he was heavily involved in their preparation. Working closely with his team of speechwriters, he ensured that each chat reflected his tone and style. The president would edit drafts himself, crossing out stiff or overly complex language, insisting on using simple, direct words that resonated with everyday Americans. His goal was clarity and relatability; he knew that a warm, conversational tone was essential for conveying his message effectively and building trust.

The style of the fireside chats was intentionally informal. Roosevelt avoided the pompous, political rhetoric typical of the time, opting instead for a friendly, reassuring tone. He used straightforward language and often began his addresses with phrases like "My friends" or "Good evening, my fellow Americans," setting the stage for an intimate and personal interaction. He aimed to make listeners feel like they were having a one-on-one conversation with him, rather than listening to a remote figure of authority.

The content of the fireside chats was carefully structured to explain complex national issues in an accessible way. Whether discussing the banking crisis, New Deal policies, or the war effort, Roosevelt broke down information into simple, understandable terms, using analogies and metaphors that the average American could relate to. For instance, when explaining banking reforms during the Great Depression, he used the analogy of a doctor diagnosing and treating an illness, a metaphor that Americans struggling with economic uncertainty could easily grasp.

The language he used was also designed to create a sense of unity and shared purpose. He frequently employed phrases like "we must," "together, we can," and "our country," reinforcing a collective identity and emphasizing that the challenges ahead required cooperation and resilience from every American. By positioning himself as part of the struggle rather than above it, he crafted an image of a leader who was in touch with the people's concerns and committed to guiding them through tough times.

Roosevelt's fireside chats were not just a communication strategy; they were a pioneering use of media to build a direct, emotional connection with the public. They helped to cement his image as a compassionate and steady leader and showcased his ability to adapt traditional political discourse to the realities and technologies of the time. Through his careful use of tone, language, and style, Roosevelt's fireside chats set a new standard for presidential communication, one that remains a model of effective public engagement even today.

Television elevated this connection to a visual experience. The Kennedy-Nixon debate in 1960 demonstrated that appearance and presentation could outweigh policy expertise in the eyes of the public. Kennedy's charm, poise, and telegenic appeal were tailor-made for the new medium, and they overshadowed Nixon's policy experience and substance.

The first televised presidential debate between John F. Kennedy and Richard Nixon on September 26, 1960, was not just a turning point in American politics; it was a dramatic unveiling of the power of television as a medium that could shape public perception. For the first time, the nation watched as two candidates, representing starkly different styles and personas, went head-to-head, and the outcome would forever alter how presidential campaigns were run. The debate, held in CBS's WBBM-TV studios in Chicago, would highlight the significance of appearance, body language, and poise over sheer policy expertise, a revelation that would echo through every subsequent election.

The debate itself focused on a series of critical issues: the Cold War, the state of the economy, and the concept of American leadership on the global stage. Moderator Howard K. Smith asked pointed questions that demanded substantive responses from both candidates. Yet, as the debate unfolded, it became clear that the substance of their answers was only part of the equation. The visual performance, projected through millions of black-and-white television screens, would become the focal point.

Kennedy, a young and charismatic senator from Massachusetts, appeared confident and composed. He had arrived well-prepared, with his campaign advisors keenly aware of the visual stakes. His dark suit contrasted sharply against the grey backdrop, making him stand out. He wore makeup that gave his skin a healthy, even tone, avoiding the harsh lighting that plagued television sets of the era. Kennedy's posture was relaxed yet attentive, and he maintained consistent eye contact with the camera, an intentional move designed to create a sense of intimacy with the viewers. When he answered questions, his facial expressions were calm, and his gestures were measured. His body language conveyed control and poise, signalling to viewers that he was a steady, trustworthy figure who could guide the country through turbulent times.

Nixon's appearance, on the other hand, told a different story. As the sitting Vice President and an experienced debater, Nixon was expected to have the upper hand. However, he made a series of miscalculations that undermined his performance. First, Nixon had recently recovered from a hospital stay, and he appeared visibly unwell. His pale complexion was accentuated by his refusal to wear makeup, resulting in an image that seemed haggard under the studio lights. Wearing a light grey suit, Nixon blended into the background, making him appear less prominent and, in contrast to Kennedy, less commanding. His nervous gestures, like wiping sweat from his upper lip, only amplified the sense of discomfort. Instead of looking into the camera as Kennedy did, Nixon often glanced at the reporters asking the questions, creating a disconnect between him and the television audience.

When Smith asked the candidates about how they would address the Soviet threat, Kennedy's response was crisp and concise. He spoke of strength, unity, and the need for America to project its power globally, framing himself as the face of a new, vigorous America. His delivery was confident and assured, creating an impression of decisive leadership. Nixon's response, while full of detail and substance, came off as rambling. He delved into specifics, referencing various treaties and Cold War strategies, yet his answers were less about projecting strength and more about explaining policy minutiae. While Nixon's knowledge was evident, his approach was not suited to the new medium. Television demanded not just answers but a visual and emotional connection, which Nixon struggled to establish.

One particularly telling moment occurred when the candidates were asked about the economy and whether the nation was moving forward. Kennedy took the opportunity to speak directly to the American people. He presented his vision in broad strokes, using simple, relatable language. His answers felt less like lectures and more like conversations, framing him as someone in touch with the concerns of everyday Americans. His body language supported this approach: his slight nods and direct eye contact created a rapport that drew viewers in.

Nixon, however, leaned into his technical expertise, listing statistics and policy specifics. Though he demonstrated his depth of understanding, his delivery felt more like a briefing than a conversation. He failed to engage the viewers emotionally. Additionally, as Nixon continued, he began to shift uncomfortably, his expression betraying the tension he felt under the hot studio lights. His physical unease was magnified each time he shifted his gaze from the camera to the reporters and back again, making him appear detached and unsure.

Another notable exchange revolved around the question of leadership and readiness to manage the escalating tensions in Cuba. Kennedy, using his body language to convey seriousness, leaned slightly forward, engaging the camera as if he were confiding in the audience. He positioned himself as a fresh leader ready to take bold action, highlighting the need for new direction and vision. His confident smile and steady gaze suggested optimism and readiness. In contrast, Nixon, who had years of foreign policy experience as Vice President, responded with detailed accounts of his work under President Eisenhower. However, instead of projecting authority, Nixon appeared defensive. His eyes darted from the camera to the floor, and he clenched his hands, a physical manifestation of his discomfort. This contrast between Kennedy's composure and Nixon's visible anxiety became one of the most memorable aspects of the debate.

Kennedy's mastery over the visual aspects of television extended beyond his composure; it was also reflected in his sartorial choices. His decision to wear a dark suit and tie was not incidental, it was a deliberate move to convey authority and seriousness, drawing a stark visual contrast with Nixon's washed-out appearance. Nixon's decision to stick with his light grey suit not only caused him to blend into the set but also diminished his presence. He looked less like the leader of the free world and more like a weary bureaucrat. Kennedy, with his tailored look and confident demeanour, appeared presidential, embodying the new American leader the nation had been waiting for.

The aftermath of the debate revealed the power of television's visual and emotional influence. Polls conducted immediately after showed a clear divide: those who listened to the debate on the radio largely believed Nixon had won, appreciating his policy depth and experience. However, television viewers overwhelmingly favoured Kennedy. His mastery of television's demands, projecting confidence, maintaining direct eye contact, and using body language effectively, allowed him to connect with viewers in a way that Nixon couldn't.

The Kennedy-Nixon debate marked a seismic shift in American politics, proving that television was not just a medium for communicating policies but a stage where the performance mattered as much, if not more, than the content. From this point on, candidates would have to be more than just politicians; they would need to be performers, image-makers, and stars of a televised spectacle.

Ronald Reagan, with his Hollywood background, exemplified this shift. His mastery of television allowed him to connect with Americans in a way that felt both personal and cinematic. Reagan's presidency was built as much on his image, of strength, optimism, and American values, as it was on his policies. The media, eager for stories that resonated with the public, often focused on these images, reinforcing the idea that charisma and character were central to presidential success.

Ronald Reagan's "Tear Down This Wall" speech, delivered on June 12, 1987, remains one of the most iconic moments of his presidency, not just for its bold message but for the personal delivery that only Reagan could achieve. Set against the backdrop of the Brandenburg Gate in West Berlin, Reagan's speech became a symbolic gesture during the final years of the Cold War. It wasn't merely the words he spoke but the manner in which he delivered them, his controlled intensity, his warmth, and his resolute tone, that elevated the moment into history.

Berlin in 1987 was still a city caught in the grip of Cold War tensions, divided physically and ideologically by the Berlin Wall. The wall, which spanned 27 miles, was a constant reminder of the chasm between East and West, oppression and freedom. Reagan's choice of location was both deliberate and daring. Standing in front of the Brandenburg Gate, a symbol of Berlin's unity before the wall severed it, Reagan faced the audience with the imposing concrete barrier behind him. The setting was chosen not only for its symbolic power but also to frame Reagan as a resolute leader standing at the frontier of freedom, speaking directly to both Berliners and the world.

It wasn't just the location that made the speech memorable; it was Reagan's delivery, honed by years of experience as both an actor and a politician. From the moment he stepped up to the podium, his demeanour was calm yet commanding. Reagan understood that this was a pivotal moment, not just in his presidency but in the broader context of the Cold War. He took his time, establishing a rapport with the crowd by acknowledging the unique history and struggle of Berlin, carefully setting the stage for the powerful climax of his speech.

His voice was steady, and his gestures purposeful. As he delivered the line, "Mr. Gorbachev, tear down this wall," his tone sharpened, firm, but not aggressive. Reagan's voice didn't waver; he didn't shout. Instead, he spoke with a resolute authority that left no room for doubt, making the line a command rather than a plea. This wasn't just rhetoric; it was a challenge issued with the confidence of a leader who believed in the cause he championed.

Reagan's background as an actor played a crucial role in how he connected with the audience. He understood the importance of pausing at key moments, allowing his words to hang in the air, creating anticipation and building emotion. His eyes scanned the crowd, making each person feel like he was speaking directly to them. Even as he addressed the wider global audience, there was a sense of intimacy in his delivery, Reagan had a knack for making a global event feel personal.

Throughout his speech, Reagan used his body language to reinforce his message. Standing tall, with his shoulders squared and his hands gripping the podium at key moments, he projected a sense of unwavering determination. His posture was open, and he often gestured outward, inviting the audience to join him in his call for unity and freedom. This physical openness conveyed both strength and accessibility, characteristics that were central to his image as a leader.

He was dressed in a dark suit, classic and conservative, with a red tie that popped against the grey of the Berlin sky and the sombre backdrop of the wall. The choice of attire was no accident; it was meant to convey authority and seriousness. His appearance was that of a leader ready to engage with the gravity of the moment, yet still accessible to the ordinary people he aimed to connect with. This careful curation of his image, combined with his deliberate delivery, transformed the event from a standard political speech into a powerful moment of theatre.

Reagan's personal delivery was met with an enthusiastic response from the West Berlin crowd, who saw in him not just an American president, but a champion for their freedom. His words, infused with the warmth and determination of his tone, resonated beyond the audience gathered at the gate. For the millions watching around the world, the speech demonstrated that the American president was not merely a distant figure issuing diplomatic statements; he was a leader who was willing to stand at the frontlines of division and make a direct, emotional appeal.

At the time, not all political commentators or advisors viewed the speech favourably. Many felt that such a direct challenge to Soviet leader Mikhail Gorbachev might provoke unnecessary tension or complicate ongoing negotiations. But Reagan's decision to keep the line was a testament to his understanding of the power of bold statements delivered with conviction. He knew the importance of not just the words but the way they were said. His advisors may have feared political consequences, but Reagan trusted that his delivery, with its careful balance of strength and warmth, would transform the phrase into a rallying cry.

In the years that followed, the speech's significance only grew. When the Berlin Wall eventually fell in 1989, Reagan's words were replayed around the world, becoming an emblem of the triumph of freedom over oppression. The delivery, Reagan's commanding yet approachable presence, his deliberate, forceful tone, ensured that the phrase "Tear down this wall" became more than just a call to action; it became an enduring symbol of hope and change.

This speech is not just remembered for its bold message but for the way it was delivered. Reagan's understanding of the power of his presence, his calculated use of tone and gesture, and his mastery of the visual elements of the speech transformed a simple plea into a defining moment in Cold War history. By making the event personal, by connecting with the audience both in Berlin and around the world, Reagan ensured that his words would resonate far beyond the immediate political moment. It wasn't just what he said, it was how he said it. That personal touch, that direct engagement, is what made the speech so powerful and so memorable.

In the 21st century, the rise of social media platforms like Twitter and Facebook revolutionized the relationship between the public and the president. Barack Obama's campaign capitalized on these platforms, using them to create a sense of direct connection with voters. His carefully curated online presence presented a modern, relatable leader, building a brand that was as much about style as it was about substance. Social media allowed Obama to reach audiences directly, bypassing traditional media filters and creating a digital persona that resonated with millions.

Donald Trump took this approach to its extreme. His unfiltered use of Twitter became a hallmark of his presidency, allowing him to dominate news cycles and create a sense of immediacy and authenticity. His persona, shaped by his television career, translated seamlessly into the digital realm. The media's focus on Trump's every tweet and statement created a spectacle that was less about governance and more about entertainment. Trump understood that in the age of instant communication, the story mattered more than the policy details behind it. The media, eager to feed the constant demand for content, amplified this approach, turning the presidency into a continuous, real-time show.

Populism vs. Expertise: A Shift in Values

With the rise of personality politics, American voters began to gravitate toward leaders who could project authenticity and relatability, often at the expense of expertise. Where once policy knowledge and experience in governance were seen as valuable assets, they are now often viewed with suspicion or disdain. The populist wave, which gained momentum in the 21st century, was a direct response to this shift in values. Voters sought leaders who appeared to speak for the common person, who seemed unencumbered by the elitism associated with policy nerds and bureaucratic expertise.

This shift is emblematic of a broader cultural trend: the celebration of the outsider, the anti-establishment figure who promises to dismantle the system rather than work within it. Donald Trump's rise exemplified this perfectly. Despite having no prior political experience, he campaigned as a man of the people, someone who would "drain the swamp" and challenge the status quo. It wasn't policy expertise that won him votes; it was the perception that he was genuine, unscripted, and a true outsider. The focus was on personality over policy, rhetoric over reality.

This is not to say that charisma and populism are inherently negative, but the consequences of prioritizing these traits over expertise have become evident. Presidents who are celebrated for their personalities are often unprepared for the complexities of governance, and the policies they enact (or fail to enact) reflect this lack of depth. When the emphasis is on being relatable rather than knowledgeable, it's no surprise that the effectiveness of governance suffers.

The Echo Chamber: Social Media's Reinforcement of Image Over Substance

Social media has not only transformed how presidents communicate but also how they are perceived and evaluated. Platforms like Twitter and Instagram have become the primary stages upon which presidents perform, and they offer a unique advantage: the ability to project an unfiltered version of themselves directly to millions. But this unfiltered connection comes at a cost. Social media, designed to engage and captivate, often amplifies personality at the expense of policy substance.

The algorithm-driven nature of social media platforms has led to the creation of echo chambers, or online spaces where users are exposed primarily to content that reinforces their existing beliefs and biases. For presidents and political leaders, this means that their messages, images, and personas are constantly reinforced and amplified among their supporters. While this allows for greater engagement and mobilization, it also deepens polarization, as each side of the political spectrum becomes entrenched in its own version of reality.

Followers of a political figure, whether it be Obama's supporters or Trump's base, often interact with content that confirms their beliefs, amplifies the leader's persona, and minimizes critical analysis of policy. The engagement metrics that drive social media, likes, shares, retweets, favour the sensational, the emotive, and the personal. In this environment, a carefully reasoned policy paper cannot compete with a charismatic tweet or a viral video.

This digital echo chamber contributes to the growing divide between perception and reality. Presidents increasingly govern through the lens of their social media personas, and voters, bombarded with personalized content, see only what they want to see. The consequences are profound: policies become secondary, and governance is reduced to soundbites and spectacles.

Public Engagement: Identity Over Policy

As a result of the emphasis on personality, voter behaviour has shifted dramatically. Public engagement with politics, particularly among younger voters, is now more about identity than policy. Voters often align themselves with candidates who reflect their own values, aspirations, and frustrations, even when those candidates' policies may not directly benefit them. This trend has led to the rise of "identity politics," where the focus is on who a candidate is rather than what they stand for.

Barack Obama's campaigns capitalized on this by building a coalition of young voters, minorities, and progressives who saw in him a symbol of hope and change. His persona transcended policy: he represented a new chapter in American history, one defined by diversity, inclusion, and possibility. Similarly, Donald Trump's appeal was not based on detailed policy plans but on his identity as an outsider and a fighter for the "forgotten" Americans. For Trump's supporters, his persona, his brashness, his willingness to speak plainly, was a form of authenticity that overshadowed any specific policy proposal.

While this kind of public engagement can be powerful, it is not without risks. When politics becomes a matter of identity, it deepens divisions and reduces the space for compromise. The presidency, as a result, becomes not just a role of governance but a reflection of cultural and social battles that extend far beyond policy.

Consequences for Governance: Charisma Over Competence
The consequence of this shift toward personality politics is that it often leaves the nation with presidents who may excel in capturing the public's imagination but fall short in effective governance. Charisma, while a powerful tool, does not necessarily translate into competent leadership. The American public's growing preference for leaders who appear genuine or relatable, rather than those with policy expertise, has profound implications for the quality of decision-making in the White House.

In the end, personality politics creates a double-edged sword. While it can mobilize voters and generate excitement, it risks prioritizing style over substance. When leaders are chosen based on charisma rather than competence, the policies they enact—or fail to enact—can have long-lasting consequences. The focus on image leaves the substance of governance obscured, and the illusion of leadership becomes a substitute for the reality of effective decision-making. The cost is a political landscape where the spectacle often overwhelms the need for sound, systemic solutions.

The Decline of In-Depth Journalism:
In the golden era of American journalism, newspapers like *The New York Times*, *The Washington Post*, and *The Wall Street Journal* served as the primary sources of in-depth analysis and comprehensive coverage of political issues. News anchors such as Walter Cronkite were seen as trusted figures, providing Americans with reliable and detailed information about the political decisions and policies that shaped their lives. Investigative journalism flourished, and in-depth reporting meant that policies, their impacts, and the nuances behind them were meticulously

examined, allowing the public to engage with politics beyond the surface level.

But today, the landscape of journalism has changed dramatically. The rise of the internet and the 24-hour news cycle has led to a significant decline in the depth and quality of reporting. Short, attention-grabbing headlines, clickbait articles, and sensationalist stories have replaced the in-depth analysis that once characterized political journalism. This shift has profound consequences for public understanding, especially when it comes to comprehending the intricacies of policy and governance. The focus on personalities, scandals, and sensationalism has overshadowed substantive reporting, leaving the public increasingly uninformed about the policies that affect their lives.

The Erosion of Traditional News Outlets

The decline of in-depth journalism can be traced back to the digital revolution. Traditional news outlets, once dominant forces in shaping public opinion, have struggled to compete with the instant accessibility and speed of online news. Newspapers that once boasted robust investigative teams and extensive editorial boards have faced declining revenues, resulting in downsizing and even closures. For those that have survived, the pressure to adapt to a digital model has meant that the priority has shifted to content that generates clicks and engagement, rather than in-depth reporting.

This transition has diluted the quality of news coverage. Today, many news websites and digital platforms focus on brevity, delivering stories in bite-sized chunks that are easy to consume but often lack depth. The proliferation of opinion pieces and commentary has also risen, with many outlets choosing to publish op-eds rather than allocate resources to fact-based investigative reporting. While opinion journalism has its place, the imbalance means that fewer resources are devoted to reporting on the details of legislation, policy initiatives, and their implications.

The erosion of traditional journalism has had a direct impact on how policies are presented and understood by the public. Detailed policy analyses that were once front-page stories or featured prominently on the evening news are now condensed into short summaries, if they are covered at all. This reduction in substantive content leaves the public without the necessary information to form a comprehensive understanding of the policies that shape their lives.

The Rise of Soundbite Culture

The emergence of soundbite culture has further exacerbated the decline of in-depth journalism. In a digital age where social media platforms prioritize engagement and brevity, complex policies are often reduced to single-sentence summaries or simplified narratives. This shift has profound implications for the way people consume and understand information. The news, instead of being a means to explore the depth and complexity of political decisions, becomes a series of quick updates, often shaped by the latest controversies or the most dramatic statements made by politicians.

For example, in the context of presidential campaigns, candidates' detailed policy proposals receive far less coverage than their soundbites or gaffes. During the 2016 and 2020 elections, the media often focused on Donald Trump's provocative statements rather than the specifics of his policy agenda. Similarly, while Joe Biden's platform included comprehensive plans on healthcare, climate change, and the economy, much of the media coverage cantered on his demeanour, his past political record, or his response to Trump's attacks. The substance of the policies was often sidelined in favour of moments that could be easily distilled into a tweet or a headline.

The prevalence of soundbites affects public understanding by prioritizing personality over policy. When the media focuses on short, sensationalized quotes rather than the underlying issues, it reinforces the perception that politics is more about entertainment and drama than governance. This shift diminishes the role of journalism as an intermediary between complex political processes and the public's understanding of them.

Social Media Journalism

The rise of social media platforms like Twitter, Facebook, and Instagram has transformed how people consume news, offering both opportunities and challenges. On one hand, social media provides an immediate, direct channel for political information, making it accessible to a broader audience. On the other hand, these platforms thrive on engagement and attention, which are often achieved through sensationalism rather than accuracy or depth. Social media algorithms amplify content that garners the most clicks, likes, and shares, usually the most polarizing and emotionally charged posts.

Politicians themselves have adapted to this landscape, bypassing traditional media channels and using social media to communicate directly with their base. This shift has made policy announcements quicker, but also more superficial. For instance, rather than presenting a detailed plan for healthcare reform, a politician might tweet a bold statement promising change, leaving the media and public to fill in the gaps. In such an environment, there is little room for the nuance and analysis that complex policy issues require.

Social media's preference for quick, digestible content further marginalizes in-depth journalism. When nuanced policy discussions struggle to capture attention in a feed dominated by provocative headlines and viral videos, the public's ability to engage with and understand these issues diminishes. The lack of depth in news consumed on social media means that voters often rely on brief impressions rather than comprehensive analyses when forming their political opinions. This shift creates a feedback loop where politicians are incentivized to prioritize spectacle over substance, knowing that it will be rewarded with more visibility and support.

The Financial Realities of Modern Journalism

The decline in in-depth journalism is not just a result of changing technology but also the financial realities facing news organizations. The traditional business model of newspapers, relying on subscriptions and advertising revenue, has been disrupted by the rise of online platforms like Google and Facebook, which dominate the digital ad market. As newspapers and other traditional media struggle to stay afloat, they are forced to cut costs, leading to smaller newsrooms and fewer resources dedicated to investigative reporting.

This financial squeeze means that in-depth policy analysis, once a hallmark of quality journalism, has become a luxury that many outlets can no longer afford. Coverage of complex issues like healthcare reform, tax policy, or international relations often requires significant time, expertise, and resources. In today's media landscape, where the demand for rapid and frequent updates is high, investing in detailed analysis can seem like a poor business decision for news organizations operating on tight budgets.

As a result, newsrooms increasingly rely on wire services like the Associated Press or Reuters for policy coverage, leading to a homogenization of news content across outlets. The same brief summary of a policy decision, stripped of in-depth analysis or local relevance, appears on multiple platforms. This lack of diversity in reporting leaves readers with fewer opportunities to engage with detailed, nuanced perspectives.

The Shift Toward Opinion Journalism

Another trend that has emerged as traditional journalism declines is the rise of opinion journalism. In-depth analysis has increasingly been replaced by commentary and punditry. Opinion journalism is less resource-intensive and more suited to the fast-paced digital environment where speed and engagement are paramount. While opinion pieces provide valuable perspectives, they often prioritize the author's viewpoint over objective analysis. This shift has led to a landscape where news is more polarized, with outlets catering to specific audiences by reinforcing their existing beliefs rather than challenging them with factual, investigative reporting.

The abundance of opinion journalism also creates an environment where policy discussions become more about framing an argument than about understanding the issue. For example, rather than explaining the complexities of a proposed healthcare reform, an opinion piece might focus on whether the reform aligns with a particular ideological stance. The public, therefore, is presented with a pre-packaged narrative rather than an opportunity to engage with the details and implications of the policy itself.

This shift contributes to the public's declining ability to critically assess policy issues. When news becomes more about opinion and less about facts, it diminishes the role of journalism as a tool for education and engagement. Without detailed reporting to provide the necessary background, context, and analysis, the public's understanding of policy issues becomes fragmented and superficial.

The Consequences: A Less Informed Electorate

The cumulative effect of the decline in in-depth journalism is a less informed electorate. When media coverage prioritizes personality, soundbites, and sensationalism, the public is left with a limited understanding of the policies that shape their lives. This has significant consequences for democratic participation and accountability. Without a deep understanding of policy, voters are more likely to make decisions based on emotion, identity, or loyalty to a charismatic leader rather than an informed evaluation of the issues at hand.

For example, during debates on healthcare reform in the United States, many voters lacked a clear understanding of the differences between proposals like the Affordable Care Act (ACA) and its alternatives. Media coverage often focused on the political battles and the personalities involved rather than explaining the specific impacts of these policies. This lack of depth left many voters making choices based on partisan loyalties rather than a nuanced understanding of how different policies would affect their healthcare access and costs.

The decline of in-depth journalism also affects political accountability. In a media environment dominated by personality-driven coverage, politicians can more easily escape scrutiny for their policy decisions. When the public lacks the information needed to critically assess the impact of policies, leaders are less likely to be held accountable for their actions. This dynamic allows for superficial or populist rhetoric to dominate, further distancing governance from substantive, fact-based decision-making.

Reviving In-Depth Journalism: Challenges and Possibilities

Reviving in-depth journalism in today's media landscape is no small feat. It requires financial investment, public demand for detailed reporting, and a shift in how news is produced and consumed. Some outlets, such as *ProPublica* and *The Intercept*, have attempted to fill the gap by focusing on investigative journalism, relying on donations and grants rather than traditional ad revenue. These efforts demonstrate that there is still an appetite for deep, rigorous reporting, but they remain exceptions rather than the norm.

Public awareness and education are also essential to reversing this trend. Encouraging media literacy and critical thinking skills can empower the public to seek out and support quality journalism. News consumers must become active participants, valuing depth over speed and quality over sensationalism. Ultimately, the decline of in-depth journalism is not just a media problem; it is a societal one. As long as quick, entertaining news is prioritized over thorough analysis, the public's understanding of policy issues will remain limited, undermining the democratic process.

The decline of in-depth journalism has reshaped the American media landscape, reducing public understanding of policy issues and transforming politics into a spectacle centred around personality. Addressing this decline will require systemic changes, including new business models for media, public education initiatives, and a cultural shift towards valuing the depth and nuance of serious journalism. Only by restoring in-depth analysis can the media reclaim its role as a vital force for an informed and engaged democracy.

Crisis Amplification: Media Amplification of Crises and the Portrayal of the President as a "Saviour" Figure

The modern presidency is often defined by its relationship with crisis. Whether it's an economic downturn, a natural disaster, a terrorist attack, or a pandemic, how the president responds can become the defining moment of their time in office. Yet, the way these crises are amplified by the media and the way the president is cast as a central, almost heroic figure in their resolution reveals much about the intersection of media dynamics, personality politics, and public expectation.

Crisis has a unique way of capturing attention, and the media, ever hungry for stories that engage viewers, has become a central player in turning moments of national peril into spectacles. In these spectacles, the president is positioned not just as a leader, but as a "saviour" figure, a person whose actions will determine the fate of the nation. This framing amplifies the visibility of the president, enhancing their public persona while simultaneously overshadowing the complexities of governance and the systemic challenges that often underlie these crises.

The Role of Media in Crisis Amplification

In the age of 24-hour news cycles and social media, the amplification of crises has become a defining feature of modern politics. When a crisis emerges, the media reacts swiftly, broadcasting live updates, expert analyses, and emotional stories of those impacted. The immediacy and intensity of this coverage create a sense of urgency, and in the rush to provide up-to-the-minute information, the media often gravitates towards focusing on a single, central figure: the president.

The president's role in a crisis, however, is complicated. While they do have the power to mobilize resources and make critical decisions, their ability to manage complex, multifaceted events is limited by institutional, political, and logistical constraints. Yet, in the heat of a crisis, the media narrative often overlooks these complexities, presenting the president as the decisive actor who can, and must, bring about resolution. This portrayal plays into the expectation that the president not only leads the nation but also embodies its hopes, fears, and aspirations.

This dynamic can be traced back to earlier moments in American history. Franklin Delano Roosevelt's handling of the Great Depression and World War II, for example, helped cement the image of the president as the nation's saviour. Roosevelt's fireside chats reassured a worried public and framed him as a guiding, paternal figure who could steer America through economic catastrophe and global conflict. This narrative, while effective in mobilizing support, also set a precedent: presidents would be expected to play a central, heroic role in future crises, regardless of the true nature of their influence.

Crisis as a Stage for Charismatic Leadership

Crisis situations create opportunities for presidents to demonstrate charisma and leadership. Media amplification of these events, and the focus on the president as the key figure, often enhances the perception of the presidency as a role not just of governance but of personal heroism. This has become a recurring pattern in American politics, where presidents are seen as the face of the nation's response to crises, whether they have a direct hand in managing them or not.

Take, for example, the aftermath of the September 11, 2001 terrorist attacks. In that moment of national tragedy, George W. Bush was portrayed as a figure of strength and resolve. His visit to Ground Zero, where he addressed rescue workers with a bullhorn, became an iconic image of leadership. The media's coverage of this event, highlighting Bush's presence and his words, transformed him into a symbol of resilience. Despite the vast complexity of the subsequent military and intelligence operations that defined the American response, the image of Bush as the "saviour" of a nation under attack persisted. This moment amplified his public persona, solidifying his role as a wartime president and demonstrating how the media, in its amplification of crisis, plays a key role in shaping presidential image.

The Pandemic Presidency: COVID-19 and Crisis Leadership

The COVID-19 pandemic offers another example of how media amplification of a crisis frames the president as the central figure. From the beginning, the media's focus on the unfolding health emergency was relentless, with constant updates, live press conferences, and expert panels dissecting the federal government's response. The crisis presented an unprecedented challenge, one that affected every aspect of American life. In such moments, the public looks to the president for reassurance, guidance, and, ultimately, solutions.

For Donald Trump, the pandemic became a defining test of his leadership. His approach, often combative and controversial, dominated media coverage. Daily press briefings, where Trump presented himself as the decisive leader in control, became spectacles. The media's focus on these briefings, and on Trump's statements and actions, reinforced the expectation that the president would be the one to "save" America from the pandemic's impact. Trump's own emphasis on his role as a central figure further amplified this narrative. Whether it was promising a vaccine in record time or challenging public health recommendations, Trump's personality and style became focal points, overshadowing the collective efforts of scientists, public health officials, and state leaders working to manage the crisis.

The portrayal of the president as a saviour figure during the COVID-19 pandemic highlights a broader issue: in crises, the complexity of collaborative governance is often reduced to the actions and image of a single individual. This reductionist view, driven by media amplification, reinforces the illusion of presidential power. It suggests that the president alone can navigate the nation through disaster, even when the reality is that systemic coordination across agencies, states, and institutions is critical. By focusing so intensely on the president, the media narrative simplifies the response into a performance, where the president's visibility and charisma are prioritized over the nuanced, collective efforts necessary for effective crisis management.

Media Narratives and Public Perception: The "Saviour" Expectation

The media's portrayal of the president as a "saviour" figure is not without consequence. It shapes public perception and creates unrealistic expectations of presidential power. When the media amplifies a crisis, portraying the president as the central actor responsible for resolving it, it cultivates a belief that the president can, and should, be able to control and manage complex situations single-handedly. This perception, however, is often at odds with the realities of governance.

The expectation that the president will act as a saviour figure during crises was evident during Barack Obama's response to the 2008 financial crisis. When the economy collapsed, the media framed Obama's actions as decisive and critical in preventing a deeper economic catastrophe. His administration's response, which included a massive stimulus package and bailouts for struggling industries, was portrayed as a heroic effort led by Obama. Yet, the reality was far more complex. The policies were the product of negotiations, compromises, and the work of numerous economists and legislators. Still, the media's focus on Obama as the face of the response reinforced the perception that it was his leadership alone that saved the economy.

The "saviour" expectation becomes a double-edged sword. When presidents succeed in portraying themselves as effective crisis managers, they receive significant public support and an enhanced legacy. However, when their response falls short or is perceived as inadequate, the media narrative can turn against them, and they may face severe backlash. The same media amplification that initially framed them as heroes can quickly shift, portraying them as failures. This volatility in public perception is amplified by the media's need for a continuous narrative, often simplifying complex crises into tales of success or failure.

The Illusion of Control and Its Consequences

The portrayal of the president as a "saviour" figure, amplified by the media, reinforces the illusion of presidential control. It suggests that the president has the power to single-handedly manage and resolve national crises. However, this portrayal is often far removed from reality. The American presidency, despite its considerable influence, is embedded within a complex system of checks and balances, bureaucratic processes, and institutional constraints. In many cases, the president's power is more about coordination and persuasion than unilateral action.

This illusion of control can have significant consequences. When the public believes that the president has near-total power in a crisis, any perceived failure is attributed solely to the individual in office. This dynamic can undermine public trust in the broader government system and deepen polarization, as supporters and detractors rally around the president's handling of a crisis as a litmus test for their leadership. It also distracts from the underlying structural issues that may contribute to crises—issues that require systemic solutions rather than the charisma or decisiveness of a single leader.

Moving Beyond the "Saviour" Narrative

The media's amplification of crises and the portrayal of the president as a "saviour" figure illustrate the complexities of personality politics in the modern era. While the focus on the president can create powerful, unifying moments, it also risks oversimplifying the nature of governance and crisis management. The emphasis on the president's role often overshadows the broader, systemic efforts required to navigate national emergencies effectively.

As crises become increasingly complex and interconnected, ranging from climate change to global pandemics to economic instability, there is a need for a shift in how the media, and the public, perceive presidential power. Recognizing that crises are not solved by one individual but through coordinated, collaborative efforts is crucial for fostering a more realistic and informed understanding of governance.

The expectation of the president as a "saviour" is both a product of media narratives and a reflection of the public's desire for a figure of strength and certainty. However, moving beyond this illusion requires a collective effort to focus not just on the spectacle of leadership but on the substantive, often less visible work that underpins effective crisis response.

Image Management: Public Persona

The role of the American presidency has evolved into one that is as much about public image as it is about governance. In an era dominated by media saturation and constant scrutiny, every aspect of a leader's appearance and behaviour is carefully curated to align with the persona they want to project. This extends not only to presidents but also to vice presidents, who play a vital role in shaping and supporting the administration's image. From hairdressers and clothing stylists traveling with them to forming strategic relationships with celebrities and tech founders, modern leaders understand that maintaining a favourable image is crucial to influence public perception and remain in the spotlight.

The Hair and Style Teams: Crafting a Polished Image

Appearances definitely matter in politics, and for the American president and vice president, this is especially true. Maintaining a consistent and polished image requires a dedicated team of professionals who work behind the scenes to ensure that every public appearance aligns with the desired image. Hairdressers and clothing stylists are integral parts of the entourage, accompanying leaders on trips and ensuring that their appearance is meticulously managed at all times.

Barack Obama, for instance, had a long-time barber, Zariff, who was part of his image team for decades, ensuring his signature close-cropped style was always immaculate. Similarly, Kamala Harris, as the first female, Black, and South Asian vice president, is acutely aware of the visual narrative her appearance conveys. Her style choices are not incidental; they are a calculated part of her public image. Harris's wardrobe, often featuring sharp blazers and professional attire, is designed to project competence, authority, and modernity. She has worked with stylists to craft a look that balances power and approachability, signalling her readiness for leadership while also connecting with diverse audiences.

Harris's hair and makeup choices are equally strategic. In a political landscape where women's appearances are scrutinized intensely, Harris has maintained a consistent, polished look that reinforces her professionalism. Her hair, always neat and carefully styled, is a visual signal of her preparedness and attention to detail, essential elements in projecting an image of a capable leader. Behind these choices is a team of stylists who travel with her, ensuring that every appearance is consistent and in line with her broader image strategy.

Donald Trump's distinctive hairstyle, too, was a topic of much media discussion, and he reportedly had a dedicated stylist who travelled with him to maintain it. The hair of a president or vice president is not just about aesthetics; it becomes a symbol of their personality. For Harris, her polished, no-nonsense look conveys both her identity as a trailblazer and her readiness to govern.

Presidential Wardrobe: The Uniforms of Power

The clothes a president or vice president wears are far more than just fabric; they are symbols carefully chosen to convey messages to the public. In formal settings, the classic navy or black suit and tie are often used to convey authority, stability, and trustworthiness. These wardrobe choices are designed to make leaders appear "presidential" or "vice presidential" in the most traditional sense—visually reinforcing their legitimacy.

However, casual outfits are strategically employed when leaders want to appear more relatable and down-to-earth. Kamala Harris has been photographed in Converse sneakers and jeans, particularly during campaign events and casual visits. This choice, which quickly became iconic, was a calculated effort to connect with younger voters and portray herself as accessible and relatable. By wearing items associated with comfort and everyday life, Harris has crafted an image that blends professionalism with a sense of authenticity and approachability.

In the political arena, women are scrutinized far more intensely for their fashion choices than their male counterparts. It's an unfortunate reality, and definitely shouldn't be the case, but appearances are still viewed as a reflection of a woman's capability, professionalism, and even morality. Kamala Harris appears to be acutely aware of this dynamic, and she, like many other high-profile women in politics, uses her appearance as a strategic tool. Her consistent, polished look, well-coiffed hair, professional makeup, and tailored outfits, are not merely personal preference but a carefully curated image, one that signals to the public that she is competent, prepared, and ready to lead. The choices Harris makes are not hers alone; behind her is a team of stylists and image consultants who ensure her appearance is always aligned with the image of a professional, capable leader.

This level of scrutiny is not new, and Harris is not the first to navigate these treacherous waters. Historical figures like Princess Diana faced similar judgment. The late Princess of Wales became an international icon not just for her humanitarian work but also for her fashion sense. Every dress she wore, every hairstyle she chose was analysed, critiqued, and praised in equal measure. But for Diana, fashion was more than just an accessory; it was a statement. Whether she was in an elegant gown or casual jeans, she understood that her appearance was a form of communication, one that could sway public opinion and project an image of relatability, compassion, or elegance, depending on the occasion. Similarly, Kamala Harris's style choices are not accidental. They are deliberate and meticulously planned to resonate with her audience and reinforce her brand as a relatable yet authoritative figure.

Comparing Harris's style strategy to Princess Catherine, the current Princess of Wales, reveals how these pressures have persisted over the years. Catherine's fashion sense is widely admired, yet every outfit choice she makes is scrutinized not only for its aesthetic but for what it might signify about her role, her status, or her mood. The press and the public analyse everything, from the designers she wears to the colours she chooses. In some cases, her choice of attire is seen as a reflection of her values, wearing sustainable fashion, for instance, is a nod to her commitment to environmental causes. However, any deviation from her usual polished look can be seen as a misstep, reflecting the narrow expectations placed on women in the public eye.

Harris's experience is much the same. The expectation is that she must appear flawless, projecting strength without appearing too assertive, maintaining femininity without being seen as frivolous. The balance is delicate. Her hair is always styled in a neat, controlled manner, often worn down, feminine, but always well-groomed. This, too, is a choice aimed at reinforcing a sense of stability and competence. By keeping her hair consistent, Harris subtly communicates reliability, a key trait for someone in a position of leadership. Her makeup, similarly, is understated but purposeful, enhancing her features without becoming a distraction. It's about striking the right balance, showing that she takes her role seriously, without appearing too focused on aesthetics.

Behind these choices, of course, is a dedicated team of professionals who understand the stakes. Stylists, makeup artists, and fashion consultants travel with Harris, ensuring that her appearance remains consistent and aligned with the image she wants to project. They adjust her look based on the occasion, whether it's a formal event, a television appearance, or a public speech, all while maintaining the central theme of professionalism and competence. The level of attention to detail is immense, and while this kind of strategic management is often unseen by the public, it plays a crucial role in how she is perceived.

Harris's style choices also include culturally significant touches that speak to her heritage and identity. For example, she has been known to wear pearls, which have historical significance as a symbol of strength and femininity within African-American sororities like Alpha Kappa Alpha, of which she is a member.

What is striking, though, is that while women like Harris, Diana, and Catherine are judged and sometimes celebrated for their fashion choices, this same attention often carries an implicit critique. Women in public life are expected to maintain an impossible standard, appear perfectly styled, yet not overly focused on fashion; display elegance, but not so much that it overshadows their professional achievements. A male counterpart, meanwhile, might only be required to wear a suit and tie to be considered appropriately dressed, his fashion choices rarely making headlines unless they deviate significantly from the norm.

Kamala Harris's style strategy, like those of Diana and Catherine, highlights the double standard that women in positions of power face. It shouldn't be necessary for a woman's appearance to be scrutinized as closely as her policies, but in the current political and cultural climate, it is. For Harris, maintaining a consistent, polished image is not just about fashion, it's about managing perception and ensuring that her professionalism is communicated in every possible way. By doing so, she not only navigates these pressures but also subtly challenges them, using her appearance as a tool to command respect and convey authority, even within a system that remains frustratingly superficial in its expectations.

Barack Obama similarly embraced the "business-casual" look, often appearing in rolled-up sleeves and khakis during town halls and campaign stops. This style helped to break down the traditional barriers between the president and the public, emphasizing accessibility. Meanwhile, Donald Trump's consistent use of power suits and bold ties projected an image of strength and dominance, reinforcing his identity as a businessman-turned-politician who embodied wealth and authority.

These wardrobe choices are not merely about appearance; they are carefully curated symbols that communicate messages of heritage, strength, and solidarity with her supporters.

Celebrities and Influencers: Building Strategic Relationships

Another key aspect of image management for presidents and vice presidents is their relationships with celebrities and influential figures. By aligning themselves with well-known personalities, leaders can enhance their image and tap into new audiences. The strategic use of celebrity endorsements and associations has become a powerful tool for modern leaders seeking to remain relevant and appealing in a culture increasingly obsessed with fame.

Barack Obama's presidency exemplified this strategy. He frequently appeared with popular celebrities, musicians, and tech moguls, blending politics with popular culture. He was photographed alongside Beyoncé and Jay-Z, invited actors and musicians to the White House, and even participated in comedic sketches with comedians like Zach Galifianakis on *Between Two Ferns*. These appearances were calculated efforts to connect with younger voters and portray Obama as a modern, culturally savvy leader.

Kamala Harris has continued this tradition. She has cultivated relationships with celebrities such as Mindy Kaling and Kerry Washington, leveraging their platforms to reach wider audiences. These connections are not coincidental; they are part of a broader strategy to engage with diverse demographics, particularly younger and minority voters. Harris's appearance on Kaling's social media, for example, where the two cooked Indian food together, was designed to showcase her relatability and highlight her heritage. By creating these moments with popular figures, Harris enhances her image as a leader who is both connected to and reflective of America's diversity.

Donald Trump's relationship with celebrities was more contentious but equally strategic. As a former reality TV star, Trump understood the power of celebrity. He maintained ties with figures like Kanye West and Kim Kardashian, using their influence to amplify his image among their massive followings. Trump's meetings with these celebrities were highly publicized, and the image of Trump with Kim Kardashian was designed to convey his openness and interest in criminal justice reform while simultaneously benefiting from the attention of Kardashian's millions of social media followers.

The cultivation of these relationships is not merely incidental; it is a calculated effort to keep leaders in the public eye, ensuring that they remain relevant and present in the cultural conversation. It blurs the lines between politics, entertainment, and celebrity culture, showing how the modern presidency and vice presidency have transformed into ongoing performances where visibility is crucial.

Leveraging Social Media: The Personal Touch

Social media has become an indispensable tool in image management for modern political figures. Platforms like Twitter, Instagram, and Facebook allow presidents and vice presidents to curate their own narratives, bypassing traditional media filters and presenting themselves directly to the public. This unfiltered access allows them to craft a persona that is both relatable and dynamic, engaging with followers in real-time.

Barack Obama was one of the first presidents to leverage social media effectively, building an online presence that highlighted his charisma, humour, and relatability. His official accounts posted images of him with his family, at casual events, and in everyday situations, presenting a humanized version of the presidency that contrasted with the distant, formal images of previous administrations.

Kamala Harris has continued and expanded this approach, using social media to showcase her work and personal side simultaneously. Her posts often feature behind-the-scenes looks at her travels, meetings with community leaders, and casual moments that highlight her approachable demeanour. By sharing moments like making cornbread for Thanksgiving or visiting local businesses, Harris crafts a relatable image that resonates with a broad audience. These posts are strategically designed to humanize her, connecting her work in the administration with the everyday lives of Americans.

Donald Trump's use of Twitter was a defining feature of his presidency. His unfiltered style, controversial statements, and direct engagement ensured that he remained the centre of media attention. His use of Twitter was nothing short of a political phenomenon, and it became a defining feature of his presidency. His unfiltered style, controversial statements, and direct engagement ensured that he remained the centre of media attention, often bypassing traditional news outlets to speak directly to millions of followers. Trump's tweets created a digital spectacle, transforming the platform into a tool for visibility, influence, and immediate reaction. Unlike his predecessors or contemporaries like Barack Obama or Kamala Harris, who used social media to connect in a more measured, polished way, Trump wielded Twitter as if it was a weapon, his posts were often provocative, inflammatory, and headline-grabbing.

However, this approach, while effective in keeping him in the spotlight, eventually led to his downfall on the platform. In the wake of the January 6th Capitol riot, Twitter permanently banned Trump's account, citing the risk of further incitement of violence. This ban was a major blow to Trump's digital presence and influence. Stripped of his preferred method of communication, he lost direct access to the platform where he had amassed over 88 million followers and, with it, a significant part of his political and media clout.

In response to the ban, Trump sought to create an alternative. In October 2021, he launched his own social media platform, Truth Social. This move was both a reaction to his expulsion from mainstream social media and an attempt to reclaim control over his messaging and audience. Truth Social was marketed as a platform that would champion free speech and provide a space for Trump's supporters who felt marginalized by Big Tech's regulations and censorship. However, while the platform attracted loyal followers, its reach paled in comparison to the global audience he once commanded on Twitter. Without the same widespread influence, Trump found himself on a smaller stage, unable to dominate the news cycle in the same way he once had.

In late 2022, following Elon Musk's acquisition of Twitter, the platform reinstated Trump's account. Musk's decision to reverse the ban was seen as a move to champion free speech, aligning with his stated mission to make Twitter a more open and less regulated space. Trump's return to Twitter, however, was not without hesitation. Initially, he expressed loyalty to Truth Social, where he had invested time and resources to build an independent platform. For a time, he resisted rejoining Twitter, framing his departure as a protest against censorship.

But as the 2024 election season ramped up, Trump recognized the strategic advantage of being on Twitter, where his reach was exponentially greater. Ultimately, the opportunity to once again tap into the platform's vast audience and its influential role in shaping political narratives was too powerful to ignore. His return to Twitter symbolized a pragmatic move to regain the digital influence and visibility that defined his earlier political career.

Trump's journey from Twitter dominance to his ban, the launch of Truth Social, and his eventual return underscores the shifting landscape of social media and politics. It highlights the challenge political figures face in maintaining influence while navigating platforms that hold the power to silence them. For Trump, Twitter wasn't just a social media account; it was a political stage, a megaphone, and a means to craft his public persona. His ability to reclaim this space reveals the critical role of social media in modern political image management and the lengths politicians will go to maintain their digital presence.

The Machinery Behind the Persona

As we have discussed, managing the image of a president or vice president is a complex, well-coordinated effort that involves a team of professionals, stylists, hairdressers, image consultants, and social media experts, all working together to shape a consistent and appealing public persona. It requires an understanding of media dynamics, public expectations, and the cultural zeitgeist. Presidents and vice presidents must not only perform the duties of governance but also navigate the demands of public attention, ensuring that every appearance, outfit, and interaction contributes to the narrative they wish to project.

The presidency and vice presidency are as much about optics as they are about policy. The ways leaders manage their public image, through style, celebrity relationships, and social media, reflect a shift in how leadership is perceived and evaluated. The public's craving for relatable, charismatic, and constantly visible leaders has transformed these offices into continuous performances, where the art of image management is not just an accessory to politics but a central pillar of political power.

The Illusion of Presidential Power

CHAPTER 4

FRAMING THE OPPOSITION AS THREATS

In 2020, then-presidential candidate Donald Trump repeatedly claimed that his opponent, Joe Biden, and the Democratic Party were not just political rivals but were actively working to "destroy the American way of life." Trump's rhetoric framed his opposition as an existential threat, suggesting that their policies would lead to economic collapse, widespread lawlessness, and the erosion of American values. This strategic narrative, amplified through social media and campaign rallies, wasn't a new tactic; it was a modern iteration of an age-old political manoeuvre.

By positioning rivals as adversaries of the state, presidents are able to consolidate power, rally their base, and justify controversial policies or actions under the guise of protecting the nation.

This approach isn't new; it finds its roots in the earliest political systems of ancient Rome and Greece. In Rome, leaders like Julius Caesar accused political adversaries in the Senate of betraying the Republic, using these accusations to justify crossing the Rubicon and seizing power. Similarly, Augustus depicted his enemies as threats to the peace and stability he promised to restore, paving the way for his consolidation of power and the transition from Republic to Empire. These tactics were mirrored in Greece, where leaders such as Pericles framed critics of his war strategies as undermining Athens' unity and democracy, rallying the citizenry to support his policies under the banner of patriotism and survival.

This historical continuity illustrates the enduring effectiveness of framing opposition as a threat. By portraying opponents as dangerous or unpatriotic, leaders can galvanize support, suppress dissent, and gain unchecked authority.

In 1968, during a time of political and social upheaval, Richard Nixon's presidential campaign used the rhetoric of "law and order" to great effect. Nixon positioned himself as the champion of a silent majority, people who were, according to his framing, under threat from the chaos and disorder caused by anti-war protesters, civil rights activists, and liberal politicians. By casting his opposition not just as political rivals but as a force undermining the stability of the nation, he created a dichotomy where voters were forced to choose between safety and security or disorder and unrest. This powerful narrative tapped into the fears of many Americans, allowing Nixon to frame himself as the guardian of American values while casting his opponents as agents of chaos. This example underscores a central theme in American politics: the art of political demonization.

Throughout history, presidents and their administrations have mastered the craft of framing their opponents as existential threats. This tactic is not merely about discrediting a rival; it is about creating an emotional narrative that resonates deeply with the public. Political demonization is a sophisticated and calculated effort to rally support, discredit adversaries, and consolidate power by appealing to fear, patriotism, and identity. In this section, we delve into the techniques and strategies used in this process, exploring how the language and imagery employed by leaders shape public perception and bolster their authority.

Techniques of Demonization

The art of political demonization is built on a few key techniques, each designed to target the emotions and psyche of the electorate. One of the most common methods is *labelling opponents as unpatriotic or traitorous*. This strategy works because it taps into a deep-seated sense of national pride and identity. By questioning an opponent's loyalty, a leader can rally the public to view them as not just wrong, but as fundamentally dangerous to the country's well-being.

For instance, during World War I, President Woodrow Wilson's administration painted critics of the war effort as traitors, even passing the Espionage Act of 1917 and the Sedition Act of 1918 to silence dissent. Wilson's rhetoric suggested that those opposing the war were aiding the enemy, aligning them with foreign threats. This framing allowed the administration to justify crackdowns on free speech and civil liberties, presenting them as necessary measures for national security. The psychological impact was profound: dissent became synonymous with disloyalty, and opposition voices were marginalized, effectively rallying the public around a united, patriotic cause.

Another effective method is *aligning opponents with foreign enemies or ideologies*. This tactic was particularly potent during the Cold War, when presidents like Harry Truman and Ronald Reagan positioned their domestic opponents as sympathetic to communism. By aligning rivals with foreign adversaries, these leaders created a stark binary: you were either with America or against it. Truman's framing of communism as an "internal threat" justified his policies and portrayed any opposition as endangering American values and security. Reagan continued this legacy, branding critics of his aggressive foreign policy as appeasers who lacked the courage to stand up to the Soviet Union. This tactic ensured that any dissenting voices could be easily discredited, not for their policies or ideas, but for their perceived lack of loyalty to the nation.

A third approach, often intertwined with the previous ones, is *suggesting that opponents pose a direct threat to societal stability and public order*. This strategy plays on fear and anxiety, portraying the opposition as an immediate danger to everyday life. Nixon's 1968 campaign is a quintessential example, but similar rhetoric has been used across the political spectrum. For instance, during the Red Scare of the 1950s, Senator Joseph McCarthy and, by extension, President Dwight D. Eisenhower's administration, depicted leftist politicians, intellectuals, and civil rights activists as dangerous radicals seeking to disrupt the American way of life. The implication was clear: supporting these individuals or even tolerating their ideas was equivalent to inviting chaos and subversion. The imagery of an America under siege, infiltrated by enemies both foreign and domestic, created a climate of fear that allowed the administration to justify restrictive and invasive policies.

Constructing the Narrative: Language and Imagery

The success of political demonization relies heavily on the language and imagery used to construct the narrative. It is not enough for leaders to simply state that their opponents are dangerous; they must craft a story that feels real and immediate to their audience. This involves the use of *emotionally charged language*, symbolic imagery, and metaphors that resonate with cultural values and fears.

Consider the language used by President George W. Bush in the aftermath of the September 11 attacks. By framing the War on Terror as a battle between good and evil, Bush positioned his administration as the defender of freedom and democracy against the forces of darkness. Critics of his policies were often labelled as unpatriotic or accused of "not supporting the troops," effectively silencing dissent. The use of terms like "axis of evil" and "with us or against us" was not arbitrary; it was a deliberate effort to create a narrative that polarized the political landscape. The simplicity of the language made it easy for the public to grasp and internalize, transforming complex political debates into a moral struggle.

The psychological impact of such rhetoric is significant. It taps into a primal fear, the fear of the 'other', and mobilizes it into action. When leaders frame their opponents as existential threats, they activate survival instincts in the electorate, pushing them to seek protection and safety. This often means rallying around the leader who promises to safeguard them, even if it involves supporting extreme or controversial measures. The effectiveness of this tactic is evident in the way Bush was able to pass sweeping legislation, such as the Patriot Act, and expand executive powers in ways that would have been unthinkable before the attacks.

Psychological Manipulation: Fear, Patriotism, and Identity

The success of political demonization hinges on its ability to manipulate psychological factors such as fear, patriotism, and identity. By framing opponents as threats, leaders can foster a sense of urgency that overrides rational debate and critical thinking. Fear, in particular, is a powerful motivator. When people feel threatened, they are more likely to seek security, even if it means sacrificing certain freedoms or accepting information without question.

Patriotism is another key element in the demonization process. By appealing to national pride, leaders can create a powerful 'us versus them' dynamic. This is why accusations of disloyalty or unpatriotic behaviour are so effective; they tap into the deep-rooted identity that many people have with their country. When leaders suggest that their opponents are working against the nation's interests, they cast themselves as the protectors of the national identity, encouraging people to rally around them as the embodiment of the country's values.

In this context, *identity politics* plays a crucial role. By aligning themselves with certain groups and positioning their opponents as enemies of those groups, leaders can create a sense of solidarity and loyalty among their supporters. For example, President Donald Trump often framed his opponents as enemies of "real Americans," a phrase that resonated deeply with his base. By suggesting that his critics were aligned with elites, immigrants, or other groups perceived as 'outsiders,' he reinforced the idea that supporting him was not just a political choice but a cultural and identity-driven imperative.

Consequences and Risks of Political Demonization

While the strategy of framing opponents as threats is effective, it comes with significant risks. When leaders rely heavily on demonizing rhetoric, they deepen political polarization, making it difficult to govern effectively or achieve compromise. By positioning themselves as defenders against an ever-present threat, they create an environment where opposition voices are not just ignored but vilified, leading to an erosion of democratic discourse.

This tactic can also backfire if the narrative proves unsustainable or if the threats appear exaggerated. For example, during the Vietnam War, President Lyndon B. Johnson and his administration initially framed the conflict as a fight against communist expansion and a defence of freedom. However, as the war dragged on and the human and economic costs became apparent, the public grew increasingly sceptical of this narrative. Johnson's credibility suffered, leading to a loss of support and a divided nation. The same tactic that initially rallied people to his cause eventually contributed to his political downfall.

The long-term effects of this strategy are also concerning. By constantly framing opposition as a threat, leaders risk eroding public trust in institutions and undermining the legitimacy of the democratic system itself. When every election becomes a battle for the soul of the nation and every opponent is depicted as an existential threat, it becomes harder for citizens to engage in constructive political debate or see politics as anything other than a zero-sum game. This deepens divisions and can lead to a cycle of escalating rhetoric, where each side feels justified in using increasingly extreme tactics.

The art of political demonization is a powerful tool that has been used by leaders throughout history to consolidate power and shape public perception. While effective in rallying support and discrediting opponents, it is a double-edged sword that, if wielded irresponsibly, can deepen polarization, erode democratic norms, and undermine the credibility of those who use it. As history and contemporary examples show, the consequences of framing the opposition as threats are profound, shaping not only the political landscape of the present but the democratic health of the nation in the future.

John Adams and the Alien and Sedition Acts
One of the earliest and most striking examples of a president framing the opposition as a threat occurred during John Adams' presidency in the late 1790s. At the time, the United States was a young and fragile nation, and tensions were high between Federalists, who supported Adams, and Democratic-Republicans, led by Thomas Jefferson. The Federalists, fearing the influence of France amidst the ongoing French Revolutionary Wars, sought to strengthen the government's grip on power. For Adams and his supporters, the opposition wasn't just a political rival, it was a potential threat to national security.

In this climate of fear and suspicion, Adams' administration passed the Alien and Sedition Acts in 1798. These laws were justified as necessary to protect the country from foreign influence and internal dissent, but their true purpose was more politically motivated. The Alien Acts, which allowed the president to imprison or deport non-citizens deemed dangerous, were aimed particularly at French immigrants, who were perceived to be sympathetic to the Democratic-Republican cause. By positioning immigrants as potential enemies and aligning them with his political opposition, Adams effectively painted the Democratic-Republicans as unpatriotic and sympathetic to foreign powers.

The Sedition Act, however, was the most direct attempt to stifle opposition. This law made it illegal to publish "false, scandalous, and malicious writing" against the government or its officials—a clear infringement on freedom of speech. Under this act, numerous Democratic-Republican newspaper editors and critics were arrested and prosecuted, their voices silenced by a government that portrayed them as dangerous agitators undermining the stability of the fledgling nation.

Adams' framing of his opponents as threats was not only an attempt to suppress dissent but also a means to secure his position amidst growing political division. By aligning his critics with foreign adversaries and portraying them as traitors, Adams sought to rally public support around his leadership and Federalist policies. His administration's narrative implied that any criticism of the government was not just opposition but betrayal, a message designed to polarize the public and strengthen his grip on power.

However, the strategy backfired. The Alien and Sedition Acts were deeply unpopular and were seen by many as a violation of constitutional rights. Rather than solidifying Adams' hold on power, they fuelled resentment and galvanized the opposition. Thomas Jefferson and the Democratic-Republicans seized on the public's discontent, framing Adams and the Federalists as tyrants. The backlash helped propel Jefferson to victory in the election of 1800, illustrating that while framing the opposition as a threat can be a powerful tool, it is also a double-edged sword that can alienate the public and undermine the very authority it seeks to protect.

Andrew Jackson and the National Bank

A few decades later, Andrew Jackson, the seventh president of the United States, also used the tactic of framing opposition as a threat, this time targeting a powerful institution rather than an individual or group. During his presidency in the 1830s, Jackson faced off against the Second Bank of the United States, an institution he viewed as a symbol of corruption and elite power. The Bank, led by Nicholas Biddle, was a central element of the American financial system, managing federal deposits and controlling much of the country's credit. To Jackson, however, it represented a threat to democracy and the interests of ordinary Americans.

Jackson's opposition to the Bank was not merely a policy disagreement; it was a full-scale political battle in which he framed the institution as an enemy of the people. He accused the Bank of being an undemocratic monopoly that wielded too much influence over the economy and politics, suggesting that it was controlled by a wealthy elite who used it to manipulate and oppress ordinary citizens. By casting the Bank as an adversary of the people, Jackson positioned himself as a populist champion fighting for the rights and freedoms of average Americans.

The rhetoric Jackson used was designed to evoke fear and distrust among the public. He portrayed the Bank as a dangerous and unchecked power that threatened the nation's economic independence. In his famous veto message against the recharter of the Bank in 1832, Jackson argued that it was unconstitutional and that it concentrated power in the hands of a privileged few at the expense of the American people. He claimed that the Bank had the potential to corrupt the government and influence elections, painting it as a force undermining the very fabric of democracy.

This narrative was effective in rallying support among his base. Jackson's portrayal of the Bank as a corrupt entity resonated with many Americans who were wary of concentrated financial power and who felt disconnected from the political elite. By framing the Bank as a threat to national interests and positioning himself as the defender of the common man, Jackson was able to justify his drastic actions, including the removal of federal deposits from the Bank and their redistribution to smaller state banks, a move that would later be referred to as the "Bank War."

Jackson's strategy of framing the Bank as an existential threat allowed him to wield executive power in an unprecedented manner. By rallying the public against a common enemy, he built a coalition that supported his controversial policies and solidified his control over the political landscape. The success of his campaign against the Bank reinforced the effectiveness of casting opposition, whether it be an institution, policy, or group, as a threat to national values and democracy.

However, as with Adams' use of the Alien and Sedition Acts, Jackson's tactics also had long-term consequences. His dismantling of the Bank led to economic instability, contributing to the Panic of 1837. The aftermath of his crusade against the Bank showed that while framing an opponent as a threat could mobilize support and consolidate power, it could also lead to unintended consequences that damaged both the presidency and the nation's economy.

The Lasting Legacy of Early Examples

The early examples of John Adams and Andrew Jackson demonstrate the power and risks of framing opposition as a threat in American politics. In each case, the presidents employed rhetoric and legislation to depict their adversaries as dangers to national security or the democratic system. This tactic allowed them to rally their supporters, suppress dissent, and justify controversial measures, all under the guise of protecting the nation's interests.

Adams' and Jackson's presidencies illustrate how framing opposition as a threat is not just a tool for consolidating power but also a method for shaping public perception. By casting their opponents as existential threats, these leaders were able to manipulate the narrative, presenting themselves as protectors of the Republic. This approach, while effective in the short term, also had the potential to backfire, as seen with Adams' loss in 1800 and the economic fallout from Jackson's Bank War.

The legacy of these early examples continues to influence American politics. The techniques employed by Adams and Jackson set a precedent for future leaders, showing that framing the opposition as a threat could be a powerful means of mobilizing public support and maintaining control. However, they also serve as cautionary tales, highlighting the dangers of overreaching and the potential backlash that can occur when the public perceives such tactics as an abuse of power.

Enter The Cold War

The Cold War Era was a time of heightened tension, fear, and political manoeuvring, where the United States faced what it perceived as an existential threat: communism. Against this backdrop, American presidents, notably Harry Truman and Richard Nixon, used the spectre of communism not only as a tool to shape foreign policy but also as a powerful domestic weapon to discredit political opponents and rally support for their administrations. The strategy was clear, by casting their critics and rivals as sympathetic to communism or, worse, as agents of foreign adversaries, these leaders could consolidate power, justify controversial policies, and manipulate public opinion to achieve their political goals. This narrative became an effective means of framing opposition as a threat, creating an "us versus them" mentality that resonated with an anxious and divided American public.

Harry Truman and the Early Cold War Tensions

In the immediate aftermath of World War II, the geopolitical landscape was rapidly shifting. The Soviet Union emerged as a powerful adversary, and the United States found itself in a global struggle for influence. President Harry Truman recognized the power of this moment, using the perceived threat of communism to reshape American politics. Truman's administration capitalized on the growing fear of Soviet expansionism by presenting the Cold War not just as an international struggle but as a conflict that could seep into the very fabric of American society.

Truman's rhetoric was designed to unify the nation and establish a clear, uncompromising position against communism. In his famous 1947 address to Congress, Truman articulated what would become known as the Truman Doctrine, declaring that the United States must support "free peoples who are resisting attempted subjugation by armed minorities or by outside pressures." While this message was aimed primarily at justifying American intervention in Greece and Turkey, it also set the stage for a broader narrative: communism wasn't just a threat abroad; it was a threat at home.

By framing the opposition to his policies as being soft on communism or failing to recognize the threat it posed, Truman effectively silenced dissenting voices. The House Un-American Activities Committee (HUAC) became a key tool in this campaign, investigating and persecuting those suspected of communist sympathies. The notion that critics of Truman's foreign policy might be secretly aligned with Soviet interests allowed his administration to sideline those who questioned the costs or efficacy of his approach. It wasn't just about preventing the spread of communism; it was about delegitimizing political opponents by casting them as dangerous or unpatriotic.

The Rise of McCarthyism

The climate of suspicion and fear that Truman helped cultivate would reach its peak with Senator Joseph McCarthy's infamous crusade against alleged communists within the U.S. government and beyond. While McCarthy was not a president, his tactics and influence were closely aligned with the broader objectives of the Truman administration. The hysteria he generated helped reinforce the narrative that communism was not merely a foreign ideology but an insidious force infiltrating American institutions.

McCarthy's approach was ruthless. By accusing government officials, Hollywood actors, and even ordinary citizens of communist sympathies, he created an environment where fear and paranoia thrived. His accusations were often based on flimsy evidence or none at all, but the very act of being accused was enough to ruin reputations and careers. Truman's administration, though not directly responsible for McCarthy's actions, benefited from the atmosphere of fear he created. The narrative of a "Red Scare" allowed Truman to justify continued aggressive actions abroad and increased surveillance and restrictions at home.

It's important to note that while Truman publicly distanced himself from some of McCarthy's more extreme rhetoric, the underlying message remained consistent: anyone questioning the government's actions or advocating for a softer approach to the Soviet Union was suspect. This tactic of framing opposition as a threat, branding critics as unpatriotic or even treasonous, was effective in stifling political dissent and rallying public support for a hardline foreign policy.

Richard Nixon and the Expansion of Anti-Communist Rhetoric

By the time Richard Nixon came to power, the Cold War had evolved, but the use of anti-communist sentiment as a political weapon remained central. Nixon, who had built his early career as a fervent anti-communist crusader during his time in Congress, was well-versed in the power of this narrative. He understood that framing political opposition as sympathetic to communism could be a potent tool for discrediting rivals and maintaining power.

Nixon's political rise was closely tied to his portrayal of himself as a staunch defender against the communist threat. In the 1940s, as a member of HUAC, he had gained national attention for his role in the Alger Hiss case, where he accused a former State Department official of being a Soviet spy. This early victory established his reputation as a hardline anti-communist and laid the foundation for his future political ambitions.

As president, Nixon continued to wield anti-communist rhetoric, but his approach became more sophisticated. Rather than simply branding opponents as communists, he expanded the definition of "threat" to encompass a broader spectrum of domestic and international actors. Nixon's administration labelled critics of the Vietnam War as unpatriotic, suggesting that opposition to the war was akin to supporting communist forces in North Vietnam. This strategy not only marginalized anti-war activists but also painted political rivals who expressed scepticism about the war effort as un-American.

The Strategic Use of the Media

Nixon's mastery of media manipulation allowed him to control the anti-communist narrative effectively. Unlike Truman, who primarily relied on speeches and congressional support, Nixon understood the growing influence of television and the press in shaping public opinion. By using media outlets sympathetic to his administration, Nixon crafted an image of himself as the protector of American interests against a vast, shadowy network of communist sympathizers.

For instance, Nixon's administration frequently leaked information to the press that painted opponents of his policies as linked to communist causes, whether that connection was real or fabricated. This strategy created a media environment where scepticism or criticism of Nixon's policies could be interpreted as support for America's enemies. The administration's use of propaganda, often cloaked as "leaks" or anonymous sources, became a vital tool in building a narrative that discredited political adversaries while solidifying public support for controversial policies.

Nixon's strategic framing extended beyond his domestic rivals. During his tenure, the United States faced growing anti-American sentiment abroad, especially in Latin America and Southeast Asia. Nixon portrayed these regions as hotbeds of communist activity, suggesting that any opposition to American intervention was aligned with the interests of the Soviet Union or China. This not only justified aggressive foreign policies but also painted those who questioned such policies as being on the wrong side of history, thus undermining their credibility and influence.

The Consequences of Anti-Communist Framing

While the use of anti-communist rhetoric was effective for both Truman and Nixon in consolidating power and rallying support, it came with significant consequences. The aggressive framing of political opposition as threats created an environment of fear and mistrust. Public confidence in democratic institutions began to erode as the narrative that enemies were lurking within the government took hold. This atmosphere of paranoia led to a widespread acceptance of invasive measures, such as increased surveillance and restrictions on civil liberties, all justified in the name of national security.

The persistent framing of opposition as dangerous or un-American contributed to the deepening of political polarization in the United States. By the late 1960s and early 1970s, the country was deeply divided, with mistrust and suspicion rampant across political lines. The fear-driven policies that arose from this environment often suppressed legitimate dissent and fostered a culture where questioning the government was equated with treason.

Nixon's eventual downfall, catalysed by the Watergate scandal, can be partially attributed to the toxic political environment his administration helped cultivate. As his anti-communist rhetoric grew more aggressive, so did his willingness to use illegal means to undermine opponents and maintain power. The narrative that framed all opposition as threats made it easier for Nixon to justify his abuses of power; after all, in his view, he was protecting the country from enemies both real and imagined.

The Legacy of Cold War Rhetoric

The Cold War era demonstrated the power of framing political opposition as threats, a tactic used effectively by both Truman and Nixon to gain and maintain power. By capitalizing on fear and suspicion, these leaders were able to justify controversial actions and silence critics. However, the long-term impact of these strategies also exposed the risks associated with such narratives. While effective in the short term, they contributed to political polarization, public mistrust, and, ultimately, the weakening of democratic institutions.

Post-9/11 and the War on Terror: Expanding the Definition of "Threat"

The attacks of September 11, 2001, marked a watershed moment in American history, reshaping not only the nation's security landscape but also the political rhetoric that followed. In the aftermath, the U.S. government's primary focus was on preventing another catastrophe, and this urgency led to an unprecedented expansion of executive power. This period saw presidents George W. Bush and Barack Obama employ the language of fear and protection to frame the war on terror, ultimately redefining who and what could be considered a "threat" to the United States. The narratives they built not only targeted foreign enemies but also extended to domestic critics and dissenters, illustrating how the boundaries of national security rhetoric can be stretched to justify controversial actions.

The War on Terror became the central pillar of George W. Bush's presidency. In his speech on September 20, 2001, he declared, "Either you are with us, or you are with the terrorists." This binary framing left no room for ambiguity. It was a powerful message designed to unite the nation under a single banner and to position any dissent as disloyalty. The simplicity of this statement effectively blurred the lines between foreign enemies, such as al-Qaeda and the Taliban, and domestic opposition to the administration's policies. It created a climate in which questioning the government's approach could easily be construed as unpatriotic, if not treasonous.

The USA PATRIOT Act, signed into law just over a month after the attacks, exemplified how this expanded definition of threat translated into policy. The Act gave the government sweeping surveillance powers, allowing agencies like the FBI and NSA to monitor phone calls, emails, and financial records with minimal oversight. The justification was clear: extraordinary threats required extraordinary measures. The Bush administration presented these powers as essential tools to prevent further terrorist attacks, positioning them as protective measures for the American people. However, the broad and vague language within the Act meant that these powers were not solely reserved for targeting foreign terrorists; they could also be directed at U.S. citizens. Activists, journalists, and even members of Congress who questioned the legality or ethics of such measures found themselves under scrutiny.

One of the most significant examples of this expanded definition of threat was the National Security Agency (NSA) warrantless wiretapping program, revealed in 2005. The program allowed the NSA to listen in on international phone calls and emails without a warrant, circumventing established legal frameworks. When the New York Times reported on this secret program, the Bush administration defended its legality by arguing that it was crucial for national security and counterterrorism efforts. Critics of the program, however, were branded as undermining the fight against terrorism. By framing these domestic opponents as potential enablers of terrorism, the administration effectively silenced critical voices that might have otherwise sparked widespread opposition or legal challenges.

This rhetoric had a chilling effect on public discourse. Citizens who spoke out against the administration's surveillance programs, the Iraq War, or the treatment of detainees at Guantanamo Bay were often painted as weakening America's resolve. Bush's use of phrases like "supporting our troops" became shorthand for supporting his policies, creating a social and political atmosphere where dissent was equated with disloyalty. In this environment, the redefinition of "threat" was not limited to physical acts of violence but extended to ideological opposition. Critics of the war on terror, even those within the United States, were portrayed as aiding the enemy through their dissent.

The Obama administration, despite campaign promises to end many of the Bush-era policies, continued to employ and expand upon the same rhetorical and strategic frameworks. While Obama's language was more measured, the underlying message remained consistent: threats to national security were multifaceted and included not only foreign militants but also those who opposed U.S. policies. This was evident in the continuation and expansion of surveillance programs under the Foreign Intelligence Surveillance Act (FISA) and the NSA's bulk data collection revealed by whistleblower Edward Snowden in 2013.

Obama's administration defended these programs as necessary for preventing terrorism, echoing Bush's argument that such measures were indispensable tools in a world where threats could materialize from anywhere, at any time. However, what made Obama's rhetoric particularly effective was his emphasis on the legal framework and oversight supposedly governing these actions. By presenting surveillance as both necessary and regulated, the administration sought to position critics of the program as not only misunderstanding the risks but also undermining the careful balance between security and liberty that the government claimed to uphold.

Even more telling was the administration's approach to whistleblowers. Under Obama, the use of the Espionage Act to prosecute those who leaked information about government activities became more frequent than under all previous administrations combined. Figures like Edward Snowden and Chelsea Manning were cast not just as lawbreakers but as threats to national security. The administration framed these individuals as putting American lives at risk, thereby rallying public and congressional support for their prosecution. In this way, the rhetoric surrounding the war on terror was further extended to include not just critics of policy but those who sought to reveal information about the policies themselves. By framing whistleblowers as adversaries, the administration silenced potential internal dissent and discouraged others from speaking out.

Obama also leveraged this expanded definition of threat to justify controversial military actions, such as drone strikes. His administration developed a doctrine that allowed for the targeting of American citizens abroad if they were deemed terrorists. The most notable example was the targeted killing of Anwar al-Awlaki in Yemen in 2011. Al-Awlaki, an American citizen, was accused of being a high-ranking member of al-Qaeda and orchestrating attacks against the U.S. The administration defended its decision without trial by emphasizing the grave and immediate threat he posed. Critics, however, raised concerns about due process and the precedent set by killing an American citizen without judicial oversight. By framing al-Awlaki's death as a necessary action to protect the homeland, the Obama administration further expanded the war on terror narrative to justify actions that would have been unthinkable before 9/11.

The power of this rhetoric lies not only in its ability to justify extraordinary measures but also in how it shapes the public's understanding of what constitutes a threat. By continuously broadening the definition of threat to include domestic dissenters, whistleblowers, and critics of U.S. policies, both Bush and Obama administrations shifted the public's perception. No longer were threats seen as solely foreign or external; they now encompassed anyone who challenged the state's narrative on security.

This expanded scope has had long-lasting implications, normalizing surveillance and curtailing civil liberties as necessary components of national defence.

The legacy of these tactics is evident in the current political climate, where the framing of opposition as a threat remains a powerful tool. The precedent set by the Bush and Obama administrations has paved the way for future presidents to employ similar strategies, using the language of national security to justify actions that would otherwise face significant resistance. By expanding the definition of threat, they have effectively blurred the lines between protecting the nation and silencing dissent, reshaping the American political landscape in profound and lasting ways.

The chapter illustrates how the post-9/11 era redefined what it means to be a "threat" in American politics. No longer restricted to terrorists or foreign adversaries, this concept now includes anyone, from whistleblowers to political opponents, who challenges the state's narrative. Presidents have used this framing to gain broad, often unchecked powers, and while the immediate impact has been to strengthen their authority, the long-term consequences are only beginning to unfold. The erosion of civil liberties, the normalization of surveillance, and the suppression of dissent have all been justified under this expanded definition, fundamentally altering the relationship between the state and its citizens.

The power of media, particularly social media, has become a formidable tool for modern leaders to shape narratives and frame their opposition as threats. The rapid evolution of communication platforms has allowed presidents and political figures to bypass traditional media, speak directly to their followers, and control the messaging in ways that were unimaginable even a decade ago. This chapter explores how contemporary leaders, notably Donald Trump and Kamala Harris, have used these platforms to not just disseminate information but to frame their political rivals as existential threats to the nation's fabric.

Fake News

The term "Fake News" is one of the most enduring legacies of Donald Trump's political career, a phrase he wielded with remarkable efficiency to frame the media narrative and consolidate his base. Since his early days on the campaign trail, Trump used "Fake News" as a rallying cry against what he perceived as biased reporting, but more strategically, as a tool to dismiss stories or criticisms that he felt were unfavourable to him. The concept has become synonymous with his brand of politics, one that pits the media against the people in a populist struggle for "truth."

Trump first began using the term during his 2016 presidential campaign, accusing major media outlets like CNN, The New York Times, and The Washington Post of bias and misinformation. As coverage of his campaign became increasingly critical, Trump doubled down, branding any negative press as "Fake News." This label served a dual purpose: it discredited unfavourable reporting and also positioned Trump as the victim of an alleged widespread conspiracy among journalists. By calling news he didn't like "fake," Trump reframed critical scrutiny as an attack not just on himself but on his supporters. This tactic allowed him to transform media criticism into an affront against the movement he was building.

For Trump, "Fake News" became a catch-all term, a flexible defence mechanism that could be applied to any narrative he deemed inconvenient or unflattering. When reports surfaced about alleged Russian interference in the 2016 election and potential collusion with his campaign, he consistently labelled these stories as "Fake News." When media outlets published polls showing him trailing behind opponents or losing support, he branded them as "fake." This consistent, repeated use of the term built an atmosphere of scepticism and distrust, particularly among his core supporters, who came to see mainstream media as an adversary rather than a source of information.

Beyond its immediate political utility, "Fake News" evolved into a rallying cry that energized Trump's base. The term gave his supporters a common enemy, the media, that united them in opposition. By painting himself as a truth-teller standing against a corrupt press, Trump cast his base as the champions of an authentic and unfiltered America. At rallies, chants of "CNN sucks!" and "Fake News!" became commonplace, turning the phrase into a badge of honour among his followers.

The effectiveness of this tactic lies in its simplicity. By repeatedly using the term, Trump created a shorthand that his supporters could easily understand and rally around. He tapped into long-standing distrust of the media among conservatives, fuelled by decades of criticism against liberal media bias. By rebranding this distrust as a battle against "Fake News,"

Trump gave it a contemporary twist that resonated deeply with voters who felt alienated by mainstream media narratives.

At a rally in Michigan during the 2024 campaign, Donald Trump claimed that Vice President Kamala Harris had diverted all FEMA funds, (funds for responding to national emergencies) amounting to billions of dollars, towards housing illegal immigrants, leaving no money for disaster relief efforts, particularly in response to Hurricane Helene. FEMA clarified that its Disaster Relief Fund, which is dedicated to emergency response and individual assistance for disasters, had not been redirected to any immigration-related programs. FEMA emphasized that the funding for disaster relief and immigration assistance are handled through entirely separate accounts. Specifically, the funds used to support migrants come from the Shelter and Services Program, which is managed by FEMA but funded through the U.S. Customs and Border Protection budget as authorized by Congress. This money has no connection to the disaster response funds allocated for hurricanes or other emergencies.

Despite these clarifications, Trump has continued to repeat the claim in his campaign appearances, illustrating a strategy he has used in the past: leveraging misinformation to discredit political opponents and fuel his campaign narrative. This tactic of repeating false information, even when corrected by authorities and media outlets, is a classic example of spreading "fake news" to manipulate public perception. By portraying Harris as mismanaging federal resources, Trump attempts to reinforce distrust in his opponents and rally his base around a narrative of governmental failure and corruption .

In fact, historical records indicate that during his presidency, Trump's own administration shifted FEMA funds to support border enforcement efforts, including transferring money from the disaster relief budget to immigration services. This makes his current accusations against Harris not only inaccurate but also could be considered hypocritical, as similar actions were taken under his administration.

For Trump, the concept of "Fake News" has numerous strategic benefits. First, it provides a convenient way to shift focus away from uncomfortable or damaging stories. When confronted with negative commentary, whether it be his tax returns, impeachment trials, or the mishandling of the COVID-19 pandemic, Trump could simply declare that the stories were "fake" and move on. This not only allowed him to dismiss criticisms without having to engage with them substantively but also created a sense of doubt in the minds of his supporters. "nothing happened!"

Second, "Fake News" became a means of delegitimizing institutions that hold power to check the president. By repeatedly attacking the credibility of the press, Trump attempted to undermine one of the pillars of American democracy: a free and independent media and a check and balance on power. In his framing, the media was not an objective institution committed to truth but rather an extension of his political opponents. This approach insulated him from scrutiny, as any investigation or report that painted him in a negative light could be labelled as biased and dismissed outright.

Third, "Fake News" functioned as a smokescreen, allowing Trump to manipulate reality and rewrite narratives. For example, during the COVID-19 pandemic, Trump often contradicted health experts about the virus, treatments, and vaccine timelines. When the press fact-checked or criticized his statements, he branded them as "Fake News," effectively casting doubt on the validity of the information. This tactic created confusion and allowed Trump to maintain control over the narrative, presenting himself as the only trustworthy source of information.

While Trump's use of the term "Fake News" could be used by his rivals as largely self-serving, there **is** some truth to the claim that the media can be biased or sensationalist. Media outlets, particularly in the 24-hour news cycle, sometimes prioritize sensational stories that attract viewers over more nuanced or less dramatic reporting. In this context, accusations of bias, whether intentional or not, have merit. Media organizations, in pursuit of ratings and online engagement, can blur the line between objective reporting and opinion, contributing to a polarized information landscape.

Trump capitalized on this reality, amplifying any instance of media misjudgement or bias to support his larger narrative. For example, when CNN or The New York Times made errors in reporting or when networks featured pundits with overt political leanings, Trump highlighted these moments to bolster his argument that the media could not be trusted. By pointing to these instances, he offered his base concrete examples that reinforced the perception of media bias, even if such instances were exceptions rather than the rule.

However, while it is true that the media is not infallible and that some outlets may demonstrate bias, Trump's use of "Fake News" is not a genuine critique aimed at reforming journalism. Instead, it is a tactical move to delegitimize all unfavourable reporting and cast himself as the sole arbiter of truth. This approach is problematic because it encourages a selective and often distorted interpretation of facts, which undermines public trust in objective information.

The broader impact of Trump's "Fake News" campaign is the erosion of a shared sense of reality. By branding any unfavourable or critical coverage as "Fake News," Trump has contributed to the fragmentation of information consumption in America. Supporters of Trump increasingly rely on alternative media sources that align with their views, further deepening ideological divides. Traditional media, on the other hand, continues to face accusations of bias and misinformation, leading to a lack of trust that affects the entire political spectrum.

This distrust has broader implications for democracy itself. When a significant portion of the public believes that the media cannot be trusted, it becomes more challenging to hold those in power accountable. Furthermore, the inability to agree on basic facts or to engage in constructive dialogue based on shared information undermines the ability of a society to function cohesively.

While Trump's use of "Fake News" has been a powerful tool for managing public perception and avoiding accountability, it has also had damaging effects on the American political and social landscape. It reveals an unsettling trend where political leaders can dismiss uncomfortable truths with a simple label, further polarizing the public and weakening the media's role as a check on power. Whether or not there is some truth in Trump's critique of the media, and we should be clear there are examples where the media definitely need to be held to higher standards, the consequences of his rhetoric have created an environment where facts are malleable, and truth itself becomes a casualty of political expediency.

The 2020 presidential election provided a vivid example of this tactic. As mail-in voting became a widely used method due to the COVID-19 pandemic, Trump repeatedly claimed that mail-in ballots would lead to massive voter fraud. Evidence was sought but as far as research I have been able to review, despite there always being some fraud in any system, none of any note was found. The Department of Justice (DOJ), under then-Attorney General William Barr, investigated claims of election fraud, including those related to mail-in ballots. In December 2020, Barr stated that the DOJ had not found evidence of widespread voter fraud that would have affected the outcome of the election. His constant repetition of this narrative on social media platforms led millions of his followers to doubt the legitimacy of the election process. Trump's framing of mail-in voting as a "rigged system" wasn't merely about casting doubt on the election; it was about painting his political opponents as part of a corrupt establishment working to steal power. His messaging wasn't subtle; he called the opposition's actions "a coup," suggesting that they were actively undermining American democracy.

This language served two key purposes. First, it rallied his base, making them feel as though they were not just supporters of a politician but defenders of their country against an internal enemy. Second, it created an atmosphere of distrust, making it difficult for any information coming from his opposition or the media to penetrate his supporters' beliefs. This tactic, framing the opposition as an existential threat, has had long-lasting effects, contributing to a deepened political divide that continues to influence the American political landscape.

Kamala Harris: The Art of Strategic Counter-Narratives

Kamala Harris, as Vice President, has employed a more nuanced approach when it comes to framing the opposition. While she does not engage in the same bombastic style as Trump, her rhetoric is nonetheless strategic. In her public speeches and media appearances, Harris has consistently framed opposition to progressive policies as not just political disagreement but as an obstacle to American progress and justice. She positions herself as a champion for equality, justice, and democracy, suggesting that those who oppose her policies are, by extension, standing against these ideals.

For instance, in the debates and discussions surrounding the George Floyd Justice in Policing Act, Harris emphasized that opposition to police reform was not merely a policy disagreement but a failure to protect Black Americans and, more broadly, a failure to uphold justice. By framing the debate in these terms, Harris transformed the opposition's stance from a political position into a moral and ethical issue. This tactic, while less overtly confrontational than Trump's, still serves to position the opposition as a threat, one that stands in the way of progress and justice for marginalized communities.

Harris has also used her platform to counteract narratives that paint her and other progressive figures as dangerous radicals. In response to conservative claims that progressive policies, such as expanding healthcare access or implementing stricter gun control, are "un-American" or "socialist," Harris has strategically framed these policies as efforts to build a fairer and safer society. By doing so, she shifts the focus from defending against attacks to redefining what it means to be truly American. In her messaging, those who resist these changes are not just holding a different view but are obstructing efforts to create a more just and equal society.

Additionally, Harris has utilized the framing of threats in her discussions about voting rights. In speeches supporting legislation like the For the People Act, she has argued that those who oppose expanding voter access are not simply protecting the integrity of elections, as they claim, but are actively working to suppress the votes of minorities and marginalized groups. She uses this narrative to cast the Republican opposition as a force undermining democracy itself. By framing the battle for voting rights as a fight between protecting democracy and succumbing to authoritarianism, Harris mobilizes her base, positioning herself and her allies as protectors of democracy.

Manipulating Media and Platforms
Both Trump and Harris demonstrate the power of media manipulation and narrative framing in the modern political arena. Trump's aggressive use of Twitter, while highly effective in galvanizing his base, also backfired by alienating moderate voters and fuelling polarization to the point where even members of his own party eventually distanced themselves from his rhetoric. His relentless attacks on the media and political opponents created an environment where it became increasingly difficult for factual information to reach all segments of the population, contributing to an erosion of trust in institutions that continues to have repercussions today.

On the other hand, Harris's approach, while more polished, also walks a fine line. Her emphasis on framing opposition as morally or ethically wrong can mobilize her base and create a strong sense of urgency around her policies. However, it can also deepen divides and contribute to a climate where political disagreement is viewed as a fundamental threat to

American values rather than a legitimate difference of opinion. By positioning opponents as obstacles to justice or equality, Harris risks alienating potential allies and making it more difficult to build bipartisan support on key issues.

The Role of Social Media in Amplifying Threat Narratives

Social media platforms have amplified these dynamics in unprecedented ways. Unlike traditional media, where narratives could be somewhat controlled and moderated, social media provides politicians with a direct line to millions of followers. Trump's tweets reached millions instantly, allowing him to set the news agenda and frame issues before mainstream outlets had the chance to respond. Harris, too, leverages social media but in a different style; her platforms focus on uplifting stories, personal anecdotes, and highlighting injustices, which she then ties to legislative priorities.

The reach and speed of these platforms mean that narratives, whether framing the opposition as corrupt, unpatriotic, or morally wrong, can gain traction almost immediately. For Trump, social media became a tool to mobilize his base, using inflammatory language to foster a sense of urgency and crisis. His declarations of "witch hunts" and "rigged elections" spread rapidly, creating echo chambers where his supporters could reinforce these messages without exposure to contradicting viewpoints.

In contrast, Harris's use of social media seeks to build a coalition by emphasizing a collective effort toward justice and equality. However, by framing opposition as actively working against these goals, she also creates an "us versus them" dynamic, which, while less overtly confrontational than Trump's, still contributes to polarization.

The Impact on American Democracy

The use of social media and modern communication channels to frame political opposition as existential threats has far-reaching consequences. It contributes to the deepening polarization of American society, making it increasingly difficult for people to engage in constructive dialogue or reach across the aisle. When political opposition is framed not as a difference in policy but as a fundamental threat to national identity or survival, compromise becomes almost impossible.

Furthermore, as leaders use these platforms to bypass traditional media and create their own narratives, the role of journalists and fact-checkers becomes diminished. Trump's "fake news" campaign effectively discredited any criticism from the press, while Harris's approach of framing her policy goals as moral imperatives can also shut down debate, as those who disagree are portrayed as standing against justice itself.

In conclusion, the manipulation of media and social platforms to frame the opposition as threats is a powerful, yet double-edged sword. While it allows modern political figures to mobilize their bases quickly and effectively, it also risks deepening divisions and undermining democratic institutions. As technology continues to evolve, so too will the tactics of political leaders, making it all the more critical for citizens to critically evaluate the narratives presented to them and for leaders to recognize the potential long-term consequences of their rhetoric.

The Erosion of Public Trust in Institutions

One of the most significant consequences of framing opposition as a threat is the erosion of public trust in democratic institutions. When presidents frame their rivals as existential dangers to the nation, they often do so by attacking the very institutions that are meant to safeguard democracy. For instance, when a president suggests that the judiciary is biased or corrupt, or that the media is spreading lies to undermine the government, they chip away at the foundations of public confidence in these critical pillars of democracy.

This tactic can be seen in recent years, where rhetoric casting the judicial system as part of a "deep state" conspiracy or labelling the media as "the enemy of the people" has gained traction. Such language not only delegitimizes the checks and balances that are designed to prevent the abuse of power but also encourages the public to distrust any information that doesn't align with the administration's narrative. The impact is far-reaching: when the electorate no longer trusts the institutions designed to protect them, the rule of law is weakened, and democratic norms begin to unravel.

When opposition parties or leaders are labelled as threats, it becomes easier for administrations to justify undermining or bypassing these institutions. Executive orders, emergency powers, and other unilateral actions can be framed as necessary to "protect" the country from the perceived threat. In reality, however, these moves erode the institutional integrity and credibility of the government, contributing to a cycle where power becomes increasingly concentrated in the executive branch, and the public grows more cynical and disillusioned with the entire system.

Deepening Political Polarization

Framing opposition as a threat also exacerbates political polarization, creating an "us versus them" mentality that divides the nation. This approach is designed to unify a president's base by appealing to their fears and anxieties. By portraying political rivals not merely as opponents with different views but as dangerous adversaries seeking to harm the country, administrations can mobilize their supporters through fear and anger. This tactic has proven effective in energizing voters, but it comes at the cost of national unity.

When political divisions become entrenched, compromise becomes nearly impossible. Legislators are incentivized to toe the party line rather than seek bipartisan solutions, fearing backlash from their base if they are perceived as cooperating with "the enemy." This gridlock impedes the legislative process and hampers the government's ability to address pressing issues, leading to public frustration and a sense of dysfunction in the political system. Over time, the perception of a broken, ineffective government fuels further polarization, creating a self-perpetuating cycle.

In addition to fuelling division, this rhetoric also demonizes entire segments of the population who may support the opposition. Supporters of rival parties are not seen as fellow citizens with different views but as traitors, extremists, or enemies within. This rhetoric turns political debates into battles over morality, identity, and patriotism rather than policy differences. The effects on the social fabric are profound; communities become divided, and citizens view each other with suspicion and hostility. When people are encouraged to see their fellow citizens as threats to their way of life, the potential for conflict, and even violence, increases, as political opponents are no longer seen as legitimate actors within a shared democratic framework.

Creating a Culture of Fear and Suppression of Dissent

The tactic of framing opposition as threats also creates an atmosphere where dissent is perceived as dangerous and unpatriotic. When administrations label their critics as threats to national security or as agents of foreign influence, they effectively signal that questioning or opposing their policies is not just wrong but potentially treasonous. This environment stifles open debate and discourages political engagement, as citizens fear that expressing dissenting opinions could make them targets of harassment or retribution.

The chilling effect on free speech and democratic participation is significant. Activists, journalists, and ordinary citizens may self-censor or retreat from the public sphere altogether, fearing consequences for their careers, safety, or social standing. Media outlets, too, may face pressures to align with the government narrative to avoid being branded as hostile or unpatriotic. As a result, the diversity of perspectives in public discourse diminishes, and the space for healthy debate and democratic deliberation shrinks.

In such an environment, policies that curtail civil liberties, such as surveillance programs, restrictions on protest rights, or punitive actions against media organizations, can be justified as measures necessary to protect the state from threats. These measures, presented as essential for national security, further curtail freedoms and concentrate power in the hands of the executive. The public, already conditioned to view the opposition as dangerous, may accept these restrictions as necessary, failing to recognize the broader implications for democratic freedom and accountability.

The Risk of Backfiring: Credibility and Authority at Stake

While framing opposition as threats can be an effective tool for consolidating power, it also carries significant risks for those who employ it. When administrations exaggerate or fabricate threats, they risk a credibility crisis if their claims are exposed or fail to materialize. Once the public begins to see these narratives as manipulative rather than truthful, the administration's authority and legitimacy can be severely undermined.

History provides numerous examples where leaders faced backlash when their fear-based narratives were revealed as exaggerated or false. In such cases, the public's trust is not only lost in the leader but also in the broader political system that allowed such manipulation to occur. The erosion of credibility can have far-reaching consequences: it may lead to electoral losses, internal party divisions, and, in extreme cases, civil unrest as disillusioned citizens demand accountability.

Furthermore, the tactic of framing opposition as threats can create a situation where leaders become trapped by their own rhetoric. Having stoked fear and suspicion among their supporters, administrations may find it difficult to de-escalate once the threat narrative is no longer politically expedient or necessary. Attempting to pivot or soften their stance may result in backlash from their base, who have been conditioned to view the opposition as a permanent danger. Thus, leaders may find themselves forced to double down on extreme measures or rhetoric, pushing the political environment into even more dangerous territory.

The Long-Term Impact on Democracy

The cumulative effect of these tactics is a slow but steady erosion of democratic norms and institutions. When opposition is consistently framed as a threat, and dissent is viewed as treasonous, the space for legitimate political competition narrows. Instead of a democracy where multiple viewpoints can coexist and compete, the political environment begins to resemble an authoritarian system where power is concentrated, and opposition is delegitimized.

As public trust in institutions declines, and as polarization deepens, the foundations of democracy weaken. Citizens lose faith in the fairness of elections, the impartiality of the judiciary, and the integrity of the media. Without these pillars, democracy becomes vulnerable, and the potential for authoritarianism increases. Leaders who employ these tactics may succeed in the short term, but they risk leaving behind a legacy of damaged institutions, divided societies, and a populace increasingly skeptical of democratic governance itself.

Consequences

The strategy of framing the opposition as threats is a powerful but dangerous tool in the arsenal of modern politics. While it can rally supporters and justify controversial policies, the long-term consequences are severe. By undermining public trust, deepening polarization, and stifling dissent, this approach risks eroding the very foundations of democracy. The consequences, as history has shown, extend far beyond a single election cycle, leaving behind a political and social landscape that is divided, distrustful, and less resilient in the face of future challenges. For presidents and administrations who wield this tool, the gains may be immediate, but the damage is often lasting, with the potential to backfire in ways that undermine their own authority and the health of the nation's democratic system.

CHAPTER 5

ECONOMIC POLICIES AND THE ILLUSION OF CONTROL

Introduction

When it comes to the economy, American presidents are often seen as the ultimate decision-makers, holding the power to create jobs, control inflation, and steer the country towards prosperity or disaster. Campaigns are built around promises of economic growth, and approval ratings often rise or fall based on the perception of economic success. The president's role in managing the economy has become a central pillar of their image. Yet, beneath the surface of these narratives lies a different reality: presidents have far less control over economic outcomes than most people believe. This chapter explores the gap between the perception of presidential power over the economy and the complex, often uncontrollable forces that actually shape economic conditions.

The belief that a president can directly influence the economy is, in many ways, a myth, a myth reinforced by media narratives, political rhetoric, and public expectations. When the economy thrives, the president is credited, and when it falters, they are blamed, regardless of their actual impact. This perception is fuelled by a desire for a clear figurehead who can be held accountable for the economy's performance. However, the reality is much more nuanced. Economic conditions are influenced by a web of factors beyond the president's reach, from the independence of the Federal Reserve to global market forces and the actions of multinational corporations.

One of the key areas where this illusion of control is most apparent is in the relationship between the president and the Federal Reserve. While the Fed plays a crucial role in managing monetary policy, impacting interest rates, inflation, and the money supply, it operates independently from the president's direct influence. The Fed's independence is designed to prevent political interference in economic decision-making, yet the public often conflates its actions with the president's policies. This dynamic reinforces the illusion that the president is responsible for economic outcomes that are, in reality, shaped by other actors.

Global markets further complicate the idea of presidential control over the economy. In an interconnected world where the U.S. economy is deeply tied to international trade, energy prices, and geopolitical events, the impact of presidential policies is often limited. Even well-intentioned initiatives, such as trade wars or tariffs, demonstrate the limits of presidential influence. The recent U.S.-China trade war, for instance, was framed as a battle that would bring manufacturing back to American shores, but the results were mixed, with tariffs impacting American consumers and businesses as much as they did Chinese counterparts.

Long-term economic issues, like the national debt and budget deficit, also reveal the bipartisan struggle to manage the economy effectively. Despite promises from both sides of the aisle, these challenges persist, showing that economic governance is not as simple as a president's campaign promises might suggest.

In this chapter, we will dive into the various factors that contribute to the illusion of presidential control over the economy.

We will examine how public perception often deviates from reality, how presidents are credited or blamed for economic conditions beyond their control, and how the broader complexities of the global economy challenge the notion that any single leader can truly steer economic destiny.

The Myth That Presidents Can Directly Control Economic Outcomes

The belief that American presidents wield significant power over the economy is deeply ingrained in the political and public consciousness. Election campaigns are filled with promises to create jobs, reduce inflation, and stimulate growth, while media coverage often attributes economic highs and lows directly to the actions or inactions of the sitting president. Approval ratings frequently hinge on economic performance, reinforcing the idea that the president is both the architect and steward of the nation's prosperity. However, the reality of presidential influence over economic outcomes is far more complex and limited than these perceptions suggest. The economy is a vast, multifaceted system influenced by global markets, independent institutions, and forces beyond the control of any single individual, even one as powerful as the president of the United States.

The Illusion of Control

The myth that presidents can directly control economic outcomes is perpetuated by several factors. First, the political system incentivizes candidates to make grand economic promises. During election campaigns, both incumbents and challengers emphasize their ability to manage the economy effectively. They promise to bring back jobs, boost GDP growth, and reduce inflation, all while painting their opponents as economically incompetent or disastrous. This narrative simplifies the complex web of economic influences into a story of individual leadership, making it easier for voters to identify whom to support or blame.

Media coverage also plays a significant role in amplifying this perception. The media often frames economic events, such as job reports or market fluctuations, as reflections of presidential success or failure. Headlines proclaim that "the president creates jobs" or "the president's policies cause inflation," even when these outcomes are the result of broader, more complex factors.

This creates a direct line of causality in the public's mind, reinforcing the belief that the president has near-total control over the economy.

In reality, however, the president's ability to influence economic outcomes is constrained by numerous factors, many of which operate independently of the executive branch. The economy is a global, interconnected system shaped by international trade, supply chains, technological innovation, demographic shifts, and the actions of independent institutions like the Federal Reserve. While the president can propose economic policies and work with Congress to implement them, the direct impact of these policies is often limited, delayed, or altered by forces beyond their control.

Jobs: The Myth of Presidential Job Creation

One of the most common economic promises made by presidential candidates is the promise to create jobs. Candidates and sitting presidents alike frequently tout their plans for job creation, linking their policies directly to employment numbers. The perception is that the president, through legislation or executive action, can significantly influence the job market. In practice, however, the relationship between presidential actions and job creation is far more tenuous.

Job creation is influenced by a multitude of factors, including consumer demand, technological advancements, global economic conditions, and corporate decision-making. While presidents can implement policies that may indirectly affect employment, such as tax cuts, infrastructure spending, or regulatory changes—the effects of these policies often take time to materialize and are mediated by broader economic trends.

For example, during the 2008 financial crisis, Barack Obama's administration implemented the American Recovery and Reinvestment Act, a massive stimulus package designed to jumpstart the economy and reduce unemployment. While the stimulus undoubtedly played a role in stabilizing the economy, it was not the sole factor in the subsequent job growth. The global economic recovery, technological innovation, and private sector initiatives also contributed significantly to job creation. Nonetheless, Obama was credited with "saving" the economy, even though the reality was that a range of factors beyond his direct control played critical roles.

Similarly, Donald Trump's presidency was marked by his emphasis on job creation, particularly in manufacturing. Trump's administration implemented tax cuts and imposed tariffs aimed at reshoring manufacturing jobs. While the economy did see job growth during his term, much of this growth was part of a long-term trend that began during the Obama administration's recovery from the Great Recession. Furthermore, the impact of Trump's trade policies, such as tariffs on Chinese goods, was mixed, with some industries benefiting while others, like agriculture and retail, faced significant challenges. Despite these complexities, the narrative persisted that Trump's actions alone were responsible for job creation or loss, depending on one's political perspective.

The reality is that while presidents can influence the conditions that may lead to job growth, they cannot control the broader economic forces that determine employment levels. Technological advancements, such as automation and artificial intelligence, play a significant role in shaping the job market, often reducing the need for traditional manufacturing jobs that candidates frequently promise to bring back. Global competition, supply chain disruptions, and consumer demand further complicate the relationship between presidential policies and job creation. Yet, the myth that presidents can singlehandedly create or destroy jobs remains a powerful tool in political discourse.

Inflation: A Problem Beyond Presidential Reach

Another area where the myth of presidential economic control persists is inflation. Rising prices have long been a concern for voters, and presidents are often held accountable when inflation surges. Political opponents and critics are quick to blame the sitting president, while the president and their administration scramble to find solutions and shift blame. However, inflation is a global phenomenon influenced by factors far beyond the reach of the Oval Office.

Inflation is typically driven by a combination of supply and demand dynamics, monetary policy set by the Federal Reserve, global energy prices, and geopolitical events. While the president may advocate for policies aimed at reducing inflation, such as addressing supply chain issues or promoting energy independence, the immediate impact of these actions is often limited.

Consider the inflation surge in the aftermath of the COVID-19 pandemic. Supply chain disruptions, labour shortages, and global energy price fluctuations contributed to rising prices across the board. While the Biden administration faced criticism for its handling of inflation, much of the issue was rooted in factors outside its control, such as global supply chain bottlenecks and the war in Ukraine, which drove up energy costs. The Federal Reserve's monetary policy, aimed at controlling inflation through interest rate adjustments, operates independently of the executive branch. Thus, while the president is often seen as the face of the nation's economic response, the reality is that their influence over inflation is limited.

The historical precedent for this disconnect is well-documented. During the 1970s, Presidents Richard Nixon, Gerald Ford, and Jimmy Carter each struggled to manage the stagflation crisis—a period of high inflation combined with stagnant economic growth. Despite their efforts, including wage and price controls and various economic initiatives, the underlying causes of inflation—such as the oil shocks and global economic conditions—remained beyond their reach. The lesson remains relevant today: while presidents may enact measures to curb inflation, they cannot control the external and structural forces that drive it.

The Limits of Presidential Influence

The limits of presidential influence on the economy become especially apparent when considering the role of global markets and international events. The U.S. economy is deeply interconnected with global supply chains, energy markets, and trade relationships, meaning that external factors often overshadow domestic policies. For instance, when the U.S. imposes tariffs or sanctions, the intended economic impact is often mitigated by the complexity of global trade networks and the responses of other nations.

The U.S.-China trade war during Trump's presidency illustrates this dynamic. Trump's administration imposed tariffs on Chinese imports, aiming to reduce the trade deficit and bring back manufacturing jobs. While the tariffs did affect certain industries, they also led to retaliatory measures from China, resulting in increased costs for American businesses and consumers. Furthermore, the global nature of supply chains meant that companies could often source materials from other countries, minimizing the impact of tariffs.

Despite the rhetoric of economic control, the outcomes were shaped as much by global responses and market adaptations as by presidential action.

Public Perception vs. Economic Reality

Despite these realities, public perception remains heavily influenced by the belief that the president has direct control over economic outcomes. Approval ratings often rise and fall with economic indicators such as GDP growth, unemployment rates, and inflation levels, even when these indicators are shaped by forces beyond presidential influence. This gap between perception and reality creates a challenging dynamic for presidents, who must manage public expectations while navigating the complexities of a global economy.

For example, during the economic recovery following the 2008 financial crisis, Barack Obama's administration was praised for stabilizing the economy, but critics pointed to slow wage growth and income inequality as failures of his policies. In reality, these issues were influenced by decades of structural economic changes, including automation and globalization, that no single administration could resolve. Similarly, Donald Trump's promise to bring back manufacturing jobs through trade policies faced obstacles due to the complex realities of global production networks and technological shifts.

The expectation that presidents can, and should, directly manage the economy often distracts from the structural and systemic issues that truly drive economic outcomes. Long-term challenges like automation, income inequality, and the impact of global trade require coordinated efforts that go beyond the influence of any single leader. Yet, the myth persists, shaping how voters assess economic performance and how presidents craft their policies and public messaging.

Economic Decisions Influenced Outside of Presidential Control

The American president is often perceived as the ultimate steward of the nation's economy. From the campaign trail to the Oval Office, the president makes promises about job creation, economic growth, inflation control, and more. However, much of the actual economic power lies beyond the president's control. One of the most critical institutions in this dynamic is the Federal Reserve, or the Fed, which operates independently of the executive branch.

The Fed's independence plays a crucial role in maintaining economic stability, but it also reveals the limitations of presidential power over economic outcomes. Understanding the Fed's function, its history, and its relationship with the presidency is essential to grasp the true nature of economic governance in the United States.

The Federal Reserve: An Independent Institution

The Federal Reserve was established in 1913 through the Federal Reserve Act, with the purpose of creating a central banking system that would stabilize the U.S. economy. Its primary responsibilities include managing the money supply, regulating banks, and overseeing monetary policy, specifically through setting interest rates. The Fed's ability to influence interest rates is particularly significant because these rates affect everything from consumer borrowing and spending to business investment and inflation.

The independence of the Federal Reserve is not accidental; it was intentionally designed this way to insulate it from political pressures. The idea was that economic policy, particularly monetary policy, should be based on long-term considerations and economic data rather than short-term political interests. The president appoints the chair of the Federal Reserve and its board members, but once appointed, these officials serve staggered terms, ensuring continuity beyond any single administration. This structure protects the Fed's decision-making process from being swayed by immediate political concerns and campaign cycles.

The Fed's autonomy means that even though the president is often seen as the face of the economy, they do not have direct control over one of the most important tools for managing economic conditions: interest rates. The president can influence fiscal policy, government spending and taxation, but monetary policy, which is crucial for controlling inflation and managing economic growth, remains firmly in the hands of the Federal Reserve. This separation underscores the complexity of economic governance and challenges the perception that the president is the sole architect of economic outcomes.

Historical Examples of Fed Independence

Throughout history, the Federal Reserve has demonstrated its independence, sometimes putting it at odds with sitting presidents. One of the most notable examples occurred during the presidency of Lyndon B. Johnson. In the 1960s, Johnson sought to finance the Vietnam War and his Great Society programs without raising taxes, a move that risked increasing inflation. To manage the economy, he pressured the Federal Reserve, then led by William McChesney Martin, to keep interest rates low. Martin, adhering to his commitment to the Fed's independence and the long-term health of the economy, resisted Johnson's pressure and raised interest rates to combat inflation. The clash between Martin and Johnson highlighted the Fed's autonomy and its willingness to act in opposition to the president's wishes when it deemed necessary.

A more recent example involves President Donald Trump and Jerome Powell, the Fed Chair he appointed in 2018. Trump frequently criticized Powell for raising interest rates, arguing that higher rates would slow economic growth and hurt the stock market—a key metric Trump used to gauge the success of his presidency. Trump's public attacks on Powell were unprecedented, with the president going as far as to suggest firing him. However, Powell maintained the Fed's independence, continuing with the rate hikes he and the Fed's board believed were necessary to prevent the economy from overheating. Powell's resistance to political pressure reinforced the Fed's autonomy, even in the face of aggressive and very public criticism from the White House.

These historical instances illustrate the Fed's commitment to its mandate, which prioritizes economic stability over political considerations. While presidents may seek to influence the Fed's actions to align with their political agendas, the institution's structure and culture have generally shielded it from succumbing to such pressures.

The Fed's Tools: Interest Rates and Beyond
The primary tool the Federal Reserve uses to manage the economy is its control over interest rates, specifically the federal funds rate. By adjusting this rate, the Fed can influence the cost of borrowing for banks, which then impacts consumer loans, mortgages, and business investment. Lowering interest rates typically stimulates economic growth by making borrowing cheaper, while raising rates can cool an overheating economy and help curb inflation. These adjustments are complex and require careful consideration of economic indicators, global market conditions, and potential long-term effects.

Presidents often desire lower interest rates to stimulate economic growth, particularly when they are seeking re-election or when the economy is sluggish. Lower rates can boost spending, create jobs, and push up stock market values, all of which are seen as positive indicators by voters. However, the Federal Reserve's role is not to serve the president's political goals but to maintain economic stability. Sometimes, this means raising rates even when doing so may be politically unpopular or damaging to a sitting president's approval ratings.

Beyond interest rates, the Fed has other tools at its disposal, such as open market operations and quantitative easing (QE). During economic crises, like the 2008 financial meltdown, the Fed implemented QE by buying large quantities of government securities and other financial assets to inject money into the economy. These actions were taken independently of presidential directives, demonstrating how the Fed operates based on its assessment of economic conditions rather than political influence. QE played a critical role in stabilizing the economy, but its implementation and the timing of its wind-down were determined by the Fed, not the White House.

Global Markets and the Limits of Presidential Influence
The globalized nature of the economy further complicates the relationship between presidential power and economic outcomes. While the president may influence domestic economic policies through fiscal measures like taxation and spending, the broader global economy is shaped by factors beyond their control. Central banks worldwide, including the Federal Reserve, operate independently to manage their economies, and their decisions often intersect with and impact U.S. economic conditions.

For instance, when the European Central Bank (ECB) or the Bank of Japan adjusts their monetary policies, such actions can have ripple effects across global markets, influencing currency values, investment flows, and trade balances. In these scenarios, the Fed's response is critical. The Fed may adjust its policies to maintain stability or respond to international financial pressures, but these adjustments are made independently, with a focus on global economic dynamics rather than presidential preferences.

The recent U.S.-China trade war under the Trump administration highlighted these complexities. While Trump's tariffs and trade policies aimed to protect American industries and reduce the trade deficit, the global market's reaction and the impact on American consumers were largely influenced by external factors beyond Trump's control. The Fed's response to the economic uncertainties created by the trade war—adjusting interest rates and monitoring inflation—showcased how the institution navigates the balance between domestic economic stability and global economic conditions, often independently of the president's economic goals.

Public Misconceptions and the Political Blame Game

Despite the reality of the Fed's independence, the public often attributes economic outcomes directly to the president. This misperception is partly due to how economic performance is framed in media and political discourse. Presidents are frequently positioned as either the heroes of economic recovery or the scapegoats of economic downturns, despite the fact that many key economic decisions are made by the Federal Reserve. The media's emphasis on the president as the face of the economy simplifies the narrative, ignoring the complexities of monetary policy and global influences.

This dynamic creates a political dilemma for presidents. They are expected to deliver economic growth, but they have limited tools to influence the broader economic landscape directly. As a result, they often pressure the Fed publicly or seek to influence its decisions, as seen with Johnson, Trump, and even Richard Nixon before them. However, the Fed's independence is designed precisely to prevent such influence, ensuring that economic policy remains focused on long-term stability rather than short-term political gain.

Guarding Against Short-Termism

The Federal Reserve's independence is vital for maintaining economic stability and credibility. If the Fed were subject to direct presidential control, it could lead to policies aimed at short-term gains rather than long-term health, particularly in election years when the temptation to manipulate economic indicators for political advantage is high. Central banks that lack independence, like those in some authoritarian regimes, often face hyperinflation or economic instability because they cannot resist political pressures to print money or lower rates unsustainably.

The structure of the Fed, with staggered terms for its board members and a long tenure for its chair, helps shield it from the volatility of political cycles.

By making decisions based on economic data and long-term objectives rather than political expediency, the Fed serves as a stabilizing force in the American economy, even when presidents attempt to sway its policies.

The Illusion of Presidential Control

The independence of the Federal Reserve reveals the limitations of presidential power over economic outcomes. While presidents are the public face of the economy and bear the political consequences of economic performance, the reality is that the most critical decisions, particularly those related to monetary policy, are made by an institution designed to operate independently. This dynamic challenges the public perception of presidential omnipotence in economic matters and highlights the complexities of economic governance in a globalized world. Understanding the Fed's role is essential to recognizing the true nature of economic power in the United States—power that is less centralized and far more intricate than presidential rhetoric might suggest.

Trade Wars

Trade wars have become a prominent tool in the political arsenal, used by presidents to demonstrate toughness, economic prowess, and an ability to put "America First." These confrontations, often framed as battles for fairness, jobs, and economic dominance, are highly visible political manoeuvres that allow presidents to showcase their leadership. However, the reality of trade wars, particularly in the globalized economy of the 21st century, is far more complex and often far less successful than the rhetoric suggests. The illusion of control and success that trade wars provide frequently masks the deeper, long-term consequences they have on both the domestic economy and global trade relationships.

One of the most notable examples in recent history is the trade war initiated by President Donald Trump against China. Trump framed the tariffs as a necessary move to reduce the U.S. trade deficit with China, bring manufacturing jobs back to American shores, and punish what he described as unfair trade practices, including intellectual property theft. His administration imposed tariffs on billions of dollars' worth of Chinese goods, aiming to force China into negotiating a more favourable trade agreement for the United States.

For Trump and his supporters, the tariffs were a bold statement of American strength and economic independence. But while these actions created the appearance of success and toughness, the consequences were far-reaching and complex.

The initial illusion of success stemmed from the perception that the tariffs were hurting China more than the United States. Trump's messaging emphasized how the tariffs would force China to the negotiating table and lead to a trade deal that would benefit American workers and industries. However, the economic reality was that the tariffs also significantly impacted American consumers and businesses. Tariffs on Chinese goods meant higher prices for imported products, ranging from electronics and clothing to agricultural machinery and raw materials. For American companies reliant on Chinese imports, these tariffs raised costs, leading to price hikes that were ultimately passed on to consumers.

The agriculture sector, in particular, was hit hard. China, in retaliation, imposed tariffs on American agricultural products, including soybeans, pork, and other commodities. American farmers, who had been major exporters to China, suddenly found their markets drying up. The U.S. government attempted to mitigate the damage with subsidies and aid packages for farmers, but these measures could not fully compensate for the lost business and uncertainty caused by the trade war. What was framed as a win for American workers and industries instead became a complex web of economic consequences, with certain sectors suffering disproportionately.

The trade war also highlighted the interconnected nature of the global economy. In the past, trade conflicts might have had more contained impacts, but in today's world, where supply chains are spread across continents and industries rely on international cooperation, trade wars create ripples that are felt far beyond the two countries directly involved. For instance, American manufacturers reliant on components produced in China had to either absorb higher costs or find alternative suppliers, which often proved expensive and logistically challenging. In some cases, companies even relocated their manufacturing operations outside the United States to circumvent the tariffs—an unintended consequence that ran counter to the administration's "America First" rhetoric.

Moreover, the long-term effects of such trade wars go beyond immediate price increases and market disruptions. They damage relationships and trust between trading partners, leading to a more fragmented global trade environment. Countries observing the U.S.-China trade war began to rethink their own economic strategies, leading some to forge closer ties with China, while others sought to minimize reliance on American markets. The shift towards decoupling and diversifying trade partnerships reflects how trade wars can, in the long run, weaken the very influence that the United States aims to assert through tariffs and trade barriers.

The ultimate agreement reached between the U.S. and China in early 2020, known as the Phase One Deal, was lauded by Trump as a major victory. Yet, upon closer inspection, it revealed the limits of what trade wars could achieve. The deal included commitments from China to increase purchases of American agricultural products and other goods, but the promised amounts were ambitious and, as it turned out, difficult for China to meet. Furthermore, the structural issues the U.S. originally raised, such as intellectual property theft and market access for American companies, were not fully addressed in the agreement. While the tariffs did lead to some concessions, they did not fundamentally alter China's economic practices, and the costs borne by American consumers and industries remained significant.

What the trade war with China ultimately illustrates is the gap between the political rhetoric surrounding trade confrontations and their economic reality. While imposing tariffs can be portrayed as a sign of strength and decisive action, the consequences are often more damaging than beneficial, particularly in a globalized economy where supply chains and markets are interdependent. Trade wars offer presidents the illusion of control and success, but they rarely deliver the long-term gains promised, leaving behind a trail of economic disruption and strained international relationships.

The Bipartisan Failure to Address Long-term Economic Issues

While trade wars capture headlines and present the image of a president taking action, another critical economic issue, the national debt and budget deficit, remains an area of consistent bipartisan failure. Both parties in the United States have, over the decades, contributed to the growing debt, yet neither has effectively addressed it.

The illusion that presidents can manage the economy often ignores the reality that long-term economic health requires difficult, unpopular decisions, decisions that are rarely made due to political expediency.

The U.S. national debt currently exceeds $31 trillion, an amount that reflects years of deficit spending by both Republican and Democratic administrations. Despite campaign promises to reduce the deficit or balance the budget, both parties have shown a tendency to prioritize short-term economic gains or political wins over long-term fiscal responsibility. Tax cuts, defence spending, social welfare programs, and emergency relief measures, while sometimes necessary or popular, have all contributed to the ballooning deficit.

Presidents often promise fiscal responsibility, yet their actions frequently tell a different story. For example, Ronald Reagan, a champion of smaller government and lower taxes, presided over a significant increase in the national debt during his presidency. His tax cuts and defence spending boosted economic growth but also led to higher deficits, a trend that continued under subsequent administrations. George W. Bush's tax cuts and the costs of the wars in Iraq and Afghanistan further accelerated the growth of the deficit, as did Barack Obama's economic stimulus package in response to the 2008 financial crisis.

The illusion of control becomes particularly evident when considering how each administration has approached the debt problem. While rhetoric often focuses on the need for fiscal restraint, the reality is that the political will to make meaningful cuts to popular programs or raise taxes is consistently lacking. Cutting entitlement programs like Social Security or Medicare, which constitute significant portions of the federal budget, is politically unpalatable. Similarly, reducing defence spending, another major budget component, is often met with resistance, particularly from defence contractors and regions economically dependent on military funding.

The Trump administration's approach was no exception. Despite campaign promises to reduce the debt, the administration passed a major tax reform bill in 2017 that reduced corporate tax rates and provided tax cuts for individuals. While these measures were framed as pro-growth policies designed to stimulate the economy, they also contributed to an increase in the deficit.

By the end of Trump's term, the national debt had grown substantially, fuelled further by emergency spending measures in response to the COVID-19 pandemic. The reality of governing often clashes with the promises made during campaigns, as the political consequences of austerity measures or tax increases outweigh the long-term benefits of deficit reduction.

Joe Biden's administration, too, has faced the challenge of managing the debt while pursuing ambitious policy goals. The American Rescue Plan, aimed at mitigating the economic impact of the pandemic, and subsequent infrastructure and social spending proposals, have all required significant government outlays. While these investments are justified by their potential long-term benefits, such as job creation and economic recovery, they also illustrate how the structural issues contributing to the deficit remain unaddressed.

What becomes clear is that the bipartisan failure to manage the debt is not solely a problem of economic policy but a problem of political will. Presidents, regardless of party affiliation, are often caught between the need to stimulate the economy and the need to control spending. The reality is that addressing the deficit would require either cuts to popular programs or increases in taxes, measures that carry political risk. As a result, the debt continues to grow, with each administration contributing to the problem rather than solving it.

The illusion of control over the economy becomes especially evident when presidents are blamed for deficits that have deep, structural causes beyond their immediate control. While a president's policies can influence the economy in the short term, the broader issue of the national debt is a long-term challenge that requires systemic solutions. The tendency to oversimplify this issue, focusing on the actions of a single administration rather than the cumulative impact of decades of policy decisions, perpetuates the myth that a president alone can rectify the situation.

Moreover, the global context of debt cannot be ignored. The United States, as a major economic power, is able to borrow at relatively low interest rates because of the stability and trust in its economy. This has allowed successive administrations to avoid immediate consequences for increasing the debt.

However, as interest rates rise or economic conditions change, the burden of servicing this debt becomes more pronounced. This could lead to significant challenges in the future, particularly if the U.S. economy faces a downturn or if other countries begin to question America's fiscal stability.

The illusion of success that trade wars present and the illusion of control over debt and deficit issues are linked by the same underlying dynamic: a desire to project strength and influence while avoiding the politically difficult realities of managing a complex economy. Trade wars, with their visible, high-stakes nature, provide presidents with a stage to demonstrate action. In contrast, the debt issue, while equally critical, is less visible and far more challenging to address within the constraints of the political system.

The Disconnect Between Political Rhetoric and Economic Reality

Trade wars and the national debt are just two examples of how presidents attempt to create the illusion of control over economic forces that are often beyond their reach. Trade wars can provide a temporary boost in perception, showing presidents as decisive actors on the global stage, yet they rarely deliver the promised economic benefits. Similarly, the bipartisan failure to address the debt reveals the limits of presidential influence when faced with systemic economic challenges that require cooperation, compromise, and a willingness to make difficult choices.

Ultimately, these economic issues illustrate the gap between political rhetoric and reality. Presidents campaign on promises of economic control and recovery, yet the interconnected and complex nature of the global economy, coupled with domestic political constraints, often limits what they can achieve.

As long as the public and the media continue to view the president as the ultimate arbiter of economic outcomes, the illusion of control will persist, shaping how presidents are judged and how policies are crafted. However, understanding the realities behind these economic challenges is essential for moving beyond rhetoric and towards meaningful, long-term solutions.

How Presidents Are Credited or Blamed Regardless of Their Actual Influence

The perception of a president's ability to manage the economy can make or break their administration. This is true regardless of how much control they actually have over the myriad factors influencing economic outcomes. Public opinion often simplifies complex economic dynamics into narratives that credit or blame the president directly.

The Simplification of Economic Complexities

Economic performance is inherently complex, driven by a multitude of factors including global markets, trade policies, technology, natural resources, the actions of multinational corporations, and the independent decisions made by entities like the Federal Reserve. Yet, in the public imagination, these complexities are often distilled into a simple question: Is the president doing a good job?

This simplification is not accidental. It serves the interests of both politicians and the media, who know that clear, straightforward narratives are more engaging and easier for the public to digest. Thus, when the economy is booming, the president is hailed as a hero; when it falters, they are blamed as a failure, even if their policies have little to do with the actual outcomes. This binary view is reinforced by media coverage, campaign rhetoric, and the public's desire for a clear figurehead to credit or blame.

How Public Opinion on Economic Performance Is Measured

Public opinion on economic performance is primarily measured through polls and surveys conducted by research organizations, media outlets, and political parties. These polls ask a range of questions designed to gauge the public's perception of the economy and their evaluation of the president's performance. Questions often include:

- "Do you approve or disapprove of the way the president is handling the economy?"
- "How would you rate the current state of the economy: excellent, good, fair, or poor?"
- "Who do you believe is most responsible for the current state of the economy?"

These questions, while seemingly straightforward, are carefully crafted to elicit responses that reflect the public's sentiments in simple, quantifiable terms. The results are then used to paint a picture of public opinion, often boiled down to approval ratings that become headline news.

Polling organizations like Gallup, Pew Research Center, and major news networks such as CNN, Fox News, and NBC conduct regular surveys to track economic approval ratings. These ratings are frequently tied directly to the president's performance, even though the economy's state is influenced by a range of factors beyond their control. The results of these polls are significant because they shape the media narrative, influence investor confidence, and, crucially, impact how voters perceive the effectiveness of an administration.

The Influence of Media in Shaping Economic Perception

The media plays a central role in shaping and amplifying public opinion on economic performance. Television networks, newspapers, online news outlets, and social media platforms all contribute to the collective narrative about the economy, often framing the discussion in ways that either credit or criticize the president.

For instance, when economic indicators like GDP growth, stock market performance, or job creation numbers are positive, the media is quick to associate these metrics with presidential success. Conversely, when indicators like inflation, unemployment rates, or economic contraction worsen, the media coverage often focuses on the president's perceived failures. This framing is powerful; it reinforces the simplistic notion that the president has direct control over the economy's health, even though their policies may only have marginal or delayed effects.

The media's focus on short-term economic fluctuations rather than long-term structural trends further distorts the public's understanding of the president's influence. Monthly job reports, stock market highs or lows, and quarterly GDP figures are presented as immediate reflections of presidential competence. However, these metrics are often the result of broader economic cycles, international developments, or independent decisions by entities like the Federal Reserve. The media's emphasis on these numbers, however, feeds the perception that the president is either fixing or failing the economy, depending on the current trends.

The Use of Statistics to Benefit Presidents

Presidents and their administrations understand the power of statistics in shaping public perception, and they often use economic data to bolster their image. This is done through carefully crafted messaging, where positive economic indicators are highlighted and negative ones downplayed or attributed to external factors.

For example, if job numbers are high, the president and their team will emphasize their policies that supposedly led to job creation. Press conferences, social media posts, and speeches will repeat statistics like "record job growth" or "lowest unemployment rate in decades." These figures are framed as direct results of the administration's efforts, even though many factors—such as technological advancements, market conditions, and decisions made by private companies, are also in play. By repeating these numbers and associating them with their leadership, presidents aim to cement a perception of economic competence and success.

Conversely, when economic indicators are unfavourable, administrations often attempt to shift the blame elsewhere. For example, when inflation rises or when there are supply chain disruptions, they may attribute these issues to global events beyond their control, such as oil price shocks, international conflicts, or the lingering effects of a pandemic. They frame these issues as temporary challenges that are being managed, rather than as failures of their policies. This approach helps maintain public confidence in their leadership, even in the face of negative data.

The use of "spin" is another tactic employed by administrations to manage public perception. Economic figures are often presented selectively to highlight the positives. For instance, an administration may focus on job creation numbers while ignoring or downplaying underemployment or the quality of the jobs created. Similarly, they might emphasize GDP growth while sidestepping issues like wage stagnation or income inequality, which also significantly impact how the average American experiences the economy. By selectively choosing which data points to highlight, presidents and their teams construct a narrative that aligns with their political goals.

The Public's Response: A Feedback Loop

Once economic data is presented and framed in the media, it creates a feedback loop that influences public opinion. When the economy is performing well, and the media highlights positive data while the administration claims credit, the public is likely to approve of the president's handling of the economy, which in turn boosts overall approval ratings. This positive feedback loop reinforces the perception that the president has direct control over economic outcomes and is effectively managing the nation's finances.

However, when the economy struggles, the reverse occurs. Even if the negative economic conditions are the result of global forces, public perception, shaped by media narratives and partisan messaging, often turns against the president. Approval ratings fall, and the opposition seizes the opportunity to highlight the administration's perceived failures, even if those criticisms oversimplify the complexity of the situation.

Public opinion on the economy is also heavily influenced by partisanship. Polling data often reveals that members of the president's party are more likely to view economic conditions favourably, while those from the opposing party are more likely to see them negatively, regardless of actual economic performance. This partisan divide indicates that public opinion on the economy is not solely based on objective data but is filtered through political allegiances and the media narratives that support them.

Case Studies: Obama and Trump
The presidencies of Barack Obama and Donald Trump provide illustrative examples of how public opinion on economic performance can be influenced by factors beyond actual control. When Obama took office in 2009 amidst the Great Recession, his administration inherited an economic crisis that had been building for years. While the economic recovery that followed was due to a combination of stimulus policies, actions by the Federal Reserve, and natural economic cycles, public opinion was divided. Supporters credited Obama with saving the economy, while detractors argued that his policies slowed growth.

Conversely, during Donald Trump's presidency, the administration frequently touted record stock market highs and low unemployment rates as evidence of Trump's economic prowess. However, many of these gains were continuations of trends that began during the Obama administration, or they were influenced by global economic conditions rather than specific policies enacted by Trump. Yet, the administration skilfully framed these positive indicators as direct results of their efforts, and the media's amplification of these statistics helped bolster Trump's economic approval ratings until the COVID-19 pandemic drastically altered the economic landscape.

The Gap Between Perception and Reality

The gap between perception and reality in public opinion on economic performance is significant. Despite the president's limited influence over many aspects of the economy, the public continues to hold them responsible for economic conditions. This dynamic is shaped by media narratives, polling methodologies, and partisan messaging that simplify complex economic realities into stories of success or failure tied directly to the president.

As long as the public craves a figurehead to credit or blame for the state of the economy, this cycle will continue. Presidents will use statistics to their advantage, media outlets will frame stories for maximum engagement, and public opinion will be shaped more by perception than by reality. Understanding this dynamic is crucial to recognizing the limitations of presidential power and the ways in which economic narratives are constructed and maintained in the political arena.

CHAPTER 6

MILITARY POWER AND THE COMMANDER-IN-CHIEF MYTH

The American presidency has long carried the weighty title of *commander-in-chief*. From the earliest days of the republic, when George Washington donned his military uniform, to the present day, the image of the president as the ultimate leader of the nation's armed forces has remained central to the American imagination. The notion of a strong, decisive leader, capable of steering the military through both crisis and conflict, is deeply embedded in the country's cultural and political psyche. It is a story Americans tell themselves, a story of power, leadership, and, ultimately, control. Yet, as compelling as this narrative may be, it often obscures the reality of how military power is actually wielded, and it masks the limits of presidential influence.

As an external observer, one can't help but notice the disconnect between the myth of the commander-in-chief and the intricate machinery that drives American military decisions. The truth is, while the president does indeed hold a significant role in shaping military strategy, the idea that they have unilateral control over all military affairs is far from accurate. The Pentagon, with its vast network of advisors, generals, and intelligence operatives, wields immense influence and so they should. The military-industrial complex, which President Eisenhower famously warned against, operates as a powerful entity with its own momentum, often pushing and pulling in directions that go beyond presidential control.

Consider, for instance, the layers of military bureaucracy. Presidents rely heavily on the expertise of their advisors, many of whom have decades of experience and agendas of their own. The president may be the face of military decisions, but behind every troop deployment, airstrike, or strategic shift, there are countless voices shaping the outcome. In practice, this means that the president's role is often one of balancing competing interests and managing the optics of decisions that have already been heavily influenced by those within the military establishment. It's a delicate dance, and one where the public perception of a single, all-powerful leader often diverges from the reality of a collaborative, sometimes contentious, decision-making process.

Then there is the matter of military interventions and proxy wars, those conflicts that unfold in places far from the eyes of the American public. From Afghanistan to Syria, U.S. military involvement often operates in murky waters, with layers of covert operations, intelligence gathering, and partnerships with allied forces. The president may authorize these actions, but the execution is complex and decentralized. These conflicts are often fought not by American soldiers alone but through alliances, proxies, and local militias. The president's authority is diluted by the intricate network of international relationships and operational tactics that no single leader can fully oversee.

In the age of drone warfare and cyber security, the traditional image of the commander-in-chief faces even greater challenges. Drone strikes, once considered a targeted, efficient method of eliminating threats, have raised ethical and strategic dilemmas that presidents struggle to manage.

While the president authorizes drone programs, the reality of their operation is determined by intelligence reports, real-time assessments, and decisions made by military personnel far removed from the Oval Office. Cybersecurity, too, complicates the commander-in-chief's role; it is a battlefield that lacks borders, where state and non-state actors collide in a space beyond the traditional chain of command. The illusion that a president can command and control these emerging forms of warfare, as they might have once controlled a battlefield or naval fleet, becomes harder to maintain.

The consequences of this disconnect are profound. When wars stretch on for years, as in Iraq and Afghanistan, the public often looks to the president for accountability. Yet, the reality is that these wars, once set in motion, operate on a logic and timeline of their own, often influenced by factors beyond the control of a single administration. The notion of the president as the architect of military success or failure is a simplification that ignores the broader geopolitical, economic, and institutional forces at play.

The Role of the Pentagon

The Pentagon, headquartered in Arlington, Virginia, is not merely a building; it represents the epicentre of American military power. It is a sprawling institution with tens of thousands of employees, including military personnel, civilian staff, and contractors. Within its walls are the Joint Chiefs of Staff, an array of defence departments, intelligence agencies, and countless advisors specializing in every conceivable aspect of warfare and national security. This structure provides the president with access to an immense pool of expertise and information, but it also means that the president is rarely the sole architect of military strategy. Instead, they are a leader navigating through the advice and recommendations of seasoned military experts whose perspectives are shaped by decades of experience, institutional priorities, and sometimes their own ambitions.

The influence of military advisors on presidential decisions is rooted in the very structure of how the American military operates. The Joint Chiefs of Staff, composed of the highest-ranking military officers from each branch of the armed forces, serve as the primary military advisors to the president. Their role is to provide professional military advice, ensuring that the president has a comprehensive understanding of the risks and possibilities associated with any military action. These advisors hold significant sway; they bring with them years, if not decades, of expertise in combat strategy, international relations, and defence policy. When they speak, presidents, many of whom lack military experience, are inclined to listen.

A classic example of this dynamic occurred during the Cuban Missile Crisis in 1962. President John F. Kennedy, faced with the Soviet installation of nuclear missiles in Cuba, found himself in a tense standoff that had the potential to escalate into nuclear war. Kennedy's military advisors, including members of the Joint Chiefs of Staff, pushed for an immediate and aggressive military response, advocating for airstrikes on Cuban missile sites. They believed that swift military action was the only way to eliminate the threat. However, Kennedy, wary of the consequences of such escalation, ultimately chose a naval blockade and diplomatic negotiations instead. This decision, which helped avert a nuclear catastrophe, demonstrated the complex relationship between a president and their military advisors. While Kennedy respected their expertise, he also recognized the need to weigh their advice against broader political considerations and the risks of full-scale war.

Another illustrative case is that of Lyndon B. Johnson during the Vietnam War. Johnson's presidency was marked by deepening U.S. involvement in Vietnam, a conflict that became increasingly unpopular and mired in controversy. From the beginning, Johnson relied heavily on the recommendations of military advisors, who assured him that incremental escalations, what came to be known as the policy of "gradualism", would lead to victory. The Pentagon and its advisors presented the president with options that seemed manageable and promised limited gains, often downplaying the likelihood of entanglement. Johnson, trusting in their expertise, authorized troop surges and bombing campaigns. Over time, however, it became clear that the military's optimistic assessments were not matching the reality on the ground, and Johnson's presidency became overwhelmed by a war that grew far beyond his control. The Vietnam War serves as a cautionary tale of how military advisors can shape presidential decisions, sometimes locking presidents into strategies that are difficult to unwind.

In more recent history, the influence of the Pentagon was evident during the presidency of Barack Obama, particularly in the decision to intervene in Libya in 2011.

Initially hesitant about military involvement, Obama faced significant pressure from his military advisors, including then-Secretary of Defence Robert Gates and top generals, who argued for a no-fly zone and airstrikes to prevent a humanitarian disaster as Libyan dictator Muammar Gaddafi threatened mass violence against civilians. Obama ultimately authorized military action, relying on the Pentagon's assurances that the intervention would be limited in scope.

However, as the situation in Libya deteriorated into chaos and civil war, it became clear that the intervention's consequences extended far beyond the limited engagement initially envisioned. The experience in Libya highlighted the tension between a president's cautious instincts and the Pentagon's confidence in military solutions, illustrating how military advisors can guide, and sometimes pressure, presidents into actions with far-reaching and unforeseen consequences.

The dynamic between presidents and their military advisors is further complicated by the Pentagon's bureaucratic culture and institutional interests. The military is an enormous and powerful institution with its own internal logic and priorities. High-ranking officers and military leaders often have long-term perspectives that may differ from the more immediate, politically driven goals of a sitting president. For instance, the military may advocate for maintaining a presence in a region to secure strategic interests or prevent a power vacuum, even when the president may seek to withdraw troops to fulfil a campaign promise or reduce overseas commitments. This was notably the case in Afghanistan, where multiple administrations struggled with the decision to draw down U.S. forces. Despite Barack Obama's efforts to end America's involvement, and later, Donald Trump's and Joe Biden's similar intentions, military leaders frequently advised caution, emphasizing the risks of a hasty withdrawal and the potential resurgence of terrorist threats. The tension between the military's long-term vision and the president's political considerations often creates a push-and-pull dynamic, one that showcases how military advisors can temper or even resist a president's strategic aims.

Moreover, military advisors wield influence not only through direct counsel but also through the Pentagon's control over information. The president depends on the intelligence and analysis provided by the military to make informed decisions. This creates a situation where the information flow is controlled and filtered through layers of military personnel and intelligence agencies, giving the Pentagon significant power to shape the narrative and options presented to the president. If advisors emphasize certain threats or present specific scenarios as likely outcomes, they can effectively steer presidential decisions in a direction that aligns with their strategic preferences.

This influence is particularly pronounced in situations involving new and emerging forms of warfare, such as drone strikes and cyber operations. In these areas, the expertise lies squarely within the military and intelligence communities, leaving the president reliant on the specialized knowledge and recommendations of advisors. For example, the Obama administration significantly expanded the use of drone strikes as a counterterrorism tool, often based on the Pentagon's assurances of precision and effectiveness. Yet, the realities of these strikes, civilian casualties, the psychological impact on local populations, and the long-term consequences, often remained obscured, leading to debates about the ethical and strategic implications of such operations. The Pentagon's framing of these technologies as clean and efficient solutions has significant influence over how presidents deploy them, shaping both military policy and public perception.

Ultimately, the role of the Pentagon and its advisors illustrates the limits of presidential power in military affairs. While the commander-in-chief is seen as the ultimate decision-maker, they operate within a complex web of influence where military expertise, institutional interests, and strategic priorities intersect. Presidents often must balance their instincts and political goals against the weight of advice from seasoned military leaders, who possess both the knowledge and the bureaucratic leverage to steer military decisions. This dynamic, while necessary for ensuring that the president is well-informed, also reveals how the image of the president as an all-powerful military leader is, in many ways, an illusion. Presidents may command the military in name, but in practice, they navigate a deeply entrenched system where influence flows in multiple directions, and where the advice of the Pentagon can be both a guiding light and a source of entanglement.

Proxy Wars and Interventions

The United States has long engaged in conflicts beyond its borders, frequently under the guise of protecting national interests or promoting democracy. But many of these conflicts do not unfold on the grand stage of a declared war; instead, they operate in the shadows, often as proxy wars or covert interventions. From Vietnam to Afghanistan, and more recently in places like Syria and Yemen, the U.S. has deployed its influence, funding, and weapons to support allied groups and local forces. Yet, despite the popular perception of the American president as a commander-in-chief who oversees every military move, the reality is that these actions may lack direct presidential oversight. They are instead managed by an intricate network of military officials, intelligence agencies, and foreign partners, creating a web of complexity far beyond the reach of any single leader.

The allure of proxy wars is straightforward: they allow nations to exert influence without the direct commitment of troops and resources, reducing the political and public backlash that often accompanies full-scale military interventions. For the U.S., proxy wars have been a tool of foreign policy since the Cold War, when the goal was to contain Soviet influence across the globe. From arming the mujahideen in Afghanistan to supporting anti-communist forces in Latin America, proxy wars allowed the U.S. to engage its adversaries indirectly. In theory, the president authorizes these actions, but the reality is that once operations begin, control often shifts away from the Oval Office and into the hands of the Pentagon, the CIA, and local allies.

Take the example of Afghanistan in the 1980s. The U.S., through the CIA's Operation Cyclone, funded and armed Afghan mujahideen fighters to combat Soviet forces. While President Ronald Reagan publicly championed the cause, portraying it as a fight for freedom, the specifics of how that support was managed, the distribution of weapons, the training of fighters, and the coordination with Pakistani intelligence, were largely conducted outside of his direct oversight. The complexity of these networks meant that once the aid flowed, the consequences became difficult to control. Eventually, these same mujahideen factions would fragment, giving rise to the Taliban and other militant groups that the U.S. would later confront as enemies. The long-term outcomes of proxy wars are rarely predictable, and the president's involvement, though crucial at the authorization stage, often becomes peripheral as operations unfold on the ground.

In more recent years, U.S. involvement in Syria illustrates the blurred lines of proxy warfare. Under the Obama administration, the U.S. began supporting Syrian opposition groups fighting against the Assad regime.

What started as a strategy to weaken Assad's hold on power and counter ISIS quickly became a complex quagmire. The CIA and Pentagon, both with their own agendas and tactics, provided support to various factions. The coordination—or, at times, the lack thereof, between these agencies led to conflicting strategies, including instances where different U.S.-backed groups ended up fighting one another. The president's role, in this case, was not one of micro-managing military strategy but of managing political fallout and navigating alliances with international partners like Turkey and Saudi Arabia, each with their own objectives in the region.

The lack of direct presidential oversight in proxy wars is not just a matter of logistical necessity; it is also a political safeguard. Proxy wars allow administrations to operate with plausible deniability, distancing the president from the direct consequences of military actions. For instance, in Yemen, the U.S. has supported Saudi-led efforts against Houthi rebels through arms sales, intelligence, and logistical support. While this involvement is significant, it is often presented as a strategic partnership rather than direct military action. This framing shields the president from immediate accountability, making it seem as though the conflict is an extension of diplomatic support rather than a proxy war under U.S. influence.

The reality, however, is that such conflicts can quickly spiral beyond the control of any single leader or administration. The decentralized nature of proxy wars means that once they begin, they operate through a complex web of intermediaries—foreign allies, intelligence agencies, and local militias—each with its own interests and objectives. The president's role becomes one of managing optics and alliances rather than directly overseeing military strategy. This distance creates the illusion of control but often leaves the president as much a spectator as the public when events escalate or go awry.

Civilian-Military Relations: The Myth of Presidential Control Over Complex Military Operations

The American president, as commander-in-chief, is constitutionally empowered to oversee the country's armed forces. This role, deeply ingrained in the American consciousness, suggests a leader who directs every military operation and oversees the country's defence with an iron grip. However, the reality of civilian-military relations is much more complex. While the president holds ultimate authority, the execution and management of military operations are often guided by the Pentagon, military advisors, and various intelligence agencies. These entities operate with a level of autonomy that can limit the president's control, creating a dynamic where the illusion of presidential omnipotence overshadows the intricate, decentralized nature of military decision-making.

The U.S. military is a vast and powerful institution, and its influence extends far beyond the chain of command directed from the White House. The Pentagon, with its hierarchy of generals and defence experts, plays a crucial role in shaping military strategy. Generals, with their years of experience and access to intelligence, often have more detailed knowledge of the situation on the ground than the president does. While the president may set the strategic vision—such as deploying troops to a particular region or authorizing military action—the details of how those operations unfold are largely in the hands of the military establishment. This separation creates a tension between the civilian leadership and military command, one that has defined American military engagements for decades.

A classic example of this dynamic is the Vietnam War. President Lyndon B. Johnson, despite his public rhetoric of control and confidence, found himself increasingly constrained by the advice and recommendations of his military advisors. Generals like William Westmoreland advocated for escalating the conflict, convinced that increased troop presence and firepower would turn the tide in America's favour. Johnson, wary of being seen as weak, often deferred to their expertise, despite his growing private doubts about the war's success. The result was a war strategy that became more about maintaining credibility and following military advice than about achieving clearly defined political goals. The illusion of control masked the reality that the war's complexity and the entrenched interests of military leaders had placed the president in a reactive, rather than directive, position.

The Iraq War under President George W. Bush further illustrates the challenges of civilian-military relations. The initial invasion in 2003 was framed as a decisive action led by the president, yet the subsequent occupation and insurgency highlighted how limited presidential control could be. Once Baghdad fell, the administration faced a chaotic situation that required rapid adaptation. Military leaders, such as General David Petraeus, spearheaded the surge strategy that was credited with stabilizing parts of Iraq. While the president authorized and endorsed these actions, the day-to-day management of counterinsurgency efforts, troop deployments, and alliances with local forces were coordinated by military officials. The president, while still central to the decision-making process, was one voice among many, navigating the recommendations of generals, intelligence reports, and political allies.

Civilian-military relations are further complicated by the Pentagon's institutional power. The Department of Defence, with its enormous budget and influence, often sets the tone for how military operations are conducted. Presidents, aware of the political and operational ramifications of defying military advice, frequently find themselves accommodating the preferences of their generals. This dynamic creates a subtle power struggle where the president's role is more about managing and mediating than commanding outright. The image of the president as a solitary decision-maker simplifies what is, in reality, a complex, collaborative, and often contentious process.

Cybersecurity presents another challenge to the myth of presidential control. Cyber operations are not confined to physical spaces and traditional battlefields; they involve state and non-state actors, hackers, and algorithms operating across a digital landscape that defies conventional military oversight. When Russia interfered in the 2016 U.S. election, it highlighted how vulnerabilities in cyberspace could undermine American interests without a clear military response. The complexity of these operations and the need for technical expertise mean that while the president may set objectives, such as countering foreign cyber threats, the execution is left to a network of intelligence agencies and cybersecurity experts. The decentralized nature of cyber operations limits the direct control the president can exert, making the image of a commander-in-chief presiding over a clear battlefield strategy increasingly obsolete.

The consequences of this civilian-military dynamic are significant, particularly when conflicts drag on or when military strategies falter. Presidents often find themselves blamed for military failures, despite the fact that their influence over day-to-day operations is more limited than the public believes. Endless wars, such as those in Afghanistan and Iraq, illustrate this disconnect. President Obama, for instance, inherited the wars in Iraq and Afghanistan and sought to end them. Yet, despite his administration's efforts to draw down troops, he found himself sending additional forces back into Iraq to combat the rise of ISIS. This cycle of withdrawal and re-engagement demonstrates how military realities often exceed the intentions or desires of the president. The Pentagon's recommendations, the situation on the ground, and the broader geopolitical context frequently dictate decisions that presidents must either endorse or risk political fallout.

The myth of presidential control over military operations is a compelling narrative, but it rarely reflects the complex and decentralized nature of modern warfare. The president, while constitutionally the commander-in-chief, is only one part of a much larger system. Proxy wars, covert operations, and the autonomy of the Pentagon and intelligence agencies create a dynamic where the president's influence, though significant, is limited by the realities of modern military power. Recognizing this gap between perception and reality is crucial for understanding how military decisions are made, and why the outcomes of these decisions often seem beyond the control of any one leader.

Commander in Chief: Films and TV

Television and film have long played a significant role in shaping public perceptions of the American presidency, especially when it comes to the commander-in-chief's role as a decisive and heroic military leader. Through decades of movies and TV shows, the portrayal of the president has evolved into a larger-than-life figure, a singular authority who not only commands the military but also serves as the nation's protector during crises, whether those crises are domestic, international, or even extraterrestrial. From political dramas to action-packed blockbusters and science fiction epics, Hollywood has reinforced the idea that the president is the ultimate military leader, wielding power over life-and-death decisions and rallying the nation during dire circumstances. Even when the threats come from beyond our planet, the president's role remains central, further embedding the illusion that the commander-in-chief is the ultimate figure of authority and control.

This portrayal is not just a matter of entertainment; it has real implications for how audiences perceive the American presidency. In a world where media and politics are increasingly intertwined, the image of the president as a heroic military leader reinforces the myth of presidential omnipotence. This depiction often blurs the line between reality and fiction, shaping the public's understanding of what the commander-in-chief is and what they should be able to do. The president, in these stories, is not just a political figure but a warrior, a protector, and a leader of men, a trope that has persisted from historical dramas to modern science fiction.

One of the most iconic and influential examples of the president as a military leader in cinema is *Independence Day* (1996), where President Thomas J. Whitmore, played by Bill Pullman, embodies the archetypal warrior-leader. When Earth faces an alien invasion of apocalyptic proportions, it is Whitmore who steps up, delivering an impassioned and patriotic speech to rally not just Americans but *the entire world*. His address, beginning with the now-famous words, "We will not go quietly into the night," serves as the film's emotional and motivational climax. This moment transforms Whitmore from a politician into a wartime hero, a symbol of unity, courage, and resilience. In this speech, he positions himself as a global leader, not just the president of the United States, emphasizing that the fight against the alien threat is a fight for the survival of humanity.

What makes *Independence Day* particularly compelling is how it elevates the president beyond his civilian role, transforming him into a warrior who takes personal action. Unlike most real-world presidents who remain far from the battlefield, Whitmore literally jumps into the fray, piloting a fighter jet and joining the fight against the aliens. This decision to portray the president as not only a military strategist but also an active combatant taps into a deeply ingrained American mythos of the president as a symbol of strength, unity, and action. It amplifies the image of the commander-in-chief to almost superhuman proportions, suggesting that the president is capable of both leading and fighting alongside his troops.

The portrayal in *Independence Day* is powerful because it simplifies the complexities of military decision-making into a narrative of heroic leadership. The movie strips away the layers of bureaucracy, military chains of command, and the multitude of advisors that typically influence presidential decisions. Instead, it frames the president as a singular hero, both the mastermind and the soldier, capable of taking direct action when others falter. It suggests that in times of crisis, the American president is not just the head of state but a warrior-leader who can be relied upon to physically defend the nation. This image is undeniably thrilling and taps into a cultural desire for strong, decisive leadership. However, it also reinforces a myth that is far from the reality of modern presidential power.

The dramatization in *Independence Day*, with its stirring monologues and action-packed scenes, effectively erases the operational complexities behind military engagements. In reality, no modern president would personally pilot a fighter jet or take direct action in a combat scenario. Presidents rely on military advisors, the Pentagon, and an entire infrastructure of decision-makers to guide and implement military actions. Yet, films like *Independence Day* present the president as both the architect and executor of military strategy, reinforcing the illusion of control and influence that far exceeds the actual capabilities of the office.

This cinematic image of the president as a wartime leader extends beyond alien invasion films. In movies like *Air Force One* (1997), Harrison Ford's portrayal of President James Marshall shows a commander-in-chief who not only negotiates with terrorists but personally fights to save hostages and reclaim control of his hijacked plane. The movie offers a high-octane image of a president who can simultaneously wield executive power and physical prowess. The narrative leaves little room for the bureaucracy or military chain of command that would realistically dictate responses in such a crisis. Instead, it frames the president as a lone hero capable of outmanoeuvring enemies and physically protecting his nation.

Television shows, too, perpetuate the myth of the all-powerful commander-in-chief. Series like *The West Wing* and *Designated Survivor* place the president at the centre of military and political crises, often portraying them as the ultimate decision-makers. In *The West Wing*, President Josiah Bartlet (Martin Sheen) is frequently shown making high-stakes military decisions, usually after consulting his circle of advisors. While the show provides insight into the complexity of political and military decision-making, it still centres the president as the ultimate authority, downplaying the decentralized reality of military command structures. Meanwhile, in *Designated Survivor*, President Tom Kirkman (Kiefer Sutherland) navigates various national security crises, often making quick, decisive military decisions to protect American interests. The show dramatizes the commander-in-chief's role in such a way that viewers are led to believe that the president has an immediate and decisive influence over every military action.

Even in science fiction films set in dystopian futures, the myth of the all-powerful, military-savvy president persists. In *The Hunger Games* series, President Alma Coin (Julianne Moore) embodies the concept of a leader directing military campaigns in a world on the brink of civil war. Despite the fictional and fantastical setting, the portrayal suggests that the president is both the orchestrator and executor of military strategy, further perpetuating the myth of the commander-in-chief as the central force in military matters.

This trend of portraying presidents as omnipotent commanders-in-chief, even in films involving alien invasions or fantastical dystopias, suggests a broader cultural fascination with the idea of strong, centralized leadership. It reflects a public desire for a figurehead who can single-handedly protect and guide the nation through crisis. However, it also misrepresents the reality of presidential power. Presidents are not lone warriors or masterminds with absolute control over military actions; they are part of a complex, often bureaucratic system that requires negotiation, collaboration, and compromise. Films and television shows, by focusing on the dramatic and heroic aspects of the presidency, create an oversimplified and misleading picture, yet it doesn't hurt the overseas view of American strength.

While these portrayals serve as entertaining escapism, they also shape public perceptions and expectations. By continually reinforcing the idea that the president is a heroic military figure capable of direct intervention, media narratives contribute to the illusion of control that presidents themselves must navigate. In reality, presidents authorize military actions but do not wield control in the ways portrayed on screen. They rely on the expertise and strategic guidance of military leaders and intelligence officials, operating within the constraints of law, politics, and global alliances.

The Consequences of Endless Wars and the broader illusion of control

Endless wars have become a defining characteristic of American foreign policy in the 21st century, and their consequences are profound, both for the presidents who oversee them and for the broader perception of presidential power. These conflicts, stretching on for years and even decades, create an illusion of control, a narrative that suggests the president, as commander-in-chief, has the capacity to manage, direct, and ultimately conclude these wars successfully. However, the reality is far more complex. The president's influence over these conflicts is often limited, constrained by the sprawling nature of the military-industrial complex, the intricacies of international alliances, and the unpredictability of local dynamics in conflict zones. This disconnect between perception and reality not only impacts presidential legacies but also exposes the broader illusion of control that surrounds the office.

Take Afghanistan, for example. America's longest war, it spanned four presidencies, each leader inheriting and passing on the conflict to the next. President George W. Bush initiated the invasion in 2001 as a direct response to the September 11 attacks, with the aim of dismantling al-Qaeda and overthrowing the Taliban regime. The initial stages of the war, marked by swift military successes, fed into the narrative of decisive presidential action. Bush, and by extension the American public, believed that the power of the presidency could decisively shape the outcome of the conflict. However, as the war dragged on, the complexity of Afghanistan's politics, tribal affiliations, and regional dynamics revealed the limitations of American influence. Bush's legacy became entangled with the decision to go to war and the failure to achieve a lasting victory, despite the perception of presidential control.

When President Obama took office, he was critical of the war in Iraq and promised to bring the "good war" in Afghanistan to a responsible end. Yet, the realities of the conflict dictated otherwise. Obama inherited a war that was already in its eighth year, and while he attempted to reduce troop levels, he eventually found himself authorizing a surge of forces to stabilize the country. This surge, while temporarily effective in reducing violence, did not bring about a lasting resolution. The Taliban continued to regroup, and the Afghan government struggled with corruption and incompetence. Obama, despite his intentions and the narrative of change that accompanied his presidency, became another leader tied to the quagmire of Afghanistan. His legacy, like Bush's, was marked by a war that could not be won but could also not be abandoned. The image of a president in control gave way to the reality of a leader bound by decisions made years earlier and by conditions beyond his influence.

President Trump entered the White House with a promise to end America's "endless wars." His rhetoric was clear, he criticized the foreign policy establishment for its entanglements abroad and vowed to bring American troops home. Yet, Trump's administration found itself similarly constrained by the reality on the ground. While he negotiated a peace deal with the Taliban, the withdrawal timeline and conditions became a matter of ongoing debate, illustrating how even a president committed to ending conflict faces significant obstacles in doing so. The military's insistence on maintaining a presence to support the fragile Afghan government and the volatile security situation showed how much of the decision-making process was out of Trump's hands.

His legacy became partially defined by the struggle to extract the U.S. from a war that had outlasted three previous administrations.

By the time President Joe Biden oversaw the chaotic withdrawal from Afghanistan in 2021, it was clear that the illusion of control had collapsed. The images of desperate Afghans clinging to American aircraft at Kabul's airport, the rapid takeover by the Taliban, and the inability to execute a smooth exit underscored how limited presidential power truly was in such a sprawling, decades-long conflict. Biden, like his predecessors, had inherited a war with no clear end and faced the dilemma of either prolonging the American presence or risking a collapse that would expose the limitations of U.S. influence. He chose the latter, and the consequences, both humanitarian and political, were severe. Biden's decision may have ended America's military involvement in Afghanistan, but it also added a chapter to his legacy that reflected the difficulty of disentangling the presidency from the consequences of endless war.

Endless wars do more than just shape presidential legacies; they highlight the broader illusion of control associated with the office. The perception of the president as an all-powerful figure capable of directing military outcomes is compelling but misleading. The reality is that wars, especially those involving insurgencies, civil conflicts, or complex regional dynamics, operate on timelines and under conditions that no single administration can manage. Generals, diplomats, intelligence agencies, and allied governments all play critical roles, often driving decisions that limit the president's options. The Pentagon, for instance, wields significant influence in these conflicts, often pushing for continued military engagement based on operational needs and strategic assessments that extend beyond electoral cycles or presidential agendas.

Proxy wars, like those in Syria or Yemen, further illustrate this illusion. These conflicts, though not involving direct American troop deployments at large scale, still operate under the banner of presidential authority. Yet, they unfold in environments where local militias, foreign powers, and shifting alliances dictate much of the action. Presidents may authorize support or funding, but the complexities of proxy warfare mean that outcomes are largely unpredictable and often outside the direct oversight of the Oval Office. The result is that presidents are left managing the optics of conflicts they cannot fully control, negotiating with allies and adversaries while the underlying dynamics continue largely unaltered by their influence.

The impact of endless wars also reverberates through the American political landscape, influencing public perception and electoral outcomes. Presidents who inherit conflicts often face the challenge of justifying continued involvement to a war-weary public. Approval ratings become tied to the perceived success or failure of military engagements, even when the president has limited capacity to affect the outcome. The wars in Iraq and Afghanistan, for instance, shaped public opinion around Bush, Obama, and Trump, illustrating how conflicts can become political liabilities regardless of their origins or evolution. This cycle, where wars begun under one administration affect the legacies and approval of subsequent leaders, underscores the difficulty presidents face in shaping their own narratives. The illusion that they control these conflicts sets up expectations that are almost impossible to meet, leading to a cycle of blame and disillusionment.

Beyond domestic politics, endless wars have significant implications for America's global standing. The prolonged nature of conflicts like those in Iraq and Afghanistan, and the inability of successive administrations to deliver on promises of victory or stability, has weakened America's credibility as a global leader. Allies question the reliability of American commitments when wars extend far beyond the timelines promised by multiple presidents. Adversaries, meanwhile, exploit these conflicts to undermine American influence, knowing that the U.S. is often mired in battles it cannot easily extract itself from. The illusion of control creates a gap between America's projected power and its actual ability to achieve its strategic objectives, weakening the image of the presidency both at home and abroad.

The expectation that the president can direct and conclude military conflicts creates a misleading narrative that obscures the institutional and geopolitical realities of modern warfare. The gap between perception and reality becomes evident as wars drag on, legacies are shaped by events beyond presidential control, and the public grows increasingly sceptical of America's role on the global stage.

The illusion of control not only sets up presidents for failure but also perpetuates a cycle where military engagement becomes both politically necessary and politically perilous. As long as the expectation persists that the president is the sole architect of military outcomes, the cycle of endless wars and their impact on presidential legacies is likely to continue.

Surveillance and the Presidency

When we think of presidential power, we often imagine the commander-in-chief directing military operations or the policymaker drafting laws. But there is another, less visible realm where the presidency exercises its authority, surveillance. In today's hyper-connected world, the ability to monitor communications, track movements, and gather vast quantities of data gives presidents a sense of omnipresence. Yet, this power is as much an illusion as it is real. For while surveillance may expand a president's reach, it also reveals the limitations of executive authority and raises critical questions about the balance between power, privacy, and democracy.

The roots of this surveillance state reach back to the mid-20th century, with the Cold War serving as a turning point in how the U.S. government engaged in intelligence gathering. Programs like COINTELPRO and Echelon set the stage for a more expansive surveillance network, initially aimed at monitoring external threats but increasingly focusing on internal surveillance as well. Presidents, from Truman to Nixon, capitalized on these systems, using them not only to gather information but also to exert control over political opponents and influence public opinion. However, the surveillance apparatus that expanded under their watch also began to escape their direct oversight, developing into an entity with its own motives and autonomy, a 'deep state' within the state.

Fast forward to the 21st century, and the presidency's surveillance capabilities have expanded exponentially. The digital revolution brought about by the internet and the rise of social media has transformed the landscape of intelligence gathering. The USA PATRIOT Act, signed into law shortly after 9/11, gave sweeping powers to the executive branch, allowing for the collection of metadata, monitoring of electronic communications, and surveillance of financial transactions, all in the name of national security. Presidents have leaned into these capabilities, understanding that they provide not just information but the perception of control and vigilance.

The public is often reassured by the idea that the president, backed by the most sophisticated surveillance technology in the world, can prevent terrorist attacks, cyber threats, and domestic violence before they occur.

But the reality is more complex. The information gathered by these vast surveillance networks often falls into the hands of intelligence agencies like the NSA, CIA, and FBI, which operate semi-independently from the executive office. While presidents might issue directives, these agencies interpret and act upon the data they collect with a level of autonomy that even the highest office in the land cannot fully control. The revelations by whistleblowers like Edward Snowden highlighted this disconnect, showing that the NSA's surveillance programs operated beyond the oversight of not just the public but also the lawmakers and, to some extent, even the president. What this reveals is that while the presidency may appear all-seeing, it is, in reality, entangled in a web of intelligence agencies that possess their own agendas and loyalties.

Moreover, surveillance technology has created a paradox for presidential power: while it enhances the ability to gather information, it also undermines the very values that the presidency is supposed to protect. The capability to monitor communications and collect vast data points has led to debates about privacy and civil liberties that presidents must navigate carefully. Democratic societies expect transparency and the protection of individual rights—principles that mass surveillance inherently challenges. When the Snowden leaks revealed the extent of NSA spying, it wasn't just a national scandal; it was an international one, damaging America's credibility as a defender of freedom and privacy on the global stage. The illusion of presidential power through surveillance is thus a double-edged sword, expanding influence while simultaneously eroding trust.

One might also argue that the expansion of surveillance has inadvertently exposed the president's vulnerabilities rather than strengthening executive power. Take, for example, the use of cybersecurity and digital intelligence to manage international conflicts. In theory, the president's access to real-time information about potential threats should create a strategic advantage. In practice, however, this has led to an increasing dependency on a digital infrastructure that is vulnerable to cyberattacks and foreign interference. The 2016 presidential election and the subsequent Russian disinformation campaigns highlighted the fragility of America's surveillance state. Despite the president's access to the most advanced surveillance technology in the world, foreign adversaries still found ways to infiltrate and manipulate American politics, proving that surveillance power does not necessarily equate to control.

Surveillance also shapes how presidents manage domestic politics. In recent years, the monitoring of social movements, such as Black Lives Matter or anti-lockdown protests during the COVID-19 pandemic, has underscored the temptation to use surveillance tools for political ends. The availability of digital monitoring technologies allows for unprecedented oversight of activists and dissenters, raising concerns about the potential misuse of power to silence political opposition or manipulate narratives. While these tools give presidents and their administrations the ability to anticipate and respond to unrest, they also create a tension between maintaining order and infringing upon the democratic right to protest. The illusion here is that surveillance grants control, but in reality, it may provoke backlash and undermine the legitimacy of the presidency itself.

Furthermore, surveillance technology has not just changed how presidents engage with external threats but also how they interact with the public. In a world where every action is recorded, presidents must constantly manage their image, knowing that surveillance, by intelligence agencies, the press, or even citizens themselves, can expose their private lives, mistakes, and inconsistencies. This perpetual visibility complicates the illusion of power. Rather than projecting strength, it makes presidents appear human, fallible, and at times, even powerless. Surveillance, therefore, not only monitors the public but also the presidency itself, contributing to the cycle of scandal and controversy that has become a hallmark of modern American politics.

The relationship between surveillance and the presidency raises a fundamental question: Does surveillance technology truly empower the president, or does it merely create the illusion of power while undermining the democratic fabric of the country? If surveillance is meant to be a tool for maintaining control, then the erosion of privacy, the expansion of state power, and the rise of political cynicism suggest that it is a tool with significant costs. Presidents who lean too heavily on surveillance may find themselves confronting the very forces they seek to control, caught in a web of public distrust, international criticism, and the overreach of intelligence agencies.

Ultimately, the story of surveillance and the presidency is a story of contradiction. The power to watch, monitor, and collect data is immense, but it does not guarantee control. It is a power that can create the illusion of strength while simultaneously revealing the limits of executive authority. As technology continues to evolve, the challenge for the presidency will be to balance the capabilities of surveillance with the values of democracy, maintaining the appearance of power without succumbing to its darker consequences.

CHAPTER 7

PARTISANSHIP AND POLARIZATION

In American politics, the notion of power has always been intertwined with perception. The office of the president, a role intended by the Founders to act as a stabilizing force within a balanced government, has become a lightning rod for partisan conflict and division. As an external observer, one cannot help but notice how, in recent decades, the intensity of partisanship has transformed not just the presidency but the entire American political landscape. The United States, often portrayed as a beacon of democracy and unity, is now increasingly defined by its divisions, what one might call a "Divided Empire."

The political fault lines that run through American society have always existed, but today they seem wider and deeper than ever. Turn on any news channel, scroll through social media, or read the latest opinion polls, and you'll see evidence of a country polarized to the point where even the notion of truth has become a partisan battleground. The president, once a unifying figure expected to govern on behalf of the entire nation, has become, instead, a symbol of division, hailed as a saviour by one side and vilified as a villain by the other. This hyper-partisan environment amplifies the illusion of presidential power, as each side invests their hopes and fears in the image of the president, casting him as either the hero who will save America or the antagonist who will destroy it.

This polarization is not just a byproduct of contemporary politics; it is also a symptom of a media environment that thrives on conflict and echo chambers. Cable news networks, talk radio, and social media platforms have all played pivotal roles in intensifying divisions, catering to partisan audiences and reinforcing preexisting beliefs rather than fostering meaningful dialogue. As a result, the American electorate has splintered into polarized camps, where citizens are increasingly isolated from views that challenge their own. It is no wonder that the presidency, viewed through such a fractured lens, appears as an epicentre of power, either wielded heroically or disastrously, depending on one's political allegiance.

This shift has profound consequences for governance. In the past, presidents operated within a framework of bipartisan cooperation, where compromise was the rule rather than the exception. Today, that framework is all but shattered. The legislative process has become gridlocked, and the ability to pass meaningful reform is often stymied by partisan agendas. Each administration faces intense resistance from the opposition, turning even routine governance into a series of high-stakes battles. The result is a government that functions less effectively, one where presidents are forced to rely increasingly on executive orders, and where partisan loyalty trumps policy substance.

This partisanship is further exacerbated by social media. In the digital age, political battles are fought not just on the floor of Congress but in the virtual town squares of Twitter, Facebook, and other platforms. These spaces amplify extreme voices, giving rise to what some call "hyper-partisan presidencies." Presidents must now navigate a landscape where their every word and action is scrutinized, dissected, and weaponized. Social media, with its algorithms favouring engagement over truth, reinforces polarized views, making it easier for misinformation to spread and harder for consensus to form.

This environment not only amplifies the personality of the president but also limits their ability to build coalitions or govern effectively.

What does it mean for the future of American governance when every policy becomes a partisan litmus test? How does this internal division affect America's role on the global stage? The erosion of bipartisanship is not merely a domestic issue; it weakens the country's stability, making it difficult for the United States to maintain its influence abroad. This chapter seeks to untangle these questions, tracing how the shift toward extreme partisanship has amplified the illusion of presidential power while simultaneously undercutting the foundations of governance and global leadership. In the end, the survival of the American "empire" may depend not on the power of its presidents, but on its ability to bridge the divides that threaten to tear it apart.

Political Echo Chambers

The role of the media in shaping political discourse in the United States has always been significant, but in recent decades, it has evolved in ways that have fundamentally altered the political landscape. The rise of partisan networks and the creation of political echo chambers have intensified divisions, amplifying the cult of personality around the presidency and other political figures. These echo chambers not only reinforce preexisting beliefs but also shape perceptions, often transforming the president into a heroic or villainous figure, depending on which side of the political spectrum one stands. As an external observer, it's impossible not to see how the media landscape in the U.S. has become a battleground of narratives, where facts are secondary to spectacle, and the most divisive content garners the most attention.

The concept of the echo chamber is not new, but the advent of 24-hour news cycles, social media platforms, and digital news outlets has expanded its reach and impact. Echo chambers are essentially spaces, physical, digital, or ideological, where people are exposed only to information, opinions, and narratives that reinforce their own beliefs. In the American context, these echo chambers are often partisan networks like Fox News, MSNBC, and increasingly popular online platforms like Newsmax or The Young Turks, which cater to specific political audiences. Within these spaces, the news is not merely reported; it is curated, framed, and sometimes manipulated to fit a specific ideological perspective.

Take Fox News, for example. Over the years, the network has cultivated a loyal conservative audience by consistently aligning itself with Republican values and candidates. Its prime-time hosts, such as Sean Hannity and Tucker Carlson, do more than report the news, they interpret it, often framing stories in ways that present conservative figures, particularly Republican presidents, as defenders of traditional American values against a hostile liberal agenda. During the Trump administration, Fox News was instrumental in creating and reinforcing the image of Trump as a populist hero. The network routinely amplified his rhetoric, downplayed controversies, and built a narrative around him as a fighter for the "forgotten Americans" who were being marginalized by coastal elites and liberal media.

For viewers who regularly consumed Fox News content, Trump's presidency became more than a political term, it became a movement, a crusade against the perceived liberal threat. The echo chamber effect was in full force: viewers were not just watching the news; they were being enveloped in a narrative that resonated with their beliefs and fears. When controversies arose, whether it was Trump's handling of the COVID-19 pandemic or his actions during the Black Lives Matter protests, Fox News often appeared to frame these issues as attacks on the president from biased media outlets and left-wing radicals. This insulated viewers from critical perspectives, reinforcing their allegiance to Trump and deepening the divide between them and those who consumed media from other, more critical sources.

On the other side of the spectrum, MSNBC and outlets like The Washington Post or The New York Times often cater to a liberal audience. The echo chamber effect works similarly here but with a different target. During Trump's presidency, these outlets frequently highlighted controversies, emphasizing his administration's alleged corruption, incompetence, and disregard for democratic norms. Shows like *The Rachel Maddow Show* dissected Trump's every move, building narratives that positioned him as an existential threat to American democracy. For viewers loyal to these sources, the portrayal of Trump was not that of a populist hero but a dangerous demagogue, a symbol of everything wrong with American politics.

This partisan divide in media coverage is not limited to television. The digital sphere has created even more potent echo chambers, particularly through social media platforms like Twitter, Facebook, and YouTube. Algorithms on these platforms are designed to maximize user engagement, often by promoting content that aligns with users' interests and past behaviours. In the context of politics, this means users are frequently presented with posts, videos, and articles that reinforce their beliefs, creating a self-perpetuating cycle of confirmation bias.

Facebook, for instance, has been criticized for its role in amplifying misinformation and polarizing content. During election cycles, users often find themselves in echo chambers where their feeds are filled with posts from like-minded individuals or groups, promoting stories that reinforce their partisan views. In the lead-up to the 2020 election, pro-Trump Facebook groups circulated stories about voter fraud and alleged corruption within the Democratic Party, while pro-Biden groups focused on Trump's mishandling of the pandemic and accusations of racism. Each side was fed a continuous stream of information that aligned with their worldview, making it increasingly difficult for users to encounter content that challenged their beliefs or presented a balanced perspective.

YouTube, another major platform, also plays a role in creating echo chambers through its recommendation algorithm. Users who watch politically charged content are often recommended videos that further entrench their views. A user watching a pro-Trump video might be recommended more content from conservative influencers, building a library of videos that praise Trump's policies, criticize his opponents, and dismiss negative media coverage as "fake news." Conversely, users viewing progressive content may find themselves in a loop of videos criticizing Republican policies, highlighting Trump's controversies, and promoting Democratic candidates as champions of progress.

The effect of these digital echo chambers is profound. They not only reinforce existing biases but also create an environment where users feel validated, their beliefs constantly affirmed by the content they consume. Over time, this leads to a hardening of political views and a decreased willingness to engage with or even acknowledge the validity of opposing perspectives. When people are surrounded by content that echoes their own beliefs, they are more likely to see political opponents not just as people with different opinions but as threats to their way of life.

This dynamic amplifies the cult of personality around political figures, particularly presidents, as they become central to these partisan narratives. Conservative echo chambers may elevate Republican presidents to near-mythic status, portraying them as defenders of American values and traditions. Liberal echo chambers, meanwhile, might present Democratic presidents as saviours of democracy and champions of progress. In both cases, the president's persona takes centre stage, overshadowing policy substance and the complexities of governance.

This phenomenon is not without consequences. By amplifying the cult of personality, these echo chambers contribute to the polarization of American politics. They create an environment where individuals are not only unwilling to engage with opposing views but are also increasingly hostile towards those who hold them. The president, as the most visible symbol of American political power, becomes a polarizing figure, beloved by one half of the country and despised by the other. This deepens the illusion of presidential power, as the media and digital platforms magnify the president's role in every issue, whether it be the economy, public health, or foreign policy, often obscuring the structural and systemic factors that play a much larger role.

The divisive impact of these echo chambers is further illustrated through specific examples of content they produce. For instance, during the George Floyd protests and the ensuing Black Lives Matter movement, conservative media portrayed the events as chaotic and dangerous, emphasizing looting and violence while positioning Trump as a law-and-order president who would restore peace. Liberal media, however, highlighted the peaceful nature of many protests, emphasizing police violence and systemic racism while portraying Trump as a divisive figure whose rhetoric and actions escalated tensions. Each side's media content not only shaped how their viewers perceived the events but also how they viewed the president's role in responding to the crisis. The result was an even deeper divide, with both sides entrenched in their interpretations of the president's actions and motivations.

The role of media and digital echo chambers in shaping and intensifying partisan divisions around the presidency highlights the complex and fragmented nature of modern American political discourse.

In this environment, the president is not just a leader but a symbol, a figurehead onto whom supporters and opponents project their hopes, fears, and frustrations. The cult of personality, amplified by these echo chambers, reinforces the illusion of presidential power, turning the office into a stage for ideological battles rather than a platform for effective governance. As long as these echo chambers persist, the divide will continue, and the perception of the president as either hero or villain will only grow more pronounced.

Polarized Electorates

The political landscape of the United States, once marked by compromise and a spirit of bipartisanship, has in recent years become a battleground for deeply entrenched partisanship and polarization. The polarization of American politics is not simply about ideological differences, those have always existed, it's about the deep, unbridgeable chasms that have formed within the electorate and the consequences these divisions have on policy, governance, and the ability of the country to function as a unified democracy. As an external observer, one can't help but see this as a slow unravelling of the very fabric that once held the United States together, a nation where, historically, political differences were hashed out through negotiation, compromise, and a shared sense of purpose. Today, it's increasingly a tale of two Americas, each with its own narrative, its own media, and its own vision of what the country should be.

The polarized electorate is, in many ways, the engine driving the current state of American politics. It's a phenomenon rooted in multiple factors: demographic shifts, economic anxiety, cultural conflicts, and a media environment that rewards sensationalism over substance. The result is an electorate that sees itself not as part of a larger, cohesive whole, but as belonging to distinct tribes, each viewing the other with suspicion, if not outright hostility. This is not simply a clash of ideas; it's a fundamental divide over identity, values, and the future direction of the country.

The impact of this polarization on policy and governance is profound. In theory, democracy functions best when different groups with varied perspectives come together to negotiate and find common ground. However, when the electorate is so deeply divided that compromise is seen as betrayal and consensus as weakness, the very mechanisms of democracy become paralyzed.

Policy-making turns into a zero-sum game, where the objective is not to craft legislation that benefits the nation as a whole, but to block or reverse the initiatives of the opposing side. As a result, gridlock has become the norm rather than the exception in Washington.

This polarized state of the electorate has given rise to what one might call hyper-partisan presidencies, where the support or opposition a president faces is intensely amplified by the deeply divided nature of the American public. The president, as the most visible and influential figure in American politics, is not merely seen as a leader to be critiqued or supported based on policy outcomes. Instead, they become an avatar of the electorate's hopes, fears, and grievances. Supporters rally around the president as a saviour of their values and identity, while opponents view the same figure as an existential threat to the nation's future. This dynamic makes it nearly impossible for presidents to govern effectively, as their every move is filtered through the lens of extreme partisan support or opposition.

Take, for instance, the presidency of Barack Obama. When Obama was elected, he was hailed by many as a transformative figure, a symbol of progress, hope, and the possibility of overcoming racial and political divisions. Yet, almost immediately, he became a polarizing figure. His supporters saw him as a new kind of leader, but his opponents, particularly on the right, painted him as a radical, someone intent on undermining American values. This intense reaction fuelled the rise of the Tea Party movement, a grassroots conservative response that viewed Obama not just as a political opponent but as a threat to the country's identity. It wasn't simply about disagreeing with his policies; it was about opposing what he symbolized.

This kind of hyper-partisan reaction was not confined to Obama alone. When Donald Trump entered the political arena, he became a lightning rod for division. His brash, confrontational style and his willingness to break with norms energized a base of voters who felt alienated and voiceless in American politics. To them, Trump represented a champion, someone who would fight the establishment, reclaim lost jobs, and assert American dominance on the world stage. But for his opponents, Trump was the antithesis of everything they believed America should be. He was seen as authoritarian, divisive, and a threat to the democratic institutions that underpin the country.

His presidency wasn't merely an administration to be opposed; it was viewed as a crisis that demanded resistance at every turn.

This extreme partisanship, where presidents are either lionized or vilified with such intensity, makes governing an increasingly fraught endeavour. Policy decisions that might once have been met with reasoned debate and compromise are now flashpoints for political warfare. Consider the battle over healthcare reform. When Obama introduced the Affordable Care Act (ACA), it was intended as a moderate reform—an effort to expand healthcare coverage while working within the existing system. However, it was met with fierce opposition, not only because of ideological differences over government involvement in healthcare but also because of what it represented. To opponents, the ACA became a symbol of government overreach and, by extension, a representation of Obama's vision for America. The debate was less about the specifics of the policy and more about the political and cultural battle lines it drew.

Under Trump, similar dynamics played out with issues like immigration and tax reform. Each policy proposal became a rallying cry for one side and a red flag for the other. Immigration policies, for instance, were not merely viewed as legislative measures but as battlegrounds for the country's identity. Supporters saw Trump's hardline stance as a necessary defence of national sovereignty, while opponents viewed it as a violation of American values and a moral crisis. The ability to engage in nuanced debate and reach across the aisle was lost in the cacophony of partisan rhetoric.

The erosion of bipartisanship is perhaps the most troubling consequence of this polarization. In a functioning democracy, compromise and cooperation are essential for passing legislation and governing effectively. Historically, even when the two parties disagreed, they found ways to work together on issues of national importance, whether it was infrastructure, defence spending, or social welfare programs. Today, that spirit of cooperation is all but gone. The filibuster, once an exceptional measure in the Senate, has become a routine tool for blocking legislation. The use of executive orders has increased as presidents, unable to secure legislative support, resort to unilateral action. This not only undermines the balance of power but also creates a cycle of instability, as each administration seeks to undo the actions of its predecessor rather than build on common ground.

The erosion of bipartisanship is not only a symptom of the polarized electorate but also a cause of further division. When Congress is gridlocked and cannot deliver meaningful policy outcomes, voters become more disillusioned and frustrated. This, in turn, drives them further into their partisan corners, reinforcing their belief that the "other side" is to blame for the dysfunction. The lack of legislative cooperation not only affects domestic policy but has profound implications for America's role on the global stage. Allies and adversaries alike watch as the U.S. struggles with internal division, raising questions about its ability to lead and maintain stable foreign policy commitments.

One need only look at recent attempts at bipartisan legislation to see the challenges polarization poses. Even in areas where there is broad agreement on the need for reform, such as infrastructure development or criminal justice—efforts to pass comprehensive bills often stall. Republicans and Democrats may agree in principle on the need for action, but the political environment makes cooperation difficult. Any attempt to reach across the aisle is often met with suspicion from one's own party, where the base may see compromise as capitulation.

Social media has played a crucial role in this erosion of bipartisanship, as it amplifies extreme voices and makes moderate positions less visible. Platforms like Twitter and Facebook prioritize content that garners engagement, and outrage is often more engaging than nuance. As a result, the loudest, most extreme voices get the most attention, drowning out calls for cooperation and compromise. Politicians who might once have championed bipartisan efforts now face the wrath of their own parties' base if they are seen as too willing to negotiate. The cycle is self-perpetuating: social media encourages extreme rhetoric, extreme rhetoric garners more support, and politicians respond by becoming more extreme themselves.

The hyper-partisan environment makes it nearly impossible for meaningful legislative cooperation to occur. Even when public support for a policy initiative is high, such as on issues like background checks for gun purchases or climate change action, the gridlock in Congress persists. Lawmakers are often more concerned with appealing to their party's base than with finding common ground. This has led to a pattern where legislative action is increasingly reliant on narrow majorities and procedural manoeuvres rather than broad-based consensus.

This erosion of bipartisanship not only affects the effectiveness of governance but also the long-term stability of the American system. The founders of the United States designed a government based on checks and balances, with the understanding that power should be distributed and that compromise would be necessary to maintain balance. As polarization deepens and bipartisanship fades, those checks and balances are threatened. The reliance on executive orders and judicial appointments to achieve policy goals bypasses the legislative branch, weakening its role in the system and making the executive branch more powerful, and more contested.

The implications of this trend for American stability are significant. The U.S. faces not only domestic challenges like healthcare, infrastructure, and economic inequality but also international pressures from rising powers like China and global issues like climate change. Addressing these complex challenges requires a functional government, one that can pass legislation, implement policies, and maintain consistency in its commitments. The inability of the American political system to function effectively due to polarization and partisanship puts all of these at risk. The country's allies may doubt its reliability, while its adversaries may take advantage of its internal divisions.

At its core, the polarization of the electorate, the rise of hyper-partisan presidencies, and the erosion of bipartisanship reveal a troubling trend: the transformation of American politics from a system of governance to a battleground of identity and ideology. The focus has shifted from policy-making and compromise to a constant struggle for dominance, where each election cycle feels like an existential battle rather than a democratic process. In this environment, the illusion of presidential power is amplified, as the electorate looks to the president not merely as a policy-maker but as a saviour or villain. This dynamic, while politically advantageous in the short term for mobilizing voters, undermines the very principles of a democratic system that requires cooperation and compromise to function.

If the United States is to overcome this deepening polarization and restore its capacity for effective governance, it will require a rethinking of how political discourse is conducted, how media influences that discourse, and how institutions can foster bipartisanship in an era of intense division.

It will mean finding ways to re-engage an electorate that sees itself as divided tribes and rebuilding the bridges that have been burned in the pursuit of partisan victory. Whether the nation can rise to this challenge remains an open question, but the stakes, both for America and for the world, could not be higher.

How internal division threatens the future of American global leadership.

The United States has long occupied a paradoxical position in global affairs, at once a beacon of democracy and a force for order, while also a nation defined by its own internal tensions and contradictions. For decades, American leadership on the world stage has rested on the twin pillars of military strength and economic power. But perhaps more importantly, it has rested on an image: that of a stable, unified country. A nation, however imperfect, that could rise above its own disputes to lead with resolve and purpose. But as political observers from abroad, it's hard not to notice that the cracks within this image are growing. America's internal divisions are not just a domestic problem; they have profound implications for its global leadership and the international order it helped create.

In the years following World War II, American leadership was largely uncontested. The United States emerged as the dominant power, not only because of its military and economic might but also because of the relative cohesion and unity that allowed it to project strength. The Marshall Plan rebuilt Europe; the Bretton Woods system stabilized global finance. American presidents, from Truman to Reagan, could take bold international actions, secure in the knowledge that, for the most part, the American public and political establishment were behind them. But the American empire that rose from those postwar decades is beginning to look fragile. The internal divisions, political, social, and economic—that have come to define the country are threatening the very foundation upon which its global leadership rests.

Political partisanship is no longer a matter of simple disagreement over policies or candidates. It has evolved into a fierce, tribal struggle where loyalty to one's party or ideology often takes precedence over national interest.

This polarization isn't just a problem for domestic governance; it undermines America's capacity to act coherently and decisively on the international stage. When American presidents are no longer seen as leaders of the entire nation but instead as representatives of a faction, either celebrated or despised by nearly half of their own country, they lose the political capital needed to make unified and effective foreign policy decisions.

The implications are clear. Take the Iran nuclear deal, or the Joint Comprehensive Plan of Action (JCPOA). Negotiated under the Obama administration, it was hailed by its supporters as a critical step toward curbing nuclear proliferation in the Middle East. But the Trump administration's unilateral withdrawal from the agreement just a few years later sent a stark message to U.S. allies and adversaries alike: American foreign policy could be subject to the whims of a deeply divided domestic landscape. This back-and-forth eroded trust, not just between the U.S. and Iran, but between the U.S. and its closest allies in Europe, who had invested diplomatic capital in supporting the agreement. If America's allies cannot trust that its commitments will hold beyond a single administration, its capacity to lead and form effective, lasting alliances is severely compromised.

For the U.S. to lead effectively, it needs more than just military power and economic influence; it needs credibility. The kind of credibility that comes from a consistent and unified approach to governance, both domestically and abroad. When international observers see political paralysis in Washington, it diminishes the perception of America as a reliable partner. When the U.S. struggles to enact its own policies, whether they relate to infrastructure, healthcare, or immigration, the message sent to the world is one of dysfunction. If a country cannot manage its own affairs, how can it manage the affairs of the world?

The consequences of this internal division are already visible in America's retreat from certain global responsibilities. The chaotic withdrawal from Afghanistan, for instance, was not merely a military failure or a logistical blunder; it was the culmination of two decades of inconsistent policy decisions driven by shifting domestic political winds. One administration sought nation-building; another pushed for withdrawal. The end result was a scene of confusion and loss that damaged America's credibility and left allies questioning its commitment to international stability.

Furthermore, the impact of internal division extends beyond geopolitical matters to the global economy. The U.S. has traditionally been a stabilizing force in global markets, its dollar serving as the world's reserve currency, and its economic policy setting the tone for international trade. However, economic policy that swings wildly depending on partisan control undermines this stability. Tariffs imposed by one administration are rolled back by the next, while tax policies shift dramatically, creating uncertainty for international businesses and investors who rely on American predictability. As America's domestic politics become more unpredictable, its role as a global economic anchor weakens.

Socially, the United States is experiencing a period of cultural and racial reckoning that is both necessary and overdue. However, this reckoning is taking place in an environment so polarized that meaningful dialogue is difficult to achieve. Issues like immigration, racial justice, and voting rights are deeply divisive, and rather than fostering compromise, they have become battlegrounds for political identity. When the world looks at America, it no longer sees a "melting pot" or a "beacon of freedom." It sees a country grappling with its own identity, a country divided not just by policy preferences but by competing visions of its very nature. This perception has serious implications for America's ability to project soft power and to lead by example, a crucial element of its influence during the 20th century.

The implications of America's internal divisions for its global leadership are profound. If the United States cannot find a way to bridge the gaps between its polarized factions, it risks losing the very stability that underpins its international influence. Allies and adversaries alike are watching closely, and they are increasingly unwilling to place their trust in a country whose political future seems so uncertain. To maintain its leadership, America must find a way to reconcile these divisions, to show the world that it can rise above partisanship and unify around common goals—both at home and abroad.

In the end, the strength of the American empire has always been its ability to adapt and reinvent itself. The country has faced division before, during the Civil War, during the civil rights movement, and it has emerged stronger. But this moment feels different. The fractures are not just along regional or ideological lines; they cut through families, communities, and institutions.

The challenge now is not just about passing legislation or winning elections; it is about rebuilding a sense of shared identity, a sense of common purpose that transcends the echo chambers and tribal loyalties that define the current political landscape. Only then can America hope to regain the stability and unity necessary for effective global leadership. If it fails, the consequences will reach far beyond its borders, reshaping the balance of power in a world that is increasingly sceptical of American dominance.

The Illusion of Presidential Power

CHAPTER 8

ALLIES AND ADVERSARIES

From an external vantage point, America's fixation on the presidency is both captivating and confounding. No other nation in the world places its leader quite so prominently on a pedestal, turning every president into a figure as scrutinized as a monarch, yet theoretically just as accountable as any other elected official. For America's allies and adversaries alike, this obsession with the personality of the president is both an opportunity and a risk. It offers a predictable cycle of highs and lows, as global leaders brace for shifts in policy and tone with each new administration. But more importantly, it raises questions about the reliability and consistency of American leadership. Can a nation, however powerful, truly lead when so much hinges on the temperament, ideology, and personality of a single individual?

Take, for instance, the transatlantic relationship. For decades, NATO allies in Europe relied on the United States as a stabilizing force, a guarantor of security and a steadfast partner in both peace and conflict. Yet, recent years have seen a shift in this trust. Under the Obama administration, relations were cordial, and a sense of continuity reassured European leaders. But the arrival of Donald Trump, with his "America First" rhetoric and criticisms of NATO allies' defence spending, sent shockwaves through Europe. Allies accustomed to American commitment suddenly found themselves wondering whether the United States was truly the reliable partner it once claimed to be. The subsequent Biden administration sought to mend these rifts, but the damage had been done. The unpredictability of American leadership, now so visibly tied to the individual holding office, left a sense of scepticism that is difficult to shake. European nations, increasingly aware of their own vulnerability in an unpredictable alliance, have started to reconsider the extent of their reliance on the United States, a shift that has global implications for power dynamics and diplomatic stability.

For America's rivals, this instability is an opportunity. China, with its long-term strategic vision, is watching closely. The Chinese government has mastered the art of patience, capitalizing on America's inward focus and its political infighting. As administrations swing from one extreme to another, abandoning global agreements one moment and rejoining them the next, China presents itself as a consistent, stable force on the world stage. By emphasizing its steady rise and projecting the image of a nation undeterred by domestic squabbles, China strengthens its position, particularly in regions where U.S. influence is waning. The Belt and Road Initiative is a prime example of how China leverages America's perceived inconsistency to expand its reach, offering infrastructure investment and partnerships while America debates its role and leadership on twitter.

Russia, too, has recognized the power of exploiting American divisions. Its disinformation campaigns are not merely attempts to sway elections; they are calculated moves to deepen the cracks in America's political fabric, weakening the country's unity and distracting it from international affairs. The more divided America becomes internally, the more it struggles to project a coherent and unified stance abroad, making it easier for Russia to expand its influence unchecked.

Even among populist leaders worldwide, the focus on American presidential shifts becomes a cue for their own political manoeuvres.

Leaders in countries like Brazil, Hungary, and Turkey watch closely, aligning themselves with U.S. policies when advantageous and distancing themselves when the tide turns. The rise of populism globally is both a reflection of America's own internal battles and a reaction to its changing leadership style. As populist rhetoric becomes more mainstream in American politics, it emboldens leaders elsewhere to adopt similar stances, often positioning themselves in opposition to, or in support of, U.S. leadership, depending on which administration holds power.

Beyond the hard power and geopolitical strategy, there's the issue of soft power, an area where America once thrived. The image of America as a beacon of democracy and stability is tarnished when the focus shifts from policy to personality. Diplomats and foreign leaders find themselves navigating not the steady, institution-driven relationships they once knew but a landscape dominated by the whims of a president's character or ideology. This shift weakens America's ability to foster long-term diplomatic ties, as alliances become contingent not on shared values or mutual goals but on the personal relationships between leaders.

The result is a more precarious global network of alliances, one that is increasingly at risk of collapsing under the weight of its own fragility. As America's adversaries capitalize on these shifting dynamics, and as its allies grow wary of the inconsistency in American policy, the nation's global influence faces a critical challenge. The world may still look to America as a leader, but it's a leadership increasingly defined by unpredictability. The reliance on personality over policy not only threatens the foundations of America's alliances but raises questions about its future role in the global order. Can America lead effectively when its allies no longer trust its consistency, and when its adversaries use its divisions as a pathway to power?

European Scepticism

European scepticism towards the United States as a reliable ally, particularly within the NATO framework, has grown markedly in recent years. This shift is deeply tied to the evolving and often unpredictable nature of American foreign policy, which increasingly appears to pivot dramatically with each administration. What was once seen as the most consistent and stabilizing force within NATO has, in the eyes of many European allies, become a source of uncertainty. As American administrations veer from cooperative multilateralism to unilateralism and back again, trust among NATO allies has eroded, raising critical questions about America's future role as a dependable leader in the alliance.

The foundation of NATO in 1949 was built on the idea that collective security and cooperation would prevent the kind of global conflicts that had torn the world apart twice in the first half of the 20th century. The United States, as the most powerful member of the alliance, was crucial not only for its military might but also for the stability and leadership it offered. For decades, this approach worked, as American administrations, regardless of party affiliation, maintained a steady commitment to NATO's principles, providing reassurance to its European partners. This consistency was essential for NATO's credibility and effectiveness; it was this unwavering American support that held the alliance together, particularly during the Cold War when the Soviet threat necessitated a unified Western defence.

However, recent years have seen a departure from this tradition of steady American commitment, with administrations adopting starkly different approaches to NATO and Europe's security. The administration of George W. Bush, particularly following the 9/11 attacks, was marked by a strong commitment to the alliance but also highlighted early cracks. The decision to invade Iraq in 2003, largely unilaterally and based on intelligence that many European allies questioned, was a turning point. Although NATO as an institution was not directly involved in the invasion, the deep divisions it caused among allies, most notably with France and Germany, set a precedent for how American unilateralism could destabilize transatlantic unity. European scepticism began to surface as allies realized that even within the NATO framework, the United States might pursue its interests without full consultation or consensus.

The Obama administration, which came into office in 2009, marked a return to multilateralism, or at least the appearance of it. Obama's approach sought to mend the fractures of the Bush years, re-emphasizing the importance of alliances and diplomatic engagement. For a time, this strategy seemed to restore some trust among NATO allies. Obama's administration committed to European security through measures such as the European Reassurance Initiative, aimed at countering Russian aggression after the annexation of Crimea in 2014. The initiative included increased deployments of U.S. troops and military resources to Eastern Europe, signalling a renewed commitment to NATO's collective defence clause, Article 5. European leaders, particularly in the Baltic states and Poland, welcomed this as evidence that the United States remained a reliable partner in the face of renewed Russian threats.

However, the seeds of scepticism had already been planted. The Obama administration's approach to the conflict in Libya, for instance, where the United States took a "leading from behind" role, showed a shift in how America was willing to engage militarily in Europe's neighbourhood. While NATO took action, the limited American involvement indicated a potential reluctance to lead in future crises. Additionally, Obama's pivot to Asia, a strategic shift aimed at countering China's rising influence, made some European allies feel that the U.S. commitment to Europe was no longer as strong as it had been during the Cold War. European leaders began to worry that, despite Obama's reassuring rhetoric, America's focus was shifting, and the alliance might be left to handle its own security challenges without the full backing of the United States.

The election of Donald Trump in 2016 exacerbated these fears. Trump's administration took a radically different approach to NATO, one that sent shockwaves through European capitals. From the start of his campaign, Trump questioned the value of NATO, calling it "obsolete" and frequently criticizing European allies for what he perceived as their failure to pay their fair share for defence. Trump's rhetoric was blunt: he suggested that if NATO countries did not meet the alliance's defence spending benchmark of 2% of GDP, the United States might not come to their defence in a crisis. This was a dramatic departure from the assurances European allies had come to expect. It suggested that America's commitment to NATO's collective defence was not guaranteed but conditional, subject to Trump's assessment of financial contributions.

Trump's approach represented not just a shift in policy but a fundamental challenge to the underlying principles of the alliance. NATO's foundation lies in the understanding that all member countries will come to each other's defence, regardless of their economic contributions at any given time. The collective security arrangement is meant to provide an unconditional guarantee of mutual defence, deterring adversaries like Russia from testing the alliance's resolve.

By questioning this commitment, Trump cast doubt on the reliability of Article 5 itself, the cornerstone of NATO's credibility. For European countries, especially those on NATO's eastern flank, like Poland and the Baltic states, Trump's statements were alarming. These nations, acutely aware of the Russian threat, had relied on the assumption that the United States would stand with them if conflict arose. Trump's comments undermined that assurance, leading European leaders to question the strength and future of the transatlantic bond.

Trump's decision to withdraw from the Paris Climate Agreement and his administration's general disdain for multilateral institutions further eroded European trust. Allies observed a pattern: America, under Trump, seemed increasingly willing to disengage from global commitments and alliances that it had previously led. The withdrawal from Syria, announced suddenly via Twitter without consultation with NATO allies, demonstrated a lack of coordination and consideration for the implications such a move would have for the region and for America's European partners who had troops on the ground. This unpredictable behaviour left European leaders in a state of uncertainty, unsure of what to expect from the United States and whether they could rely on America's word in future conflicts or cooperative efforts.

When Joe Biden assumed office in 2021, many European leaders breathed a sigh of relief, hoping that the new administration would restore the traditional American approach to NATO and multilateralism. Biden, who had long championed the importance of alliances, immediately set about reassuring NATO partners of America's commitment. The rhetoric was familiar, invoking the language of shared values and unity. However, the damage done by the Trump administration's unpredictability could not be so easily undone. Even with Biden's promises, European allies remained cautious. The swift change from Trump's hostility to Biden's warmth highlighted the volatility of American foreign policy, dependent now on the personality and politics of whoever occupied the Oval Office rather than the institutional commitment to the alliance.

The chaotic withdrawal from Afghanistan in August 2021 became a critical test of Biden's credibility. Despite his assurances of multilateral cooperation, the manner in which the U.S. executed the withdrawal left European NATO allies scrambling.

Many felt blindsided by the speed and disorganization of the pullout, particularly those who had troops deployed as part of the NATO mission. The hurried exit, coupled with the failure to coordinate adequately with European partners, led to questions about whether Biden's promises of cooperation were backed by real, meaningful action. If even a supposedly multilateralist administration like Biden's could mismanage such a significant operation, how could European allies trust American consistency in more direct NATO missions?

The cumulative effect of these events, Bush's unilateralism in Iraq, Obama's pivot to Asia, Trump's open hostility to NATO, and Biden's missteps in Afghanistan, has led to a palpable shift in how Europe views the United States. Trust, once a given in the transatlantic relationship, is now more conditional. European leaders increasingly discuss the need for "strategic autonomy," a concept that seeks to build up Europe's own defence capabilities so that it does not have to rely solely on the United States. French President Emmanuel Macron has been particularly vocal about this, advocating for a stronger, more unified European military presence that can act independently of the U.S. when necessary. This is not just rhetoric; it's a response to the perception that America's involvement in Europe's security is no longer guaranteed.

The rise of populist movements within Europe itself has complicated the relationship. European leaders, particularly those with populist leanings, have found themselves aligning with or opposing U.S. policy based on the alignment with their own political fortunes rather than a sense of shared values or long-term strategy. This fragmentation within Europe, partially influenced by America's own polarized politics, makes it difficult for NATO to present a united front. When U.S. leadership is seen as transient or unreliable, European countries may begin to *hedge their bets*, exploring diplomatic and economic relationships beyond the traditional Western alliance framework.

The future of NATO and American leadership in Europe is at a crossroads. Can America lead effectively when its allies no longer trust its consistency? The answer lies in whether the United States can demonstrate a commitment that transcends the changing winds of domestic politics. For now, the scepticism among European NATO members is not just a temporary reaction but a structural shift. Europe's quest for strategic autonomy signals a recognition that the U.S. may no longer be the stabilizing force it once was. For America to regain its role as a trusted leader, it will need to rebuild not just policies but the trust that has eroded over years of inconsistent leadership. Without that, America's capacity to lead in Europe, and perhaps beyond, may continue to diminish, altering the balance of power in a world increasingly uncertain of American intentions.

The Special Relationship

The relationship between the United States and the United Kingdom, often referred to as the "special relationship," has long been a pillar of international diplomacy, forged through shared history, language, and values. From the trenches of World War I to the beaches of Normandy in World War II, and through the Cold War, the UK and the USA have stood side by side. This alliance has not only been strategic but also deeply symbolic, representing a unified front of Western democracy and power. However, as global dynamics shift and American foreign policy becomes increasingly unpredictable, the question arises: is the special relationship still as special as it once was? Is the United States finding other, perhaps more convenient or beneficial, partners?

Historically, the UK has often aligned itself closely with U.S. foreign policy, even when other European nations opted for a different course. One of the most significant examples of this alignment was the Iraq War in 2003. Under Prime Minister Tony Blair, the UK chose to support President George W. Bush's decision to invade Iraq, despite widespread scepticism and opposition from several key European allies, including France and Germany. Blair's staunch support of the United States, despite controversy at home and abroad, was emblematic of the special relationship, a willingness to prioritize transatlantic unity over European consensus.

However, the decision to back the U.S. in Iraq came at a high cost for the UK, both domestically and internationally. The war was unpopular among the British public, and Blair's credibility suffered as intelligence about weapons of mass destruction was later discredited. Within Europe, the UK's decision to support Bush created a sense of distance between Britain and its European counterparts, who had opted for a more cautious approach. This marked the beginning of a period where the UK's role within Europe and its relationship with the U.S. were increasingly at odds, setting the stage for future complications in the special relationship.

In the years following the Iraq War, the special relationship has endured, but not without strains and challenges. The UK's close alignment with the U.S. remained consistent during the Obama administration, as the two countries coordinated efforts in Afghanistan and worked together on issues such as counterterrorism. However, Obama's pivot to Asia, a strategic focus aimed at countering China's rise, led to some anxiety in the UK about its role in American foreign policy priorities. While Britain was still considered a vital ally, it was no longer at the centre of America's strategic focus. Europe's importance in American foreign policy seemed to diminish, and with it, the UK's role as America's closest partner.

The Brexit referendum in 2016 added another layer of complexity to the relationship. When the British people voted to leave the European Union, the UK's position on the global stage shifted dramatically. The decision to exit the EU meant that Britain could no longer be seen as America's conduit to Europe; its influence within the European bloc was no longer guaranteed. For the United States, which had often valued the UK's role as an influential voice within the EU, Brexit presented a challenge. The UK's ability to shape European policy and align it with American interests was now in question.

Under President Donald Trump, the special relationship took on a new and somewhat unpredictable dynamic. Trump and UK Prime Minister Boris Johnson, often compared for their populist rhetoric and unconventional leadership styles, appeared to have a personal rapport. Trump was one of the few world leaders to openly support Brexit, and he frequently praised Johnson's leadership, referring to him as "Britain's Trump." This alignment seemed, on the surface, to be a reaffirmation of the special relationship, with Trump promising a comprehensive free trade agreement that would bolster the UK's post-Brexit economy.

However, the reality was more complicated. While the Trump administration's rhetoric was supportive, its actions were often inconsistent and transactional. The much-promised trade deal never materialized, as negotiations stalled over regulatory and agricultural standards. The UK's decision to allow Huawei, the Chinese telecommunications giant, to participate in its 5G network also created friction, with Trump's administration pressuring Johnson's government to exclude Huawei over national security concerns. Although Johnson eventually reversed the decision, the episode highlighted how the special relationship was no longer the unshakeable alliance it once was but was increasingly subject to geopolitical competition and American priorities that did not always align with Britain's.

The Trump years also demonstrated that while the UK was a close ally, it was not always the most favoured one. Trump's foreign policy often prioritized relationships with other countries based on transactional benefits. For instance, his administration worked closely with Saudi Arabia, seeing it as a vital partner in the Middle East and a lucrative market for American arms. Similarly, Trump's emphasis on strengthening ties with Israel and India suggested a shift in U.S. foreign policy that saw the Middle East and South Asia gaining precedence over traditional European allies.

Trump's scepticism towards NATO, his criticism of member states' defence spending, and his broader "America First" policy left many European countries, including the UK, uncertain about America's long-term commitment to their security. The UK, which had consistently met NATO's defence spending target, found itself in the uncomfortable position of defending American criticisms while simultaneously trying to reassure its European neighbours of its continued commitment to European security.

When Joe Biden took office, there was optimism in the UK that the relationship could return to a more traditional footing. Biden, a strong supporter of NATO and multilateralism, seemed more aligned with Britain's foreign policy approach. However, despite the warmer tone, the Biden administration's focus was, again, shifting towards Asia and the Indo-Pacific. While the UK remains an important ally, especially in the intelligence-sharing Five Eyes alliance, the broader strategic focus of the United States is clearly evolving.

The chaotic withdrawal from Afghanistan in 2021 underscored these shifting dynamics. The UK, alongside other NATO allies, had troops deployed as part of the mission in Afghanistan, and the sudden decision by the Biden administration to withdraw troops left Britain and its allies scrambling to respond. The lack of coordination and consultation between Washington and London was stark, leading to criticism from UK leaders, including Defence Secretary Ben Wallace, who expressed deep disappointment at the U.S.'s handling of the situation.

For many in the UK, the Afghanistan debacle was a clear indication that the special relationship, while still important, no longer guaranteed the level of consultation and cooperation that had once been a given.

Moreover, Biden's focus on reinforcing alliances in Asia, such as the AUKUS pact with Australia and the UK, illustrates the United States' prioritization of countering China's influence in the Indo-Pacific region. While AUKUS is undoubtedly a reaffirmation of the special relationship, it is also indicative of how American strategic interests are evolving beyond the traditional transatlantic alliance. The UK is still seen as a valuable partner, but primarily in areas that align with the U.S.'s broader geopolitical strategy. This pivot suggests that while the special relationship remains intact, it has become more conditional, more tactical, more one-way, and less central than it once was.

The special relationship between the UK and the United States has faced significant tests over the past two decades. While the UK has often chosen to align itself closely with American foreign policy, even at the expense of broader European unity, the shifting priorities of U.S. administrations have exposed the fragility of this alliance. Brexit, changing American foreign policy focuses, and instances of poor coordination have all strained the relationship. The UK remains a key ally, but its position is not as central or as influential as it once was. As America's strategic interests pivot to Asia and its alliances become more transactional, the special relationship appears increasingly conditional, leading to a reassessment of Britain's role and its global partnerships. Whether the UK can maintain its status as America's closest ally or whether it will need to navigate a new, less exclusive, and less predictable partnership or indeed find new allies itself, remains an open question.

China's Long Game: How China capitalizes on American political instability.

China's strategic approach to global dominance is often characterized as the "long game." This term encapsulates Beijing's focus on patient, calculated moves designed to secure its influence not just for today, but for decades, and even centuries, to come. Unlike many Western nations, whose policies are often constrained by electoral cycles and shifting political landscapes, China has the advantage of a centralized, authoritarian government that can plan long-term strategies without fear of internal opposition or public opinion shifts. This approach has enabled China to effectively capitalize on American political instability, exploiting divisions within the United States and leveraging its own growing economic and military power to expand its influence globally.

To understand how China capitalizes on American political instability, it's crucial to first acknowledge the extent of that instability. In recent decades, the United States has become increasingly polarized, with deepening divisions between Democrats and Republicans, and a media environment that amplifies this partisanship. Policy reversals are common as administrations change, creating a sense of unpredictability in U.S. foreign policy. This inconsistency provides fertile ground for China to advance its own agenda, as it can predict that American policies may shift drastically with each new administration.

One of the key ways China exploits this instability is by positioning itself as a stable, reliable partner in regions where American influence has waned. In Asia, Africa, Latin America, and even parts of Europe, China presents itself as a consistent, long-term player, offering infrastructure investment, development loans, and trade deals through initiatives like the Belt and Road Initiative (BRI). The BRI, launched in 2013 by President Xi Jinping, is a massive, multi-trillion-dollar global development strategy aimed at building infrastructure and boosting trade across Asia, Africa, and Europe. This project serves as a powerful tool for China to project its influence and cultivate relationships with countries that may feel disillusioned by America's inconsistent policies.

China's ability to fill the void left by American unpredictability is especially evident in Asia. While the United States has vacillated in its approach, sometimes prioritizing the region, as seen with President Obama's "pivot to Asia," and other times appearing disengaged or inconsistent, such as under President Trump, China has steadily built up its influence. Through economic engagement, strategic partnerships, and military expansion in the South China Sea, China has asserted itself as the dominant power in the region. American allies like the Philippines and Thailand, who traditionally relied on the U.S. for security assurances, have increasingly turned to Beijing for economic cooperation and, in some cases, security partnerships.

China's ability to present itself as a stable force in the face of American unpredictability has proven attractive to many nations in the region that seek stability and economic growth over political alignment.

The Trump administration's unpredictable approach to foreign policy gave China even more opportunities to capitalize on American political volatility. Trump's "America First" agenda, which often took a transactional approach to international relations, alienated traditional U.S. allies and undermined the perception of the United States as a dependable partner. Trump's trade war with China, while aimed at curbing Chinese economic practices seen as unfair, also highlighted the unpredictability of U.S. policy. The back-and-forth nature of the trade negotiations, coupled with the imposition of tariffs that were often announced or lifted with little notice, created uncertainty in global markets and weakened U.S. alliances. Countries caught in the crossfire, particularly those reliant on trade with both the United States and China, increasingly saw Beijing as the more stable and predictable partner.

China's response to the trade war showcased its long-term strategic patience. While the United States imposed tariffs, China retaliated but also worked to strengthen its ties with other global players, including the European Union, African nations, and countries in Latin America. Beijing took steps to position itself as a champion of globalization and free trade, in stark contrast to the protectionist rhetoric coming from Washington. In doing so, China presented itself as a reliable alternative to American unpredictability, further consolidating its influence.

Additionally, China's focus on technological and economic dominance highlights how it takes advantage of American political divisions. In areas like 5G technology, artificial intelligence, and green energy, China has rapidly advanced, sometimes outpacing the United States. The Chinese tech giant Huawei, for example, became a leader in developing and exporting 5G technology. While the Trump administration took steps to block Huawei's influence, labelling it a security threat, the approach was often reactive and inconsistent. The lack of a cohesive strategy and the absence of a united front among U.S. allies allowed China to continue exporting its technology to various parts of the world, embedding itself further in the technological infrastructure of many nations.

Furthermore, China has also been adept at exploiting the polarization within the United States to its advantage. Beijing has recognized that the deepening divisions between Democrats and Republicans provide opportunities to undermine American democracy and distract U.S. policymakers. China has engaged in cyber operations and disinformation campaigns aimed at sowing discord, amplifying existing tensions, and weakening public trust in American institutions. By fuelling division within the United States, China effectively diverts American attention away from its international ambitions, allowing Beijing to expand its influence with minimal resistance.

A clear example of China's strategy to exploit American political instability can be seen in its handling of the COVID-19 pandemic. As the virus spread, the Trump administration was criticized for its inconsistent messaging, failure to coordinate with allies, and focus on blaming China rather than developing a cohesive international response. In contrast, China, despite its initial mishandling of the outbreak, launched a massive global effort to provide medical supplies, equipment, and vaccines. Through "mask diplomacy" and later "vaccine diplomacy," China positioned itself as a global leader in crisis response, filling the void left by what many perceived as American retreat and dysfunction. Countries that might have otherwise aligned with the United States found themselves turning to China for assistance, further cementing Beijing's influence.

The Biden administration's efforts to restore multilateralism and reassert American leadership, while welcomed by many U.S. allies, have not been sufficient to fully counter China's long-term strategy. Despite Biden's emphasis on alliances and the importance of democracy, the rapid withdrawal from Afghanistan and the hasty formation of the AUKUS pact without consultation with European partners signalled to many allies that American foreign policy remains inconsistent. China, on the other hand, continues to leverage such instances as evidence that the United States is an unreliable partner. Beijing's media outlets and diplomatic messaging frequently highlight U.S. policy reversals and its internal political struggles to cast doubt on America's ability to lead globally.

China's ability to maintain a stable and consistent foreign policy, combined with its emphasis on economic and technological development, allows it to present itself as a more dependable partner to countries seeking long-term growth and stability. While the United States deals with internal polarization, shifting policies, and economic uncertainty exacerbated by COVID-19, China continues to invest in its infrastructure projects through the BRI, expand its military presence, and deepen its technological reach worldwide.

Another critical aspect of China's strategy is its efforts to undermine the cohesion of Western alliances, particularly NATO. China recognizes that a unified Western front poses the greatest challenge to its ambitions. By capitalizing on American political instability and using its economic clout, China has been able to pull some European countries closer to its sphere of influence. Investments in critical infrastructure projects, such as Greece's port of Piraeus and Italy's participation in the BRI, show how China has succeeded in gaining footholds within NATO countries. These moves have led to tensions within the alliance, as some members grow increasingly dependent on Chinese investment while others, particularly the U.S., advocate for distancing from Beijing.

The pattern is clear: China's strategy is not one of overt confrontation but rather of patient exploitation. It watches and waits as the United States, mired in political and social divisions, shifts its focus inward. China's long game capitalizes on American inconsistencies, presenting itself as a predictable, stable, and increasingly powerful alternative. As the United States struggles with domestic polarization, its adversaries are steadily positioning themselves to take advantage of the instability.

China's long game is built on exploiting the gaps left by American unpredictability. While the United States grapples with polarization and inconsistent foreign policy, China uses its stable governance structure and strategic patience to expand its global influence. It presents itself as a reliable partner, offering economic opportunities and technological advancements to countries that may feel sidelined or disillusioned by American leadership.

Whether through economic investment, technological prowess, or targeted information campaigns, China's approach is designed to steadily shift the global balance of power in its favour, capitalizing on the internal divisions and erratic behaviour that increasingly characterize American politics. For the United States, this presents a profound challenge: unless it can restore a sense of consistency and unity in its foreign policy, it risks ceding ground to a rising power that plays a long game far more effectively than any administration tied to the short-term cycles of electoral politics ever could.

Russia's Influence: Exploiting America's internal divisions through disinformation campaigns.

Russia's influence on American politics and society, particularly through disinformation campaigns, has become one of the most pressing and visible threats to Western democracy. Over the past decade, Russia has strategically exploited America's internal divisions, using its state-sponsored media and sophisticated cyber operations to deepen partisan divides and undermine trust in democratic institutions. The aim is not merely to sway elections or public opinion but to destabilize the United States from within, rendering it less effective on the global stage. This strategy has had far-reaching consequences, not just for America but for international stability as a whole. One of the most significant outcomes of this disinformation-fuelled instability has been its impact on Russian President Vladimir Putin's confidence to invade Ukraine in 2022, as he calculated that a fractured and distracted United States would be less capable of mounting a united response.

Russia's tactics are rooted in its long-standing tradition of using propaganda and influence operations as instruments of statecraft. Since the days of the Soviet Union, the Kremlin has understood the power of information as a tool to manipulate, control, and destabilize. The collapse of the USSR did not end this strategy; instead, it evolved with the digital age, becoming more sophisticated and expansive. The rise of social media platforms and their vast, largely unregulated reach provided a perfect opportunity for Russian operatives to infiltrate and influence American society. By creating fake accounts, bots, and propaganda campaigns, Russia has effectively used these platforms to amplify divisive content, target vulnerable groups, and deepen political polarization.

The 2016 U.S. presidential election marked a watershed moment in Russia's disinformation campaign. The Internet Research Agency (IRA), a Russian state-backed organization, was at the forefront of these efforts. It created thousands of fake social media profiles across platforms like Facebook, Twitter, and Instagram, masquerading as American citizens and activist groups. These profiles posted incendiary content, not only promoting one candidate over another but, more significantly, sowing discord and conflict across a wide array of social and political issues. By targeting issues such as racial tensions, immigration, gun control, and police brutality, Russian operatives managed to inflame debates, incite anger, and provoke violent confrontations.

The impact of these disinformation campaigns was multifaceted. They not only influenced public discourse but also shaped the perception of legitimacy around the election itself. For many Americans, the sheer volume of divisive and often contradictory information created confusion and mistrust. The narrative that the election was "rigged" or "stolen", a sentiment that gained further traction in the 2020 election—originated, in part, from Russian efforts to undermine confidence in the democratic process. This loss of faith has had long-lasting consequences, diminishing America's ability to present a united front, both domestically and internationally.

The divisions amplified by Russia's disinformation campaigns also laid the groundwork for further political violence, such as the January 6th insurrection at the U.S. Capitol. While there is no direct evidence that Russia orchestrated this attack, the atmosphere of mistrust and polarization it had helped foster created fertile ground for such an event. Russia's objective was not to control every narrative but to ensure that chaos and division became the dominant themes of American politics. By doing so, it weakened America's democratic institutions and global standing.

Vladimir Putin's strategy in exploiting these internal divisions was not just about weakening America from the inside but also about expanding Russia's geopolitical influence. For years, Putin has sought to reassert Russia's dominance on the global stage, viewing the disintegration of the Soviet Union as a great historical catastrophe. A weakened and distracted United States, torn apart by internal strife, presented an opportunity for Putin to push his agenda with greater impunity. Russia's annexation of Crimea in 2014, for example, was a calculated move, made possible by the perception that the West, particularly the U.S. under the Obama administration, was unwilling to respond decisively. American hesitation in enforcing its "red lines" in Syria and the subsequent inaction regarding Crimea signalled to Russia that U.S. resolve was waning.

In the years that followed, Russian operatives continued to test and deepen America's divisions. The political polarization fuelled by disinformation campaigns did not dissipate after the 2016 election; instead, it intensified, creating a cycle of distrust and alienation. This ongoing effort made it difficult for the United States to unify its citizens, weakening both domestic governance and its international credibility. By keeping American politics in a state of turmoil, Russia effectively reduced the capacity of the United States to focus on foreign policy, particularly in Eastern Europe, where Putin's ambitions were becoming more apparent.

The instability within the United States was a significant factor in Putin's decision-making process regarding Ukraine. By 2022, Russia's assessment was that the United States, beset by internal divisions, political instability, and a chaotic media environment, would struggle to respond effectively to an invasion. The perception that America was too fractured to mount a unified and coherent response was likely a key calculation for Putin, who believed that he could act with limited consequence.

Moreover, the legacy of the Trump administration's ambivalence towards NATO and alliances reinforced this perception. Trump's repeated questioning of NATO's value and his administration's threats to withdraw American support unless allies increased their defence spending sent a message that the U.S. commitment to collective defence was no longer guaranteed. This erosion of trust within NATO, combined with the internal discord in the United States, emboldened Putin to test the alliance's resolve.

The Biden administration's chaotic withdrawal from Afghanistan in 2021 further added to Putin's confidence. The images of American troops withdrawing under pressure, the hasty evacuation, and the lack of coordination with allies reinforced the narrative that America was both unreliable and inward-looking. For Russia, this was another signal that America's influence was waning, and that now was the time to exploit that weakness.

When Russia invaded Ukraine in February 2022, it was not just an opportunistic move; it was a calculated risk based on years of observing and contributing to American instability. Putin's miscalculation, however, lay in underestimating the global response. While the United States did indeed face challenges in rallying a quick and unified response, it ultimately succeeded in coordinating with NATO allies to impose sanctions and provide military aid to Ukraine. Nonetheless, the slow response and initial hesitations reflected the degree to which Russia's strategy of division had succeeded in sowing doubt and caution among Western allies.

Russia's disinformation campaigns, therefore, have been more than just attempts to influence elections; they have been part of a broader strategy to weaken American influence globally. By deepening divisions within American society, Russia has aimed to reduce America's capacity for effective governance, thereby weakening its international standing and making it more difficult for the U.S. to engage in global crises. The invasion of Ukraine was the culmination of this strategy, an attempt to capitalize on perceived American weakness.

In the broader context, Russia's influence through disinformation has not only affected the United States but has also targeted other Western democracies, aiming to disrupt the unity of NATO and the European Union. The Kremlin's support for far-right and far-left parties in Europe, its involvement in the Brexit referendum, and its backing of populist leaders are all part of this broader campaign. By weakening America's closest allies, Russia seeks to isolate the United States further and prevent a coordinated Western response to its actions.

Looking forward, the implications of Russia's influence on American stability and global leadership are profound. The erosion of trust in democratic institutions and the deepening of partisan divides leave America vulnerable, both internally and on the world stage. As the United States continues to grapple with these divisions, Russia will likely continue its efforts to exploit and deepen them, seeking to maintain an international environment in which it can act with relative impunity.

The challenge for the United States is to recognize the broader strategy at play and respond with resilience, not only by countering disinformation campaigns but by addressing the underlying divisions that make such efforts effective. For America to reclaim its global leadership position, it must first restore trust in its democratic processes and unify its society. Only by doing so can it effectively counter Russian influence and rebuild the credibility that has been compromised over the past decade.

Global Reactions to American Populism: How populist leaders elsewhere react to U.S. leadership changes.

The ripple effects of American populism, particularly in recent years, bear striking parallels to the later years of the British Empire, when the UK's global influence began to wane amid political shifts and domestic instability. At its height, the British Empire was the model for

185

governance, stability, and global influence, much like the U.S. has been for decades. However, as British politics grew more volatile, with leaders attempting to maintain the image of strength while struggling to manage growing dissent at home and abroad, the empire's influence became more inconsistent and reactive rather than strategically cohesive.

In the late 19th and early 20th centuries, Britain, like modern America, found itself at a crossroads. The rise of nationalism and independence movements across the empire mirrored today's populist surge, where leaders in regions like the Middle East and South America react not just to policies but to the personality and style of the prevailing power. For instance, Britain's shifting approach to its colonies, whether through appeasement or forceful repression, influenced nationalist leaders who adjusted their strategies based on the perceived strength or weakness of British rule.

When Britain showed signs of inconsistency or disunity, such as with the contentious debates around Irish Home Rule or the ambivalent response to uprisings in India or Egypt, local leaders sensed an opportunity to push their own agendas. Similarly, today's populist leaders, from the Middle East to South America, perceive shifts in U.S. policy or style not just as policy changes but as windows to assert their own power or realign alliances based on how the U.S. presents itself globally.

Just as British instability provided fertile ground for colonial leaders to either challenge or align with British interests based on their own objectives, American populism now prompts other leaders to react to the fluctuations of U.S. politics. The difference is that while Britain's empire ultimately fractured, the U.S. commands, even if declining, a vast and interconnected influence network. Yet, the pattern remains: when a dominant power shows signs of internal volatility or a shift from a stable, strategic approach to a personality-driven, populist style, it forces leaders around the world to adapt, often leading to unpredictable and varied alliances or conflicts.

In essence, American populism today, much like British political volatility in the twilight of its empire, creates a scenario where global leaders no longer see the dominant power as a consistent or reliable partner. Instead, they treat it as a variable that must be navigated carefully, often turning to other allies or playing off the dominant power's unpredictability to achieve their own ends.

This dynamic reflects the vulnerabilities inherent in relying on personality over policy, a lesson Britain learned as it struggled to maintain its influence amidst internal and global shifts.

In the Middle East, a region with complex geopolitical dynamics and historical ties to the United States, the rise of populist leaders like Donald Trump had a particularly significant impact. Trump's administration, marked by its departure from traditional diplomatic protocols and its embrace of direct, sometimes inflammatory rhetoric, was a gift to many Middle Eastern leaders who shared similar approaches. Figures like Turkey's Recep Tayyip Erdoğan, Egypt's Abdel Fattah el-Sisi, and Saudi Arabia's Mohammed bin Salman (MBS) found in Trump a leader whose populist instincts aligned with their own.

The relationship between Trump and MBS was perhaps the most illustrative example of how Middle Eastern leaders reacted to American populism. Trump's emphasis on transactional diplomacy, a "you scratch my back, I'll scratch yours" approach, resonated with MBS, who was eager to establish Saudi Arabia as a major player on the global stage and to modernize its economy while consolidating his power. The U.S. president's willingness to overlook human rights abuses, such as the murder of journalist Jamal Khashoggi, signalled a shift in American priorities that empowered MBS to act with greater impunity. This marked a departure from previous U.S. administrations that, while still strategic partners with Saudi Arabia, had at least nominally upheld human rights standards as part of their foreign policy. Trump's focus was on maintaining Saudi Arabia's support in the region, particularly in counterbalancing Iran, and securing lucrative arms deals rather than pressing for internal reforms.

The populist synergy between Trump and MBS extended beyond rhetoric. Trump's withdrawal from the Iran nuclear deal in 2018, a key move in his administration's populist appeal to its base, had significant ramifications in the Middle East. It was applauded by Saudi Arabia and Israel, both of whom viewed Iran as a primary threat. The decision demonstrated to regional populist leaders that Trump's America was a reliable partner in combating their adversaries, even if it meant upending international agreements and isolating allies in Europe who had worked hard to maintain the deal.

It was an example of how U.S. populism could embolden regional leaders to push harder against their perceived threats, knowing they had the backing of a U.S. administration willing to eschew traditional diplomatic norms.

In Israel, Prime Minister Benjamin Netanyahu's relationship with Trump was similarly significant. Netanyahu, himself a populist figure who has repeatedly leaned on nationalistic and security-focused rhetoric to rally his base, found in Trump a leader whose views on the Middle East closely aligned with his own. The two leaders formed a close bond, reinforced by Trump's unprecedented decisions, such as moving the U.S. embassy to Jerusalem and recognizing Israeli sovereignty over the Golan Heights. These actions were cheered by Netanyahu's supporters and presented as evidence of his ability to influence U.S. policy to Israel's advantage. The populist nature of Trump's foreign policy, which prioritized immediate wins and symbolic gestures over long-term strategy, provided Netanyahu with opportunities to strengthen his position domestically and like Russia to find the confidence to enact their own foreign policy.

However, the departure of Trump and the election of Joe Biden, a more traditional and diplomatic figure, prompted unease among some Middle Eastern populists who had grown accustomed to the U.S. populist approach. Biden's emphasis on human rights and multilateralism signalled a potential return to the old ways of American diplomacy, where transactional relationships might give way to more conditional support based on values and international norms. For leaders like Erdoğan and MBS, this shift meant recalibrating their strategies. Erdoğan, who has often used anti-Western rhetoric to bolster his domestic support, found himself balancing between maintaining relations with a now less friendly U.S. administration and leveraging ties with other powers like Russia. The confidence that Trump's populism had provided these leaders began to wane under Biden's more measured and critical stance.

The Middle East was not the only region where American populism had far-reaching consequences. In South America, populist leaders also drew inspiration and encouragement from the American political climate, using the U.S. as a model for their own tactics or as a justification for their governance styles. In Brazil, for example, President Jair Bolsonaro often drew comparisons to Trump, both in style and substance.

Bolsonaro, who campaigned on a platform of nationalism and anti-establishment rhetoric, mirrored Trump's approach by promoting himself as an outsider willing to confront corruption and the political elite. His handling of the COVID-19 pandemic, characterized by denialism and downplaying of the virus, further aligned with Trump's populist disregard for expert advice and scientific consensus.

The relationship between Bolsonaro and Trump was more than just ideological alignment; it was a demonstration of how U.S. populism could embolden similar movements abroad. Bolsonaro frequently praised Trump, and the two leaders developed a rapport based on their shared political playbooks, which included a focus on deregulation, nationalism, and confrontation with the media. Bolsonaro's frequent attacks on the press and his framing of himself as a victim of a corrupt system were strategies directly influenced by Trump's playbook. The Trump administration's open support for Bolsonaro, despite international concerns about deforestation in the Amazon and the erosion of democratic norms in Brazil, sent a message that populist leaders could count on the backing of the United States as long as they presented themselves as allies in the global fight against socialism and corruption.

In other parts of South America, the reaction to American populism was varied, depending on the existing political landscape and the interests of leaders. In Venezuela, Nicolás Maduro used Trump's aggressive stance as a rallying cry against American imperialism, framing his own regime as a victim of U.S. interventionism. By portraying Trump as the face of an imperialist agenda that sought to undermine Venezuela's sovereignty, Maduro reinforced his narrative that Venezuela's struggles were not due to his own mismanagement but rather to external meddling. This reaction demonstrates how American populism, particularly when characterized by antagonism toward Latin American governments, can be used as a tool by leaders to consolidate power and shift blame away from their own administrations.

In contrast, other South American leaders viewed American populism as an opportunity to strengthen ties with the United States, especially if they shared an ideological alignment with Trump. In Colombia, President Iván Duque, a conservative and close ally of the United States, welcomed Trump's hardline stance on Venezuela and the war on drugs.

Duque's government sought to maintain and strengthen military and economic cooperation with the Trump administration, seeing it as a chance to secure American support for Colombia's regional policies. The alignment with Trump's populist rhetoric, particularly on issues like fighting narcotrafficking and countering leftist regimes in the region, reinforced the U.S.-Colombia partnership. However, this relationship was also fragile, as it was largely built on personal and ideological ties rather than long-term strategic planning.

The shift to the Biden administration, much like in the Middle East, signalled a potential departure from the populist dynamic that had shaped relationships with South American leaders. Biden's focus on human rights, climate change, and anti-corruption efforts introduced a new set of priorities that some populist leaders found difficult to navigate. In Brazil, Bolsonaro, who had enthusiastically aligned himself with Trump, faced increasing isolation as Biden's administration expressed concern over Brazil's environmental policies and human rights record. Bolsonaro's reliance on the special relationship he had built with Trump left him in a vulnerable position, demonstrating the risks that come with aligning too closely with a U.S. leader whose populist approach may not endure beyond one administration.

The global reactions to American populism illustrate a complex web of alliances, strategies, and adaptations. For some leaders, American populism has been an opportunity to find common ground and strengthen ties through ideological alignment. For others, it has been a challenge, prompting them to either resist U.S. influence or capitalize on anti-American sentiment to bolster their own legitimacy. In the Middle East, populist leaders like MBS and Netanyahu found ways to benefit from Trump's approach, but the unpredictability of American politics under populist influence has also led to scepticism and uncertainty.

As the United States continues to navigate its internal political dynamics, the global community watches closely. American populism has shown that U.S. foreign policy can be heavily influenced by the persona of the president rather than institutional consistency, making it both a source of opportunity and instability for other nations.

For populist leaders, the appeal of an American leader who mirrors their own style is undeniable, but the volatility that comes with it also poses risks, as alliances formed on populist rhetoric and personal relationships may prove to be fleeting. As the world adjusts to changing American leadership, it remains to be seen whether the effects of U.S. populism will be short-lived or whether they will leave a lasting imprint on global politics, reshaping alliances and regional dynamics for years to come.

CHAPTER 9

THE RISE OF CORPORATE LOBBYING

Lobbying and corporate interests are often the silent architects of American policy. They work in the shadows, far from the scrutiny of the public eye, and yet their fingerprints are all over the legislation, regulations, and decisions made by the government. The American presidency, often seen as the ultimate seat of power, is not immune to these influences; in fact, it is a primary target. The image of the president as a singular force, steering the ship of state with decisive control, is appealing. But the reality is far more complicated. Behind the scenes, presidents are courted, cajoled, and sometimes even coerced by powerful corporate and lobbying interests that shape their agendas and, by extension, the direction of the nation.

From an external observer's perspective, it's striking how much American democracy, which prides itself on the ideals of freedom and representation, is inextricably intertwined with corporate money and lobbying efforts. It's a system where power is not just voted into office but bought, negotiated, and secured through backroom deals. The rise of corporate lobbying has been swift and transformative. In the early 20th century, lobbying was a minor industry, with only a handful of firms operating in Washington, D.C. Today, it is a multi-billion-dollar enterprise. Lobbyists represent every sector imaginable, from big tech and pharmaceuticals to fossil fuels and defence contractors, each wielding substantial influence over the policy landscape. The question isn't whether presidents are influenced by these interests; it's how much they are and what that influence looks like in practice.

Take, for example, the issue of campaign finance. Running for president in the United States is an expensive endeavour. Candidates need millions, often billions, to make it to the finish line. Corporate donors and Super PACs have become indispensable in financing these campaigns, giving them an unparalleled level of access and influence. When corporations funnel money into political campaigns, they are not merely supporting a candidate; they are buying a stake in the policymaking process. This money often comes with strings attached, ensuring that certain industries—whether it's oil, pharmaceuticals, or tech—have a seat at the table when critical decisions are made. The reality is that no matter how independent or altruistic a candidate may seem, their reliance on corporate donations invariably shapes their priorities once in office.

The revolving door phenomenon is another aspect of this intricate relationship between corporate power and governance. The movement of individuals between high-ranking corporate positions and government roles is not just common; it's almost an expectation. Executives from pharmaceutical giants or energy conglomerates frequently find themselves in key advisory or leadership roles within government agencies meant to regulate those very industries. Once their tenure in public office is complete, many return to lucrative positions within the private sector. This constant shuffle creates an environment where corporate interests and government policy become indistinguishable, blurring the lines between public service and private profit. It's a cycle that raises serious questions about whether presidents are truly making decisions based on the national interest or on the advice of individuals whose loyalties lie elsewhere.

Specific industries, such as pharmaceuticals and fossil fuels, have mastered the art of lobbying, using their vast resources to shape policies that align with their interests. The pharmaceutical industry, for instance, spends millions each year lobbying for favourable legislation, often influencing drug pricing policies, patent laws, and regulations around healthcare. The oil and gas sector, similarly, has deep ties to policymakers, ensuring that environmental regulations remain lenient and favourable to their operations. For presidents, aligning with these interests often provides political and financial advantages, but it also leads to policies that may not reflect the best interests of the public or the environment.

This dynamic creates the illusion of presidential independence. The president appears to be at the helm, making independent decisions that guide the nation's future. But in reality, these decisions are often shaped by powerful lobbying groups that work tirelessly behind the scenes. It's a carefully constructed façade, one that hides the extent to which external forces hold sway over the nation's most powerful office.

The Rise of Corporate Lobbying: How lobbying groups have become a powerful force in shaping national policy.

In American politics, there's a saying that money talks. And nowhere is that more apparent than in the corridors of power where corporate lobbyists roam. As an external observer, it's impossible to ignore the grip that these lobbyists have on the American political system. The rise of corporate lobbying, the influence of campaign finance, and the pervasive role of money in politics paint a picture of democracy that looks more like an oligarchy, a system where power is concentrated not in the hands of the people, but in the boardrooms of major corporations. The story of corporate lobbying in America is a tale of how money, influence, and power intertwine to shape policy, and, ultimately, the presidency itself.

To understand how lobbying became such a formidable force, we need to look back to the late 20th century, a time when the political landscape in the United States was undergoing significant transformation. While lobbying has existed in various forms since the country's founding, it wasn't until the 1970s and 1980s that corporate lobbying really began to consolidate its power.

This period saw the emergence of influential lobbying groups like the Business Roundtable and the Chamber of Commerce, organizations that brought together the might of the country's largest corporations under a common banner: to influence legislation in favour of business interests.

The catalyst for this shift was a landmark memo written by Lewis Powell, a corporate lawyer who would later become a Supreme Court Justice. In 1971, Powell penned a memo to the U.S. Chamber of Commerce, warning that American capitalism was under attack and that businesses needed to organize politically to protect their interests. Powell's words were a call to arms for corporations, urging them to invest in lobbying, legal challenges, and media influence to counteract what he perceived as a growing anti-business sentiment. The memo marked the beginning of a new era in American politics, one where corporate interests would become inextricably linked to policymaking.

The results of this shift are evident today. Lobbying has evolved into a multi-billion-dollar industry. In 2022 alone, lobbying spending in Washington, D.C. amounted to over $4 billion, with corporations and trade associations leading the charge. Pharmaceutical companies, tech giants, defence contractors, and energy firms, these are the groups that dominate the lobbying landscape, wielding their financial power to shape national policy to their advantage. When we think about the legislative process today, it's hard to ignore that many bills, particularly those related to healthcare, the environment, or financial regulation, are influenced, if not entirely crafted, by corporate lobbyists.

Take the pharmaceutical industry, for instance. Big Pharma has long been one of the most influential sectors in Washington. Lobbying efforts by pharmaceutical companies have shaped drug policy for decades, it could be argued often to the detriment of public health. The United States, unlike most other countries, does not regulate the price of prescription drugs. This is not an accident. The lobbying power of the pharmaceutical industry has ensured that every attempt to introduce price controls has been met with fierce resistance. During the Obama administration, when the Affordable Care Act was being drafted, pharmaceutical lobbyists played a pivotal role in shaping the final legislation. The industry agreed to support the bill, but only under the condition that price negotiations for Medicare would be off the table, a move that protected their profit margins but kept prescription drug prices high for millions of Americans.

This example highlights a critical aspect of corporate lobbying: it is not just about influencing specific legislation; it is about creating an environment in which corporate interests are consistently prioritized over public good. Lobbyists work not just by pushing for certain laws but by building long-term relationships with lawmakers. They fund political campaigns, host lavish fundraisers and offer lucrative post-political careers to those who support their agendas. This revolving door between politics and lobbying is not just a feature of American politics; it's a defining characteristic. Senators and representatives often leave office and immediately join lobbying firms, leveraging their insider knowledge and connections to further corporate interests.

But it's not just legislators who are influenced; the executive branch is deeply enmeshed in this web as well. Presidents, despite their power, are not immune to the influence of corporate lobbying. From the early days of campaigning, presidential candidates are aware that winning the race to the White House requires enormous sums of money, money that often comes from corporate donors with vested interests. The relationship between campaign finance and corporate influence is symbiotic. Corporations provide the funds necessary for campaigns, and in return, they expect access, influence, and policy outcomes favourable to their industries.

The Citizens United Supreme Court decision in 2010 further solidified this relationship. By allowing unlimited corporate spending in political campaigns, the ruling gave corporations even more power to shape political agendas. Super PACs, political action committees that can raise and spend unlimited amounts of money, sprang up almost overnight, funded by wealthy individuals and corporations eager to influence elections and, by extension, national policy. The floodgates were open, and corporate money poured into campaigns, transforming the political landscape into one where big donors have an outsized voice in who gets elected and, more importantly, who governs.

This brings us to the presidency itself. When corporate money plays such a pivotal role in campaign finance, it's inevitable that presidential priorities are shaped, if not dictated, by corporate interests. It's not uncommon for industries to heavily back a candidate who aligns with their goals. Consider the energy sector, which has consistently poured money into Republican campaigns, banking on the party's opposition to strict environmental regulations.

When Donald Trump ran for office, fossil fuel companies saw an opportunity. They invested heavily in his campaign, and once elected, Trump's administration rolled back numerous environmental protections, including regulations on methane emissions and protections for public lands. The energy industry got what it paid for.

On the other side, tech companies and financial institutions have often aligned with Democratic candidates. Barack Obama's administration, while progressive in many areas, was notably friendly to Silicon Valley. Major tech companies like Google and Facebook donated millions to his campaigns, and in return, they enjoyed an administration that was largely hands-off when it came to regulating their growing power. This trend has continued with subsequent administrations, where corporate interests often overlap with presidential priorities, creating a landscape where policy is, at best, influenced and, at worst, dictated by the very entities that fund campaigns.

The effect of corporate lobbying is not just felt in specific policies but in the overall direction of American governance. Presidents, regardless of party affiliation, must navigate a system where corporate interests are deeply entrenched. Campaign promises to tackle issues like healthcare costs, environmental protection, or financial regulation often clash with the reality of corporate influence. Even when a president may genuinely want to challenge corporate power, they face a formidable lobbying machine capable of mobilizing vast resources to oppose any reforms that threaten their interests.

This is why, despite the rhetoric of change, substantive reform on issues like campaign finance, pharmaceutical pricing, or climate change remains elusive.

The influence of corporate lobbying is not only a domestic issue; it also extends into foreign policy. Defence contractors, for instance, are some of the most powerful lobbying groups in Washington. Companies like Lockheed Martin and Raytheon spend millions each year to maintain their influence. Their lobbying efforts shape defence budgets and military policies, and if you read commentary on the internet you might assume they could be encouraging a hawkish foreign policy that benefits their bottom lines. Presidents, aware of the power of these defence contractors, frequently adopt stances that align with the interests of the military-industrial complex. The influence is subtle yet pervasive; it's not about pushing for war, but rather ensuring that defence spending remains a priority, keeping contracts flowing and profits high.

It is striking how this corporate influence has come to define the American political process. The concentration of power among lobbying groups raises fundamental questions about the nature of American democracy. The notion of "government of the people, by the people, for the people" becomes increasingly difficult to reconcile with a system where corporate dollars hold so much sway. It's not that the American people are without a voice, but their influence is often drowned out by the sheer volume of corporate lobbying.

In the end, the rise of corporate lobbying and the influence of campaign finance reveal the limitations of the presidency itself. Presidents, despite their symbolic power, operate within a system where money often dictates policy. The illusion of presidential power persists, but the reality is that corporate interests frequently pull the strings. Understanding this dynamic is crucial to understanding American governance today. Lobbying isn't just about influencing a single policy; it's about maintaining a system where corporate power is preserved, arguably at the expense of the public good.

The way forward remains uncertain. Campaign finance reform, while frequently proposed, faces the very obstacle it seeks to dismantle: money. Corporations and lobbying groups will resist any effort that threatens their influence, pouring funds into campaigns to defeat candidates who advocate for reform. The entrenchment of corporate power is deep, and dismantling it would require not just legislative action but a cultural shift in how money is perceived and managed in American politics. It would also require the public to demand transparency and accountability, to push back against the influence of corporate dollars in the legislative process. I am not sure they care.

In this landscape, the role of the media is critical. Corporate influence often hides in plain sight, embedded within the political system, and it takes investigative journalism and critical reporting to expose its extent. The American people deserve to know the depth of lobbying's impact and how it shapes the very policies that affect their daily lives.

For a democracy to thrive, the influence of money must be transparent, and power must be accountable to the people, not the corporations that fund campaigns and write legislation. Only then can the United States move closer to the ideals on which it was founded, in my humble opinion.

Revolving Doors

The relationship between corporate power and government in the United States has long been a defining feature of its political landscape. From the early days when business elites held political sway to the current era of multinational corporations and lobbying giants, the ties between commerce and politics have only deepened. In modern American politics, this relationship is evident through what is often called the "revolving door" phenomenon, a continuous cycle where individuals move between top positions in the corporate world and influential government roles, each side benefiting from the other's influence. From an external perspective, it's difficult not to see how this pattern undermines the notion of independent governance. The idea that a president or lawmaker can act solely in the national interest becomes harder to accept when considering the deep-rooted ties between corporations and policymakers. By looking closely at specific industries such as fossil fuels, pharmaceuticals, and firearms, we see how this influence shapes policy and challenges the integrity of the political system.

The revolving door is not limited to one political party or administration; it is a structural feature of the American political economy. As corporations have grown larger and more powerful over the decades, they have become increasingly adept at embedding their interests within the government. Executives from major industries often take up key government roles, bringing their industry expertise, and, critics argue, their loyalties. When their government tenure ends, they frequently return to the private sector, where their connections and insider knowledge make them even more valuable. This mutually beneficial arrangement creates an entrenched system of influence that is difficult to untangle.

The fossil fuel industry is perhaps the most striking example of this revolving door phenomenon. Key figures with ties to this sector have often held influential regulatory roles, advocating for policies that favour industry interests over environmental concerns. For example, individuals previously involved in legal battles against environmental regulations have later taken up regulatory positions where they work to roll back the very protections they once fought.

After their time in government, many return to executive positions within the industry, having furthered their sector's interests while holding public office. Such patterns reveal a system where corporate influence remains intact regardless of changes in administration.

But this phenomenon extends beyond the energy sector. The pharmaceutical industry has similarly benefited from this back-and-forth movement between corporate boardrooms and government. Major healthcare reforms have been shaped by officials with ties to pharmaceutical companies. After leaving government service, these individuals often transition back into the industry, taking on lucrative roles and leveraging their government experience to further industry aims. This pattern has ensured that pharmaceutical companies retain a powerful voice in shaping legislation, often to the detriment of affordable healthcare and access to essential medicines.

The pharmaceutical industry's influence is reinforced by extensive lobbying efforts. It is among the biggest spenders in Washington, ensuring that its interests are represented regardless of which party is in power. Through lobbying, pharmaceutical companies have been successful in blocking or delaying regulations that would allow the government to negotiate drug prices or support cheaper generic alternatives. This maintains high drug prices, with presidents and lawmakers often constrained by the powerful lobbying efforts behind the scenes.

Another industry with a significant influence over American politics is the gun lobby. Organizations representing this sector wield substantial power over gun legislation, primarily due to their ability to mobilize voters and make substantial campaign contributions. Their involvement in politics has ensured that any attempt to introduce stricter gun control legislation faces fierce resistance.

This influence creates a political climate where even moderate proposals, such as background checks or limits on certain types of firearms, struggle to gain traction.

The influence of this sector has shaped the response to numerous incidents of gun violence. Despite public support for reforms, lobbying efforts and pressure campaigns from this sector have successfully prevented significant legislative change. Their influence extends beyond financial contributions; they have built a loyal base of supporters who view any form of regulation as an infringement on their rights. This deep-rooted connection between the gun industry and a significant portion of the electorate gives these organizations outsized influence over policymakers, who must weigh the political costs of opposing such a powerful group.

The illusion of independence becomes even clearer when examining environmental policy. The fossil fuel industry's power is reinforced through lobbying and strategic placement of allies in key government roles. Even administrations that have emphasized green agendas have had to navigate the influence of corporate interests. Despite promises to limit fossil fuel expansion and tackle climate change, policy outcomes often reflect the compromises made to placate industry stakeholders with deep financial resources and a strong influence over policymaking.

This dynamic raises a critical question: can any administration truly act independently when powerful interests are so deeply embedded in the system? Corporate influence extends beyond campaign contributions; it's about creating a system where business and political power are deeply intertwined. The revolving door phenomenon is a central feature of this system, ensuring that individuals with industry ties maintain influence at the highest levels of government. These individuals bring their perspectives and priorities from their corporate backgrounds, shaping policies that align with industry interests.

When examining the pharmaceutical, fossil fuel, and gun industries, it's evident that these sectors have developed sophisticated methods to maintain their influence. Whether through direct lobbying, financial contributions, or placing allies in government roles, these industries ensure that their interests are consistently represented. This is their job and they do it well. Regardless of the administration in power, presidents must navigate this landscape, often finding that their ability to act independently is limited by entrenched corporate power.

The public, meanwhile, is often presented with the illusion of independence. Campaigns promise change and a stand against powerful corporations, but once in office, presidents face the reality of negotiating with these entrenched interests. The revolving door phenomenon reveals how deeply corporate power is embedded within the political system, affecting policies and decisions in ways that are often hidden from public view.

This dynamic erodes public trust in institutions. When people see executives moving seamlessly between corporate and government roles, it becomes increasingly difficult to believe that policies are being made in the public's best interest. This erosion of trust weakens democratic engagement, as citizens become cynical about the political process and its ability to deliver real change.

From an external perspective, the revolving door phenomenon and the illusion of independence are not merely features of American politics, they are central to its current operation. The integration of corporate and political power ensures that business interests remain deeply embedded within the government, influencing policy decisions in ways that risks prioritizing industry over public welfare. Whether it's environmental regulations, healthcare pricing, or gun legislation, these powerful industries and their ability to embed themselves in the halls of power present significant challenges to independent governance.

The question, then, is whether there is the political will to address these challenges. Efforts to regulate lobbying, limit campaign contributions, and enforce stricter rules around conflicts of interest have been attempted, but they often fall short. The scale of corporate influence and the incentive structure allowing executives to move between government and private sector roles remain deeply entrenched. As long as this cycle continues, the notion of an administration acting solely in the public interest will remain an illusion, overshadowed by the powerful interests operating behind the scenes.

CHAPTER 10

THE GLOBAL ECONOMY AND THE LIMITS OF PRESIDENTIAL IMPACT

The global economy is a beast that even the most powerful nations struggle to tame, and yet, in American political discourse, it often seems as if the president alone holds the reins. From campaign promises to televised addresses, presidents routinely speak about their power to create jobs, influence markets, and strengthen the economy. But the truth is more complicated. For all the grand claims and bold policies, the president's power is, in reality, often overshadowed by the vast, interconnected forces of the global economy, forces that make the United States just one player in a much larger game.

Imagine the economy as a web, with each nation a node interconnected by threads of trade agreements, multinational corporations, currency exchanges, and geopolitical alliances. Presidents can pull on one of those threads, perhaps imposing tariffs or negotiating a trade deal, but the ripple effects are far beyond their control. A single tug can cause unintended shifts that resonate far beyond the White House, affecting global supply chains, influencing international markets, and impacting everyday people halfway across the world. The power of a president, no matter how determined or strategic, is diluted in this vast and complex system.

The roots of this limitation can be traced to the era of globalization that took off in the latter half of the 20th century. As markets opened up and supply chains stretched across continents, the economic fates of nations became increasingly entwined. Suddenly, the decision to impose a tariff wasn't just about American steelworkers or protecting domestic industries; it had global repercussions. An executive order aimed at boosting one sector could upset international alliances or ignite retaliatory measures from trading partners. The world's largest corporations, more powerful and wealthier than some countries, are not bound by borders; they adapt, relocate, and recalibrate faster than national policies can adjust. The result is a global economy that is beyond the reach of any single nation's leader.

Consider the power multinational corporations hold in this equation. With headquarters in one country, factories in another, and supply chains that crisscross the globe, these entities operate with agility and leverage that can easily sidestep national policies. When a president pledges to bring jobs back home or stimulate local manufacturing, multinational corporations may simply shift operations to more favourable markets. Their power, and their influence, frequently outstrip the reach of any presidential decree. This dynamic creates an ongoing challenge: presidents must navigate the demands of global business while appeasing domestic voters, knowing full well that their policies might not produce the intended effects.

This dilemma extends beyond trade and multinational businesses. Economic policies are also influenced by the volatility of currency markets and inflation, which can be manipulated by foreign powers outside of the president's control. Take currency wars, for example. When another nation devalues its currency to make exports cheaper, it directly challenges U.S. economic interests, pushing American products out of competitive reach.

The president may respond with tariffs or sanctions, but these measures often have unintended consequences—rising prices for American consumers or retaliatory actions that further strain international relations.

Economic sanctions are another favoured tool of presidential power. On paper, they appear decisive and strong, demonstrating a leader's ability to control international behaviour through economic pressure. Yet, the reality is more complex. Sanctions can be circumvented by rogue states finding new trading partners, and their impact can be slow, sometimes taking years to see results, if any at all. For every successful example, like the pressure exerted on Iran to negotiate its nuclear program, there are others where sanctions have failed to curb behaviour, exposing the limits of their effectiveness. The illusion of control is maintained, but the actual leverage is often tenuous.

And then there are trade agreements. These are complex negotiations involving multiple countries, each with its own interests and demands. The process can take years, spanning multiple administrations, and often leaves a president with little ability to claim immediate success or failure. Take NAFTA, for instance. The agreement, which shaped North American trade for decades, involved years of negotiation and continued to evolve long after it was signed. More recently, the Trans-Pacific Partnership (TPP) and its eventual replacement under the Trump administration illustrated how trade deals are political tools as much as they are economic ones—used to signal strength or renegotiation but often more symbolic than substantive in the short term.

Presidential economic policies, especially those designed for short-term gains, also come with long-term consequences that can unravel the illusion of control. Tariffs, for example, are frequently employed to boost domestic production, yet they can backfire, resulting in higher costs for American businesses and consumers. While the immediate narrative might celebrate protecting American jobs, the long-term reality often includes supply chain disruptions, increased prices, and strained international relations. It is a high-stakes game where short-term victories are often dwarfed by the complexities that emerge over time.

So, when we look at the American president's role in the global economy, it is essential to recognize the limits of that power.

The interconnectedness of today's world means that the decisions made in Washington, D.C., do not exist in a vacuum. They ripple out, impacted by multinational corporations, global market forces, and foreign policies. The image of a president as an economic saviour may be appealing for campaign rhetoric, but in reality, they are navigating a vast web where every pull of a thread brings unforeseen consequences. Understanding this helps us see the presidency not as a position of absolute power but as a role of negotiation, adaptation, and often compromise.

Globalization's Impact

To fully grasp how globalization and multinational corporations limit the power of the American president, we must first delve into the historical and structural shifts that have created this current economic reality. The narrative of presidential power, particularly in economic affairs, has long been central to American politics. It serves as a convenient and compelling story: a strong leader at the helm, able to pull the levers of policy to create jobs, control markets, and maintain prosperity. But in a world where economies are intricately intertwined, where supply chains stretch across continents, and where corporations often operate beyond the reach of national governments, this narrative is increasingly outdated. The reality is more fragmented, complex, and, for a president, far less controllable.

The post-World War II era marked the beginning of a new economic order. The United States emerged as a global superpower and led the charge in creating institutions and agreements that would facilitate international trade and cooperation. The Bretton Woods Conference of 1944 laid the groundwork for institutions like the International Monetary Fund (IMF) and the World Bank, which aimed to stabilize and grow the global economy. These were followed by the General Agreement on Tariffs and Trade (GATT), and later, the establishment of the World Trade Organization (WTO) in 1995. These institutions and agreements collectively promoted a vision of economic integration, reducing trade barriers and fostering a global marketplace where goods, services, and capital could move more freely.

For the United States, globalization brought significant benefits. American companies could expand their markets beyond domestic borders, accessing new consumers and resources. The growth of global supply chains meant that products could be produced more cheaply by taking advantage of labour and manufacturing efficiencies abroad.

Technology companies, automobile manufacturers, and agricultural producers all capitalized on these opportunities, driving American economic growth for decades.

But globalization also came with vulnerabilities. As American companies began outsourcing manufacturing and other operations to countries with cheaper labour and fewer regulations, the American economy became increasingly dependent on global networks. The once-local production of goods, from cars to electronics, became fragmented across continents. A car assembled in Michigan, for instance, might rely on parts manufactured in Mexico, Japan, and South Korea. This interdependence made the American economy, and thus the president's influence over it, more tenuous.

The Changing Nature of Presidential Economic Power

In the early 20th century, presidents had more direct control over the economy. The domestic focus of industries meant that policies such as tariffs, labour laws, and infrastructure investments could have an immediate impact. Franklin D. Roosevelt's New Deal, for example, used federal spending and regulation to build infrastructure, create jobs, and stabilize markets. Even Dwight D. Eisenhower's Interstate Highway System in the 1950s had clear, measurable effects on the economy, linking cities and towns across America, and spurring commerce and mobility.

Fast forward to the late 20th century, and the picture looks different. The presidency of Ronald Reagan in the 1980s marked a shift towards a more globalized economy. Reagan, an advocate of free-market policies, pushed for deregulation and reduced trade barriers, laying the groundwork for the further integration of the American economy into the global marketplace. This shift was not solely the work of one administration; it was part of a broader bipartisan consensus that spanned several decades. The North American Free Trade Agreement (NAFTA), signed into law by President Bill Clinton in 1993, is another example of a policy designed to deepen economic integration. The agreement eliminated trade barriers between the United States, Canada, and Mexico, boosting trade but also accelerating the offshoring of manufacturing jobs to Mexico, where labour was cheaper.

NAFTA's legacy illustrates the double-edged sword of globalization. On one hand, it facilitated economic growth and expanded markets; on the other, it led to the decline of manufacturing in the American Midwest, resulting in job losses and economic dislocation for many communities. While presidents are often credited or blamed for such outcomes, the reality is that these changes are the result of broader structural shifts in the global economy. Presidential policies can influence the trajectory, but they are rarely the sole determining factor.

The Power of Multinational Corporations

The rise of multinational corporations (MNCs) is one of the most significant consequences of globalization. These entities, some of which are more economically powerful than entire nations, operate with an agility and reach that national governments struggle to match. Apple, Amazon, and ExxonMobil are just a few examples of American corporations whose influence extends far beyond U.S. borders. These companies have global supply chains, international customer bases, and the ability to shift operations to wherever conditions are most favourable, whether that means lower taxes, cheaper labour, or less stringent environmental regulations.

For a president, managing the economic impact of these corporate giants is a challenge. On one hand, MNCs contribute significantly to the American economy, creating jobs, paying taxes, and driving innovation. On the other, their global operations mean that their loyalties are often divided. When an American president enacts policies aimed at encouraging domestic investment, such as tax cuts or incentives for American production, MNCs may respond favourably, but only when it aligns with their broader global strategies. When it doesn't, these companies have the power to shift resources and operations elsewhere.

The Case of Apple: A Multinational Giant Beyond Presidential Reach

Apple provides a compelling example of how multinational corporations navigate the global economy and elude national control. Although Apple is headquartered in Cupertino, California, its production network spans the globe, with key manufacturing sites in China, India, Vietnam, and beyond. The company's reliance on Chinese manufacturing, particularly through its partnerships with firms like Foxconn, demonstrates how deeply integrated Apple is into the global supply chain.

This integration means that when U.S. presidents make moves like imposing tariffs on Chinese imports, as Donald Trump did, the effects ripple out in ways that often undermine the intended goals.

In response to Trump's tariffs, Apple explored shifting some of its production out of China. But instead of moving manufacturing back to the United States, which would have fulfilled the administration's objectives, the company diversified its operations to other countries like India and Vietnam. This shift demonstrates the limits of presidential influence. Multinational corporations like Apple prioritize efficiency and cost-effectiveness, responding to global market conditions rather than national policies. The president's influence is just one factor in their decision-making processes, often secondary to the demands of their global operations.

Oil, Gas, and the Global Energy Market

Another sector where the global economy and multinational corporations limit presidential power is energy. The U.S. has long been a major player in the global oil market, and the domestic shale boom of the past two decades has further solidified America's position as an energy superpower. However, even as the U.S. produces more oil and gas, the global nature of energy markets means that prices and supply chains remain volatile and beyond the control of any single administration.

Consider the impact of global oil prices. While the president may advocate for increased domestic production or energy independence, the reality is that oil prices are set on international markets influenced by factors like OPEC's production decisions, geopolitical tensions, and global demand. The shale boom, while a boost for the U.S. economy, was driven by private companies making market-based decisions rather than presidential directives. When oil prices crashed in 2020 due to the COVID-19 pandemic, no amount of presidential intervention could stabilize an industry whose fortunes were tied to global demand, not domestic production.

Similarly, when presidents attempt to use energy policy as a tool of foreign policy, such as imposing sanctions on countries like Iran or Venezuela, the global nature of the oil market often complicates these efforts. While sanctions can restrict the flow of oil from these countries, the interconnected global market allows them to find alternative buyers, and oil prices can fluctuate in ways that negate the intended economic pressure. The global energy market is a stark reminder that even as presidents claim authority over American energy policy, their actual control is limited by global factors beyond their reach.

Tech Giants: Operating Beyond Borders

The technology sector further illustrates the power imbalance between multinational corporations and national governments. Companies like Google, Amazon, Meta (formerly Facebook), and Microsoft operate at a scale that transcends borders, influencing economies and politics around the world. These companies are not only powerful economic actors but also have access to vast amounts of data, making them influential in ways that governments struggle to regulate.

For example, Amazon's supply chain network is a global enterprise that connects consumers and suppliers across continents. The company's ability to deliver goods quickly and efficiently is due to a complex logistical operation that integrates warehouses, shipping hubs, and transportation networks around the world. When the U.S. government tries to regulate Amazon's labour practices or antitrust behaviour, the company can leverage its global operations to push back. Amazon's influence is not confined to American politics; it lobbies governments across the globe to maintain favourable conditions for its business model.

The tech giants' ability to navigate and influence the global economy also has implications for data privacy and regulation. Governments around the world are increasingly concerned about how companies like Google and Meta collect, store, and use data. While the European Union has implemented strict regulations through the General Data Protection Regulation (GDPR), American policymakers have struggled to create a unified approach. When the U.S. government attempts to impose regulations, tech companies often lobby heavily, using their economic clout to push for favourable legislation. The global nature of their operations allows these firms to sidestep national regulations by operating in jurisdictions with more lenient laws, further demonstrating the limits of presidential power in a globalized economy.

The Pharmaceutical Industry and COVID-19

The COVID-19 pandemic highlighted the power of multinational pharmaceutical companies and their central role in the global economy. Companies like Pfizer and Moderna, headquartered in the United States, developed vaccines at unprecedented speed, becoming critical players in the global health crisis. While the American government played a role in funding and facilitating vaccine development through initiatives like Operation Warp Speed, the companies themselves operated within a global framework, producing and distributing vaccines around the world.

When the Biden administration pushed for waiving intellectual property rights to expand vaccine access in developing countries, pharmaceutical companies resisted. Their argument was that such a move would not only undermine innovation but also disrupt the complex global supply chains needed for vaccine production. The episode illustrated how multinational corporations can push back against presidential initiatives, especially when their global interests do not align with national policy objectives. Despite the urgency of the pandemic, the influence of these companies limited the reach of presidential power, underscoring the complexity of managing a globalized economy.

Trade Agreements: The Limits of Presidential Achievements

One area where the global economy most clearly constrains presidential power is in trade agreements. Trade deals are often touted as significant achievements or failures of administrations, but the reality is that these agreements are the result of years of negotiation, often spanning multiple presidencies. The Trans-Pacific Partnership (TPP) and its subsequent replacement, the United States-Mexico-Canada Agreement (USMCA), serve as examples.

The TPP, initiated under the Obama administration, was designed as a multilateral agreement to open markets, strengthen labour standards, and counter China's growing influence in Asia. However, the agreement faced resistance both domestically and abroad. The Trump administration ultimately withdrew from the TPP, framing it as a victory for American workers. But this withdrawal did not occur in a vacuum; it was the product of complex economic and political forces, including opposition from labour groups, multinational corporations, and international partners.

The USMCA, which replaced NAFTA, was similarly complex. While the Trump administration framed it as a significant renegotiation that put American interests first, the final agreement contained many provisions already negotiated under the TPP framework. The lengthy and intricate nature of trade negotiations means that presidents often take credit for deals shaped by their predecessors and influenced by international partners. Trade agreements are rarely the product of unilateral presidential action; they are negotiated outcomes shaped by multiple stakeholders, illustrating the limits of presidential influence in a globalized economy.

The Reality Behind the Illusion of Control

The interconnected nature of the global economy has fundamentally altered the dynamics of presidential power. While the president remains a central figure in American economic policy, their influence is increasingly tempered by the realities of globalization and the power of multinational corporations. These corporations operate with agility and scope that far exceed national boundaries, making them difficult to regulate or control through traditional means.

Globalization has created a world where American policies must account for international supply chains, global financial markets, and the influence of multinational corporations that do not answer to any single government. This complex environment forces presidents to operate with the awareness that their decisions, no matter how bold or decisive they may seem, are only one factor in a much larger economic web.

The American public, however, still clings to the myth of presidential economic power. It is a comforting narrative, one that provides a clear hero or villain in an increasingly complex world. But as the economy continues to globalize and the influence of multinational corporations grows, it is crucial to recognize the true limits of presidential power. The era of national economic control is waning, and the path forward requires a more nuanced understanding of how the American economy fits into a global system. Without this recognition, the illusion of presidential power will persist, masking the intricate and interconnected reality that defines the 21st-century economy.

Currency Wars & Inflation

Currency wars and inflation are two powerful forces that reveal the limitations of presidential power in managing the economy. While presidents may champion policies to bolster economic growth, stabilize inflation, or protect American jobs, the influence of external economic forces, such as currency manipulation by other countries, can often undercut these efforts. In a globalized economy, where the value of a nation's currency is influenced by the actions of foreign governments, international investors, and geopolitical events, the idea that a president can maintain control over inflation and exchange rates is more illusion than reality.

To understand how currency wars and inflation intersect with presidential power, we need to consider the mechanics of global trade and international finance. Currency manipulation occurs when a country artificially adjusts the value of its currency, usually to gain a competitive edge in international markets. By keeping its currency undervalued, a nation can make its exports cheaper and more attractive, boosting its trade surplus at the expense of trading partners. This tactic can have ripple effects, leading to inflation and economic instability in other countries, including the United States. Despite the American president's attempts to combat these issues, the interconnected nature of global markets means that their ability to counteract these forces is limited.

The Mechanics of Currency Manipulation

Currency manipulation is not a new phenomenon. It has been a tool of economic policy for centuries, used by governments to gain advantages in international trade. China is one of the most frequently cited examples. Over the past few decades, China has been accused of keeping the value of the yuan artificially low to make its exports more competitive. By intervening in foreign exchange markets and buying up foreign currencies, China could suppress the value of its own currency, ensuring that its goods remained cheap and attractive to consumers abroad, particularly in the United States.

For American presidents, this manipulation presents a significant challenge. An undervalued yuan means that American manufacturers face stiff competition, often making it difficult for U.S.-based companies to compete on price. This dynamic has been a recurring theme in American politics, with presidents from both parties promising to crack down on currency manipulation to protect American jobs and industries. But despite their efforts, the complexities of international finance and the independence of global markets make it difficult for any administration to fully counteract these tactics.

During the Obama administration, for example, there were frequent calls from Congress and industry leaders to label China a "currency manipulator." The administration, aware of the consequences such a designation could bring, opted for a more diplomatic approach, engaging with China through multilateral channels and pushing for reforms. The aim was to encourage China to allow its currency to appreciate gradually rather than imposing immediate penalties that could escalate into a trade war. While some progress was made, the issue remained unresolved, illustrating the difficulty of combating currency manipulation through diplomatic means alone.

The Trump Administration and Currency Wars

The Trump administration took a more aggressive stance on currency issues, particularly with China. Donald Trump repeatedly accused China of manipulating its currency to gain a trade advantage, and his administration sought to confront this through tariffs and threats of additional sanctions. Trump's approach was to create leverage by imposing tariffs on hundreds of billions of dollars' worth of Chinese goods, in part to force China to make concessions on currency policies.

However, this strategy highlights the complexities of using presidential power to manage global economic dynamics. While the tariffs were intended to pressure China into adjusting its currency practices, the outcome was not as straightforward as the administration had hoped. The tariffs led to retaliatory measures from China, escalating tensions and impacting American consumers and businesses. Furthermore, currency values are influenced by a wide array of factors beyond simple government intervention, including market sentiment, international investment flows, and economic data. The yuan's value did fluctuate during Trump's trade war, but it was as much a result of investor reactions and economic uncertainty as it was a response to U.S. policy.

The interplay between currency values and tariffs also complicates the issue of inflation. When tariffs are imposed on imported goods, like those from China, the cost of those goods often rises. American businesses that rely on imported materials face higher costs, which are typically passed on to consumers in the form of higher prices. This dynamic creates inflationary pressure within the United States. While the president's intention might be to curb unfair trade practices, the unintended consequence is often a rise in domestic prices, which can lead to political backlash.

The Role of the Federal Reserve

While presidents are often the face of economic policy, particularly when it comes to addressing inflation, the reality is that the Federal Reserve (Fed) holds significant influence over inflationary control. The Fed's mandate includes maintaining stable prices, and it uses tools like interest rate adjustments to manage inflation. However, when external forces such as currency manipulation or global commodity price spikes drive inflation, the Fed's efforts can only do so much.

For example, when countries devalue their currencies to boost exports, it can flood the market with cheaper foreign goods, impacting domestic industries and adding to inflationary pressures. The Fed might respond by raising interest rates to cool inflation, but this, in turn, can slow down economic growth and increase borrowing costs for businesses and consumers. The president may push for fiscal policies that aim to counteract these effects, such as stimulus spending or tax cuts, but these measures take time to have an impact and may not fully address the underlying global forces at play.

A clear example of this complex dynamic is the 2011-2012 currency dispute between the United States and Brazil. Brazil accused the United States of engaging in a "currency war" by implementing policies that weakened the dollar and artificially boosted American exports. The Brazilian government argued that U.S. policies were destabilizing other countries' economies and creating inflationary pressures abroad. In response, Brazil began to take steps to control the appreciation of its own currency. This back-and-forth illustrates the tangled web of global currency politics, where the actions of one country often provoke reactions from others, creating a cycle that no single president can effectively control.

The Impact of Currency Devaluation on Inflation

Currency manipulation by foreign countries can also exacerbate inflation domestically in ways that are difficult for presidents to manage. When other countries devalue their currencies, it makes American exports more expensive abroad, reducing demand for U.S. goods. Simultaneously, it makes imports cheaper, encouraging American consumers and businesses to buy foreign goods instead of domestically produced ones. This dynamic can hurt American manufacturers and lead to job losses in sectors that are sensitive to international competition, such as steel, textiles, and electronics.

To combat these effects, American presidents may propose policies designed to protect domestic industries, such as tariffs or subsidies for American companies. However, as discussed earlier, these measures often lead to higher prices for consumers, contributing to inflation. Presidents face a difficult balancing act: protecting American industries without triggering inflation that can harm the economy as a whole.

The Euro and Transatlantic Currency Tensions

Currency wars are not limited to U.S.-China relations; they extend to other global relationships as well. The value of the euro, for example, has long been a source of tension between the United States and the European Union (EU). The euro is the second most traded currency in the world, and its value relative to the dollar affects global markets and American exports. When the euro weakens against the dollar, European goods become cheaper for American consumers, while U.S. goods become more expensive for European buyers. This dynamic can harm American exporters and create inflationary pressures as the trade balance shifts.

During the Obama administration, the eurozone crisis of 2010-2012 created significant challenges for U.S. economic policy. As the economies of Greece, Italy, and Spain struggled, the value of the euro fell, which impacted U.S. trade and economic stability. While the U.S. government could express concern and engage in diplomatic efforts, it had limited power to influence the economic policies of EU member states or the European Central Bank. The fluctuations in the euro and their impact on the American economy were largely beyond the control of the U.S. president, highlighting how interconnected global currencies are.

The Limits of Presidential Power in Addressing Currency Manipulation

While currency manipulation remains a concern for American policymakers, presidents have limited tools at their disposal to combat it. The most frequently used tools are tariffs, sanctions, or labelling a country a "currency manipulator," which can trigger diplomatic and economic consequences. But these actions, while politically powerful, often fail to achieve the desired economic outcomes. Tariffs can lead to retaliatory measures, hurting American consumers and businesses.

Sanctions can isolate countries economically, but they can also push them to form new alliances and find alternative markets, minimizing their effectiveness.

For example, the Trump administration's approach to labelling China a currency manipulator was as much about signalling to domestic audiences as it was about influencing Chinese policy. While it garnered headlines and demonstrated a tough stance, the economic effects were less clear-cut. The Chinese government's control over its currency, combined with its ability to shift its trade networks, meant that the U.S. actions had only a limited impact. The interconnected nature of the global economy makes it difficult for any single nation, even one as powerful as the United States, to control the behaviour of another's currency.

Inflation: A Global Challenge

The issue of inflation is similarly complex. It is not solely a domestic phenomenon; it is influenced by global supply chains, commodity prices, and currency fluctuations. Presidents can implement policies aimed at curbing inflation, such as reducing tariffs, increasing energy production, or adjusting fiscal policies, but their success depends heavily on external factors. If oil prices spike due to geopolitical tensions or if a major trading partner devalues its currency, these external forces can negate or undermine presidential efforts.

The COVID-19 pandemic provides a stark example of these challenges. Global supply chain disruptions and rising energy prices contributed to inflationary pressures worldwide. While the Biden administration implemented policies to address these issues, such as releasing strategic oil reserves to lower fuel costs, the scale of the problem was beyond the control of any one administration. Inflation remained a persistent issue, driven by global factors like energy shortages and supply chain bottlenecks. The limitations of presidential power were clear, as economic realities dictated by international events and market forces shaped the American economy.

The Illusion of Control

Currency wars and inflation illustrate the illusion of presidential control over economic outcomes. While presidents can implement policies and use diplomatic tools, the interconnected nature of the global economy often dilutes their impact. Currency manipulation by other countries, fluctuations in global commodity prices, and international supply chain disruptions all highlight the limits of executive power. Presidents may claim victories or assign blame, but the reality is that their influence is only one piece of a much larger, interconnected puzzle.

The narrative of presidential control is appealing because it simplifies the complexities of a globalized economy into a story of leadership and accountability. But understanding the realities behind currency wars and inflation reveals a more intricate picture—one where the forces shaping the economy are as much external as they are domestic. Presidents may be the face of economic policy, but their power is constrained by a global system that operates beyond the reach of any one leader.

The Long-term Consequences of Short-term Policies:

How policies designed for short-term gains (e.g., tariffs) can have long-term detrimental effects.

The modern political landscape is often characterized by the push for quick wins. Politicians, especially presidents and prime ministers, face relentless pressure to deliver immediate results, whether it's to bolster approval ratings, secure re-election, or respond to crises in ways that appear decisive. But these short-term policies, designed with immediate gains in mind, frequently come with long-term consequences that are far less advantageous. For every policy that seeks to show immediate strength or competence, there's often a hidden cost, a ripple effect that extends far beyond the immediate impact. This dynamic is especially evident in economic policies, where actions taken to stimulate or protect domestic markets can lead to unintended consequences that undermine both national and global stability over time.

The Illusion of Immediate Gains

In democratic systems, leaders are often judged on the here and now. Campaigns are built on promises of swift action, creating jobs, reducing inflation, protecting industries, or responding to international threats with economic sanctions. The problem, however, is that the economic environment is rarely responsive to such quick fixes, particularly in a globalized world where trade, supply chains, and markets are deeply interconnected. When leaders enact short-term policies aimed at securing immediate benefits, they frequently overlook or underestimate the long-term consequences that these policies can create.

The decision to impose tariffs, for instance, is often framed as a bold move to protect domestic industries. But while tariffs may provide temporary relief or a brief spike in domestic production, they can set off a chain reaction that disrupts international markets, triggers retaliatory measures, and harms consumers. And while the impacts of tariffs are sometimes subtle and unfold over years, the ultimate costs can be significant.

The Tariff Trap: European Steel and Aluminium

One example of short-term policy thinking can be seen in the United States' decision to impose tariffs on steel and aluminum imports in 2018 under President Donald Trump. These tariffs, justified under the pretext of national security, were aimed at revitalizing American steel production and protecting American jobs. On the surface, this might have appeared as a strong, decisive measure to shore up a struggling domestic industry. However, the long-term implications were far more complex, especially for Europe.

The European Union, one of the primary exporters of steel and aluminium to the United States, found itself suddenly facing tariffs that raised the costs of doing business. The EU quickly retaliated, imposing tariffs on a variety of American products, from whiskey to motorcycles, creating a tit-for-tat economic conflict. While these moves were intended to pressure the United States into rescinding its tariffs, they also set off a series of disruptions that extended beyond the immediate economic sphere.

European industries dependent on steel and aluminium imports from the United States saw their costs rise. Companies such as Germany's automobile manufacturers, which rely heavily on steel imports for car production, were forced to adjust their supply chains and absorb higher costs, making their products less competitive globally. The ripple effect of these tariffs extended throughout the European economy, straining industries that relied on both the export and import of affected goods. As costs increased, businesses faced difficult decisions, including layoffs, downsizing, and relocating production outside of Europe.

Meanwhile, in the United States, while there was a temporary boost in steel production, the long-term benefits were more elusive. Industries dependent on steel, such as construction and automotive manufacturing, faced higher prices for materials, leading to reduced profitability and job losses in those sectors. Additionally, as European and other international producers adjusted to the new tariff environment, they began to explore markets outside the U.S., reducing American exports in other areas and further dampening any long-term economic benefit from the tariffs.

The Energy Crisis and Short-Term Reactions in Europe

Another contemporary example is the energy crisis in Europe, exacerbated by the Russia-Ukraine conflict. In an attempt to rapidly reduce dependency on Russian gas, several European countries implemented policies to secure alternative energy sources and boost domestic production. On the surface, these policies, including subsidies for renewables and increased investments in LNG (liquefied natural gas) terminals, appeared to be necessary short-term responses to an urgent situation. However, these actions have also revealed the long-term complexities and consequences of shifting energy strategies so quickly.

Germany, in particular, illustrates the trade-offs involved in short-term policymaking. Historically, Germany has relied heavily on Russian gas, building its energy strategy around affordable and abundant imports. Following Russia's invasion of Ukraine, Germany faced a sudden and severe energy crisis as Russian supplies were curtailed. The immediate response was to scramble for alternative supplies, including LNG imports from other countries like the United States and Qatar. While this diversification helped avert an immediate catastrophe, it also exposed the country to new vulnerabilities, such as fluctuating global LNG prices and competition for limited supplies.

Additionally, the decision to ramp up coal-fired power plants temporarily, to offset the loss of Russian gas, clashed with Germany's long-term environmental goals. This short-term fix, aimed at maintaining energy security and stabilizing the domestic economy, undermined years of progress toward reducing carbon emissions and transitioning to renewable energy. As a result, Germany now faces the challenge of aligning its long-term climate objectives with the realities of its short-term energy needs, illustrating the delicate balance policymakers must strike.

The Long-Term Impact of Subsidy Policies in France

France's decision to cap energy prices in response to the energy crisis offers another case study in short-term policy solutions with potential long-term ramifications. The French government, facing public pressure over rising energy costs, introduced a price cap on electricity and gas to shield consumers from the full impact of market fluctuations. While this measure was politically popular and prevented immediate hardship for many households, it also came at a significant financial cost. The government had to allocate billions of euros to subsidize energy prices, increasing public spending at a time when debt levels were already high.

This policy, while effective in the short term, may have detrimental long-term effects. By insulating consumers from the real cost of energy, the government reduces the incentive for both households and businesses to adopt energy-efficient practices or invest in renewable energy solutions. Furthermore, the reliance on subsidies as a quick fix could strain public finances, leading to budget deficits that will have to be addressed through spending cuts or increased taxes in the future. In essence, while the price cap policy allowed the government to appear responsive and decisive, it deferred the deeper, structural changes needed to create a sustainable energy economy.

The Impact of Agricultural Subsidies in Spain and Italy

Short-term agricultural policies in Europe have also had long-term consequences. In Spain and Italy, for example, governments have frequently implemented subsidies for certain crops to stabilize prices and protect farmers during periods of economic uncertainty. While these subsidies provide immediate relief, they often distort market incentives and discourage diversification. Over time, this has led to environmental degradation, as farmers continue to grow water-intensive crops like olives and almonds, despite severe drought conditions that make such practices unsustainable. The emphasis on short-term economic stability has thus come at the cost of long-term environmental and agricultural resilience.

The broader implications of these agricultural subsidies extend beyond national borders, affecting European Union policies as a whole. The Common Agricultural Policy (CAP), which was designed to ensure food security and support rural economies across Europe, has increasingly come under scrutiny for its environmental impact. In prioritizing subsidies for certain types of agriculture, the CAP has encouraged practices that contribute to deforestation, soil depletion, and water scarcity, undermining the EU's broader sustainability goals. Here again, the focus on immediate stability and political expediency has led to long-term consequences that are difficult to reverse.

The Broader Economic Impact of Short-Termism

Short-term policies, while often politically advantageous, tend to undermine the economic stability they are meant to protect. The European examples demonstrate how policies designed for immediate relief—whether it's capping energy prices, imposing tariffs, or providing agricultural subsidies—can create dependencies, distort market incentives, and lead to unintended long-term consequences that complicate future policymaking.

In the United States, similar dynamics play out. For instance, tax cuts and stimulus packages are often introduced to provide quick economic boosts or to respond to crises, but they also add to the national debt, creating fiscal challenges down the line. The tax cuts introduced by the Trump administration in 2017 aimed to stimulate economic growth by reducing the corporate tax rate, but the longer-term consequences included a ballooning deficit that subsequent administrations must now contend with.

The short-term focus that drives many of these policies is reinforced by electoral cycles and the constant pressure for leaders to demonstrate immediate results. Politicians operate within a system where long-term planning is often sacrificed for short-term gains, leading to a cycle of policy decisions that prioritize immediate benefits over sustainable solutions. This creates a political environment where the true costs of policy decisions are deferred or ignored, only to emerge years later as entrenched problems that are far more difficult to resolve.

In recent years, the United States has implemented several short-term policies that have had significant ripple effects across Europe and, in turn, have reverberated back to impact the U.S. economy. These policies, often enacted with immediate strategic or political gains in mind, reveal the complex interdependence between the U.S. and Europe, and the unintended consequences that can arise when short-term objectives overshadow long-term planning.

The Impact of Digital Tax Policies

An example of a short-term U.S. policy affecting Europe, and ultimately boomeranging back to the United States, involves the issue of digital taxation. Several European countries, frustrated by the minimal taxes paid by large American tech firms like Google, Apple, Facebook, and

Amazon (the so-called GAFA companies), began implementing digital service taxes. These taxes targeted revenue generated within their borders by these tech giants, rather than taxing profits, which are often funnelled through low-tax jurisdictions.

In response, the Trump administration launched an investigation under Section 301 of the Trade Act, threatening retaliatory tariffs against European goods if these taxes were not rescinded. The Biden administration continued to pressure European governments, emphasizing that the taxes unfairly targeted American companies. While the U.S. aimed to protect its tech industry and signal that it would not tolerate discriminatory trade practices, this short-term approach led to heightened tensions with key European allies like France and Italy.

The impact was twofold. First, European countries dug in their heels, pushing forward with digital tax measures despite U.S. threats, which strained transatlantic relations. This response also led to a delay in reaching a consensus within the Organisation for Economic Co-operation and Development (OECD) on a global digital tax framework. Second, American tech companies, caught in the middle, faced the dilemma of either absorbing the additional taxes or passing the costs onto consumers in Europe, potentially damaging their market share and brand reputation.

Ultimately, the standoff led to retaliatory measures and countermeasures that affected not just the digital economy but also other sectors. American wine and bourbon exporters faced European tariffs, complicating the trade environment and creating uncertainty for businesses in both regions. The U.S. administration's short-term approach to defending its tech giants inadvertently resulted in economic consequences for other American industries, showing the interconnected nature of these policy choices.

Agricultural Policy and the European Response
Another area where U.S. policy has reverberated back involves agricultural trade. The Trump administration's aggressive approach to international trade led to disputes with multiple regions, including Europe. One notable example was the imposition of tariffs on European agricultural products such as cheese, wine, and olives in response to the EU's subsidies to Airbus, a competitor to American aerospace giant Boeing.

While this short-term policy aimed to pressure the EU into compliance with World Trade Organization (WTO) rulings, the effect on both sides was significant. European farmers and agricultural producers faced market disruptions, as tariffs made their products less competitive in the U.S. market. In response, Europe implemented its own tariffs on American agricultural exports, targeting politically sensitive sectors like American soybeans, whiskey, and corn.

These retaliatory tariffs affected American farmers who had already been dealing with the fallout from the U.S.-China trade war. The compounding effect of lost markets in both Europe and China led to an increase in subsidies and aid packages from the U.S. government to support struggling farmers. What started as a short-term policy to protect one sector—American aerospace—ended up creating a ripple effect across the agricultural industry, requiring further intervention and government spending to mitigate the impact.

Pharmaceutical Policy and Vaccine Diplomacy

During the COVID-19 pandemic, the United States was quick to secure a massive supply of vaccines for its population through Operation Warp Speed, a policy designed to prioritize American vaccine needs first. This "America First" approach was initially successful in vaccinating millions of Americans, but it also led to vaccine shortages and delays in Europe. While the U.S. administration's short-term focus was on quickly vaccinating its own citizens, the global implications of this approach became evident as Europe faced public backlash over delayed vaccine rollouts.

European governments criticized American pharmaceutical companies for prioritizing U.S. orders, breaking their word and their contract, despite their contracts with European nations. This tension was further heightened when the U.S. administration blocked the export of crucial vaccine ingredients, slowing down European production capabilities. While the short-term policy aimed to protect American interests, it led to a deterioration in transatlantic relations, and European leaders called for more independence from American pharmaceutical supply chains.

The consequences were felt in the U.S. as well. European pushback led to delays in collaborative efforts on vaccine development and distribution, and criticism of American pharmaceutical companies grew, affecting their global operations. The perception of vaccine hoarding also tarnished America's image abroad, as critics argued that U.S. policies were contributing to global vaccine inequity.

The examples of short-term policies reveal a pattern: while these actions may secure immediate benefits or appear strong and decisive in the moment, they often lead to long-term repercussions that reverberate back to the United States.

The complex interdependence of global markets means that policies designed with short-term objectives can disrupt alliances, create economic instability, and ultimately require further intervention to address the fallout. As the world becomes increasingly interconnected, the challenge for U.S. policymakers will be to balance immediate political and economic gains with the long-term implications of their actions, especially when those actions have the power to impact allies and domestic interests alike.

Moving Beyond Short-Term Thinking

The long-term consequences of short-term policies illustrate the need for a shift in how economic policy is approached, not just in the United States but globally. The challenge lies in creating policies that balance immediate needs with sustainable, long-term solutions. This requires leaders who are willing to look beyond the next election cycle, and a public willing to accept that some of the most effective policies may not yield instant results.

Addressing issues like energy security, trade imbalances, and agricultural sustainability will require a more comprehensive approach that considers the interconnected nature of the global economy. It will also require cooperation between nations and a willingness to engage with the complexities of economic interdependence. Without such a shift, the cycle of short-term gains leading to long-term challenges will continue, perpetuating the illusion that quick fixes are enough to manage the complexities of a globalized world.

To navigate this, political leaders and the public alike must be willing to engage in a more honest and nuanced dialogue about the trade-offs involved in economic policymaking. Only by moving beyond short-term thinking can we begin to address the deep-seated issues that truly shape the economic landscape.

CHAPTER 11

THE OPTICS OF POWER

Staging the Presidency

In the theatre of American politics, the presidency is the ultimate performance. It's not just about policies and governance; it's about crafting an image, a persona that resonates with the public and commands authority both domestically and on the world stage. The illusion of power that surrounds the office of the president is meticulously constructed, and it's no accident. It's the result of a highly coordinated effort involving speechwriters, set designers, communications teams, and an array of specialists whose job it is to choreograph every moment of a president's public life. It's about staging, the calculated use of visuals, locations, and symbolism to convey strength, leadership, and control.

The American president does not simply deliver speeches; they perform them. And every performance is an opportunity to reinforce the aura of authority that defines the presidency. From the White House Rose Garden to the Oval Office, from the grandeur of state dinners to the impromptu press conferences held in the corridors of power, every event is carefully scripted, every backdrop chosen with intention. The settings are not mere details; they are essential elements in the construction of presidential power. They serve as visual narratives that tell a story of strength, stability, and leadership. But it's more than just aesthetics—it's a calculated manipulation of perception, designed to turn the president into a figure of near-mythic proportions.

The Role of Speechwriters, Set Designers, and Communications Teams

In the age of 24-hour news cycles and social media, every word a president utters and every gesture they make is magnified. The stakes are high, and the room for error is minimal. Enter the army of behind-the-scenes experts, speechwriters, set designers, communications strategists, whose task it is to create a flawless image. These professionals are not just support staff; they are the architects of presidential power. They understand the importance of optics and how the smallest detail can influence public perception.

Take the speechwriters, for example. A presidential speech is more than a string of policy points; it's a narrative crafted to evoke emotions, to inspire, to unify, or sometimes, to rally against a common enemy. The language is chosen not just for clarity but for impact. In 1961, John F. Kennedy's inaugural address, with its memorable call to "ask not what your country can do for you, ask what you can do for your country," was the result of careful planning. It was designed to evoke a sense of collective responsibility and patriotic duty, creating an image of Kennedy as a unifier, a leader for a new generation. The speechwriters behind such words understand that they are not just drafting policy statements; they are creating a narrative that will become part of the president's legacy.

Set designers and communications teams play a similarly crucial role. When a president delivers a speech, the backdrop isn't incidental; it's strategic. The Oval Office, with its elegant decor and history-laden ambiance, is used for moments of grave importance, while the Rose Garden provides a more relaxed, yet still authoritative, outdoor setting that connects the president to the public. During the COVID-19 pandemic, President Joe Biden's frequent use of symbolic locations, like vaccine distribution centres, was intended to project his administration's commitment to solving the crisis. The visual optics of a president among healthcare workers or scientists dressed in lab coats creates a powerful narrative: the president as a hands-on leader, deeply engaged with national issues.

Even the choice of lighting, camera angles, and the way the podium is set up are meticulously planned. The communications team ensures that the president is always positioned as the focal point, often with a dramatic backdrop, such as the American flag, to reinforce patriotism and authority. Every visual element serves a purpose, building an image of strength, stability, and, above all, control.

Iconic Locations: The Oval Office, Air Force One, and the Symbolism of Power

When a president speaks from the Oval Office, it's a signal that the nation is facing a moment of consequence. The Oval Office, with its deep history and iconic architecture, is not just an office; it's a stage. Its very shape, a circle, suggests unity and continuity, while the Resolute Desk, steeped in history, is a reminder of past leaders who have faced and overcome crises. When a president sits behind that desk, they are not just a politician; they become part of an unbroken lineage of American leadership. The weight of history and the power of tradition are harnessed to enhance the authority of the moment.

Air Force One, too, serves as a mobile stage of power. It's not merely a mode of transportation; it's a symbol of American strength and reach. Every time a president steps off the plane, saluted by military personnel, the image is one of command and global dominance. The aircraft itself is an icon, a flying Oval Office that projects American power wherever it lands. The president descending the stairs of Air Force One, often with the backdrop of international landscapes, sends a message: America's influence knows no borders. It is a carefully curated moment designed to reinforce the idea that the president is a global leader, moving seamlessly between nations, commanding respect on every continent.

The White House itself is the ultimate stage for presidential power. From the State Dining Room to the East Room, its grand spaces are not just rooms; they are settings for statecraft, diplomacy, and ceremony. The White House is a symbol, not just of American democracy, but of power—an enduring, almost mythic representation of stability and control.

When the president hosts foreign dignitaries in the Blue Room or addresses the nation from the Cross Hall, the message is clear: the president stands at the heart of American power, a living symbol of its continuity and strength.

The Art of Presidential Fashion and Body Language

Even the clothes a president wears and the way they carry themselves are part of this carefully crafted image. A well-tailored suit projects professionalism and authority, while a more casual look, like rolled-up sleeves, can signal a down-to-earth, hands-on approach. This balance between formality and relatability is key. In a moment of crisis, the president might be shown in casual attire, projecting the image of a leader who is not above the fray but actively working to solve the problem alongside ordinary citizens.

Body language is equally important. A firm handshake, a confident stride, or an upright posture all contribute to the aura of authority. Presidents are coached on how to interact with world leaders, how to gesture during speeches, and even how to position their hands when making statements. The goal is to convey confidence, strength, and control, regardless of the actual situation.

Throughout history, different presidents have used their body language to define their leadership style. Franklin Delano Roosevelt, despite his physical limitations, mastered the art of projecting strength through his facial expressions and gestures during his fireside chats. Ronald Reagan, with his background as an actor, used his expressive face and confident posture to embody the role of the "Great Communicator." And in the digital age, presidents like Barack Obama and Donald Trump have used their presence and gestures on social media to project an image of engagement, whether it be a confident stride onto the global stage or a thumbs-up to signal triumph.

National Crises as Stages for Presidential "Showdowns"

Crises, whether natural disasters, terrorist attacks, or economic downturns, provide the perfect stage for presidents to demonstrate their power, or at least the illusion of it. In these moments, the image of the president as the "saviour" figure comes into full force. The nation looks to the president not just for leadership but for reassurance.

They are expected to be both the commander-in-chief and the consoler-in-chief, roles that are as much about optics as they are about action.

The imagery of a president visiting a disaster site, surrounded by survivors, conveys empathy and strength. George W. Bush, standing on the rubble of the World Trade Center with a bullhorn, was a moment carefully crafted to symbolize resilience and determination. The visual was one of unity, designed to portray a nation rallying together under a strong and decisive leader. Similarly, Barack Obama's image in the Situation Room during the operation that led to Osama bin Laden's death was a display of command and focus, a leader orchestrating a critical moment in American history. These images are seared into public memory, not because they necessarily represent the entirety of presidential action, but because they are powerful symbols of leadership during moments of crisis.

Yet, this choreography of crises also exposes the limitations of presidential power. While the imagery is potent, the actual control a president has over complex situations, like natural disasters or economic meltdowns, is often limited. What the public sees is a well-managed performance, carefully scripted to give the impression that the president has everything under control. But behind the scenes, the reality is far more chaotic, with various agencies, advisors, and departments scrambling to respond. The president, in these moments, becomes both an actor and a symbol, staged to convey an illusion of command that may not align with the complexities unfolding in real time.

The Optics of International Summits vs. Domestic Events

The stagecraft of the presidency differs significantly when the backdrop changes from domestic to international. At home, the president's image is shaped by familiar locations and symbols, flag-draped podiums, the Rose Garden, or a tour of a factory floor. But abroad, the president's image becomes one of global influence and power. International summits, for example, are designed to showcase the president as a key player in world affairs. The optics are carefully managed to present a sense of unity and cooperation, even when tensions run high behind closed doors.

The choreography of these events includes everything from the positioning of national flags to the seating arrangements that imply equality among leaders. The handshakes and photo-ops are calculated moments, projecting the idea of a strong and cooperative United States. However, the reality is that these images often mask the complex negotiations and disagreements that occur beyond the cameras. The performance is designed to reassure the public and allies alike that the U.S. president is an influential leader on the global stage, regardless of the actual outcomes of these summits.

Domestic events, on the other hand, aim to connect the president directly with the American people. The optics shift from global power to personal engagement, visiting schools, touring disaster sites, or appearing at rallies. These events are designed to make the president seem accessible, a leader who understands the struggles of ordinary Americans. This duality, projecting power abroad while showing relatability at home is essential to maintaining the illusion of a presidency that is both powerful and empathetic.

The Use of Optics in International Diplomacy

Presidential staging reaches a peak during international diplomatic events, where every handshake, every podium, and every flag arrangement is meticulously planned. These summits are not just about policy negotiations; they are as much about optics as any domestic event. The president's image as a global leader is reinforced through carefully choreographed encounters that are designed to project American strength and unity.

Consider the carefully staged handshake between North Korean leader Kim Jong-un and Donald Trump at the Demilitarized Zone (DMZ). The optics of the American president stepping into North Korean territory, an unprecedented move, was a powerful image of diplomacy in action. Regardless of the outcome of the negotiations, the image was broadcast globally, projecting a message of strength and bold leadership. It was a high-stakes performance meant to convey that America, under its current leadership, was fearless and willing to engage with adversaries directly.

Similarly, the optics surrounding G7 and G20 summits often focus on the president's interactions with other world leaders. The seating arrangements, the group photos, and the bilateral meetings are all designed to present an image of cooperation and international leadership.

When Joe Biden attended the G7 summit in Cornwall, the images of him standing shoulder to shoulder with European leaders were intended to signal a return to multilateralism and a commitment to rebuilding alliances. The visual message was clear: America was back, and its president was once again a central figure on the global stage.

However, these carefully staged international optics also expose the limits of presidential power. The images may suggest unity and strength, but the reality is often more complicated. Behind the scenes, disagreements over trade, climate change, and defence spending may be intense, with the visuals crafted to mask these complexities. The images of solidarity, while powerful, often belie the challenges of negotiating with diverse global interests. The president, as the figurehead, is the face of these efforts, but the true power lies in the diplomatic machinery and the long-term negotiations carried out by diplomats and advisors behind closed doors.

Controversies Surrounding the Staging of Power

While the optics of the presidency are designed to enhance the image of strength and control, they can also become sources of controversy when the public perceives them as insincere or overly manufactured. The careful choreography that goes into staging power can sometimes backfire, revealing the very illusion it seeks to create.

One such instance occurred in the aftermath of Hurricane Katrina, when President George W. Bush flew over the disaster area rather than visiting the ground. The aerial photographs of him looking out of Air Force One's window became iconic, but not in the way his communications team had hoped. Instead of conveying a sense of command and concern, the images highlighted a sense of detachment and distance. The public response was critical, as many felt the president appeared out of touch with the suffering on the ground. It was a stark reminder that the optics of power must be carefully managed to avoid conveying the wrong message.

More recently, Donald Trump's controversial photo-op in front of St. John's Church during the 2020 protests in Washington, D.C., also demonstrated the risks involved in staging presidential power. The image of Trump holding up a Bible in front of the church, after protesters had been cleared from the area with tear gas, was intended to project strength and resilience.

However, the incident was widely criticized as a blatant attempt to manipulate public perception, with many seeing it as a crude and forced display of power. The backlash underscored the delicate balance between using optics to reinforce authority and overreaching in ways that damage credibility.

Even subtle manipulations can backfire. When Joe Biden received his COVID-19 vaccine on live television, the intention was clear: to project transparency and confidence in the vaccine rollout. However, critics quickly seized on the framing and camera angles, suggesting that the image was too staged, too perfect, and that it did little to address the real concerns about vaccine distribution inequalities. The incident demonstrated that even when intentions are good, the optics must be carefully managed to avoid accusations of political theatre.

The Influence of Technology on Presidential Staging

As technology advances, so too do the tools available for managing the optics of power. Augmented reality, deepfakes, and digital editing tools are beginning to play a role in how presidential images are crafted and disseminated. The ability to manipulate images and create entirely new visual narratives in real time has transformed how presidents can engage with the public. It's no longer just about live television broadcasts; it's about crafting digital experiences that can be shared, re-shared, and repurposed across platforms.

For example, digital events that place presidents in virtual environments, whether giving a speech to a digital audience or using backdrops created entirely through augmented reality, are becoming increasingly common. These technologies allow presidents to control every aspect of the visual narrative, eliminating unpredictable elements and ensuring that every detail aligns with the intended message.

While these technological advancements offer new opportunities, they also present new challenges. The line between reality and fiction becomes increasingly blurred when digital manipulation is used to create presidential events that may not have occurred as presented. This has led to debates about authenticity and the ethics

The First Family: Dynasties, Spouses, and Influence

The American presidency, a role often mythologized as the pinnacle of individual achievement and power, is rarely a solitary endeavour. Presidents may appear to stand alone at podiums, signing bills or addressing the nation, but behind the scenes, the influence of their families, spouses, children, and extended relations, plays a crucial, if often unacknowledged, role. The so-called "First Family Factor" adds layers of complexity and nuance to our understanding of presidential power, revealing how familial ties, personal relationships, and dynastic legacies can shape both policy and public perception.

First spouses, for instance, are more than just ceremonial figures; they are often influential advisors and public symbols in their own right. From Eleanor Roosevelt, who redefined the role of the First Lady by championing civil rights and using her position to influence policy, to Melania Trump, whose fashion choices and public statements were scrutinized as carefully as any policy speech, the influence of presidential spouses is a potent force. They serve as extensions of the president, projecting either empathy, strength, or even glamour, depending on the needs of the administration and the image they wish to convey. Yet, the true extent of their influence often remains hidden from public view, leading to a fascinating tension between their public personas and private power.

Political dynasties, such as the Kennedys, Bushes, and Clintons, further illustrate how family influence extends beyond the immediate presidency, creating an illusion of continuity, stability, and control. These families have woven themselves into the fabric of American politics, making the presidency seem not just an elected office, but a legacy passed from one generation to the next. The power of these dynasties lies not only in their shared last names but in the networks, wealth, and influence they wield, which can sway policy long after a family member leaves office. The Kennedys, with their "Camelot" aura, or the Bushes, with their carefully curated image of Texan pragmatism, create a narrative that extends beyond individual presidencies, reinforcing the perception of power that spans generations.

Presidential children also play a significant role, sometimes as symbols of innocence and hope, and other times as political actors themselves.

Ivanka Trump's prominence in her father's administration, for example, blurred the lines between familial loyalty and political responsibility, while Hunter Biden's business dealings have been the source of both controversy and speculation. Similarly, the Bush daughters, the Kennedy clan, and Chelsea Clinton have each, in their own ways, shaped the public's perception of their family's legacy. These children, whether reluctantly or enthusiastically, become public figures themselves, their actions and choices scrutinized as extensions of their parent's presidency.

The presence of a presidential family serves another purpose as well: humanizing the president and reinforcing their authority. Photos of presidents surrounded by their spouses and children, celebrating holidays or greeting visitors at the White House, are strategically deployed to present a more relatable, personable image to the public. These moments, often carefully staged, serve to soften the harsh realities of politics, portraying the president not just as a leader but as a family person, someone who embodies the same values as ordinary Americans.

Yet, for all their visibility, the influence of these family members often remains opaque. Behind the scenes, they may wield significant sway over policy and decision-making, providing counsel and shaping opinions that the public never sees. Spouses and children may act as intermediaries, conveying messages between powerful allies or dissenting voices, and advising on crucial matters of state. This behind-the-scenes influence underscores the reality that the presidency is not just about one person but is instead a complex web of relationships, loyalties, and advice, some of which remain deliberately out of the spotlight.

The First Family Factor is a double-edged sword, revealing both the humanizing and the complicating effects of familial influence. It raises critical questions about accountability: to what extent should the public know about the influence wielded by those closest to the president, and how much of that influence should remain private? In examining the role of spouses, children, and dynastic legacies, this chapter unpacks the layers of complexity that the First Family brings to the presidency, revealing yet another facet of the illusion of presidential power.

CHAPTER 12

PUSHING THE BOUNDARIES

In the architecture of American democracy, the president was designed to be but one part of a balanced system, checked by the powers of Congress and the judiciary. Yet, the reality of presidential authority has, over centuries, diverged from the framers' blueprint. The office has morphed into something far larger and more influential than originally intended, with presidents often pushing the limits of their authority, manoeuvring through legal and constitutional constraints to expand their reach. It's a phenomenon as old as the Republic itself, but one that has become particularly prominent in modern times. From declaring national emergencies to making recess appointments, presidents have tested the boundaries, sometimes in the name of progress, other times in the pursuit of political gain.

The evolution of executive power can be traced through the stories of individual presidencies, each one adding a chapter to the ever-growing narrative of what it means to wield authority in the United States. Andrew Jackson, with his defiant response to the Supreme Court's ruling in *Worcester v. Georgia*, famously scoffed at the checks on his power, and Franklin D. Roosevelt, faced with a resistant judiciary, attempted to reshape the courts themselves. Fast forward to modern times, and the pattern persists. President Donald Trump's national emergency declaration to secure funding for a border wall in 2019 showed how the presidency can be used as a tool to override Congressional decisions, while Barack Obama's interventions in Libya without Congressional approval demonstrated how presidents justify military actions under the banner of the War Powers Resolution.

The recurring theme in these stories is the complex interplay between necessity, power, and ambition. When presidents bypass Congress to enact policy or influence the judiciary, they often frame their actions as essential responses to national emergencies, moments when time and circumstance demand swift, unilateral decision-making. Indeed, sometimes they are. Lincoln's actions during the Civil War and FDR's expansive New Deal programs exemplify how presidential overreach has, at times, been justified by the exigencies of history. Yet, each instance also chips away at the delicate balance of power that defines the American system.

It's important to recognize that the expansion of presidential power doesn't just occur in grand, sweeping gestures; it is often in the smaller, procedural manoeuvres that executive authority grows. Executive orders, veto threats, and signing statements, these are the quieter tools that, while seemingly benign, incrementally expand the president's influence. Take, for instance, the practice of executive orders, which has evolved from an administrative mechanism into a tool for circumventing legislative approval. Or the strategic use of national emergency declarations, which allow presidents to bypass the legislative process altogether, as seen in the Trump administration's approach to border security.

This chapter dives into these cases, offering a closer look at how presidents, throughout history, have navigated the limits of their authority and reshaped the contours of American democracy. It's a narrative of power that is not only about the presidents themselves but also about the systems they operate within, the Congress that seeks to limit them, the courts that attempt to rein them in, and the public that ultimately judges them. In this dynamic dance, the illusion of presidential control often obscures the real power struggles taking place behind the scenes. By examining these stories, we can better understand how the actions of individual leaders can both strengthen and strain the institutions meant to contain them.

Expanding Presidential Power: Budget and Emergency Authority

The expansion of presidential power through budget control and emergency authority is a phenomenon that has been unfolding throughout American history. In a system originally designed to separate powers and ensure checks and balances, presidents have increasingly used specific tools to bypass Congress, exerting executive influence over budget allocations, national emergencies, and appointments. This expansion not only alters the immediate policy landscape but also sets lasting precedents that reshape the boundaries of executive authority for future administrations.

Budget Manipulation: Shifting Funds and Bypassing Legislative Blocks

A prime example of how presidents manipulate budgetary authority is Donald Trump's 2019 declaration of a national emergency to secure funding for his promised border wall. When Congress refused to allocate the requested $5.7 billion for the wall, Trump sought alternative means to achieve his agenda. Declaring a national emergency allowed him to divert funds from other federal budgets, particularly from the Department of Defence, to finance the construction. By invoking this power, he bypassed the traditional legislative process, overriding Congressional authority in a way that, while legally contested, highlighted the ability of presidents to exploit budgetary control mechanisms when legislative opposition arises.

The strategic use of budget manipulation is not unique to Trump; it is a tool that has been wielded by other presidents facing legislative resistance. The power of the purse is constitutionally granted to Congress, but presidents have found ways to use executive authority to shift funds from one area to another, effectively bypassing the checks and balances system. For instance, during Ronald Reagan's administration, funds initially appropriated for humanitarian aid were redirected to support Contra rebels in Nicaragua, an operation later revealed as the Iran-Contra Affair. These actions illustrate how presidents leverage budgetary control as a means of expanding executive influence, setting precedents that future administrations can cite when faced with similar legislative hurdles.

National Emergencies: Expanding Executive Power

The National Emergencies Act of 1976 was intended to limit executive powers by requiring the president to renew emergency declarations annually and for Congress to have the ability to terminate an emergency with a joint resolution. However, the law has had the unintended consequence of providing a framework that presidents can exploit. Since its enactment, presidents have declared more than 60 national emergencies, many of which remain in effect today. The broad discretion given to the president to define what constitutes an emergency has enabled the use of this power as a political tool, bypassing Congress and creating legal and constitutional ambiguities.

Presidents like George W. Bush and Barack Obama expanded the use of national emergencies to address issues such as terrorism and international conflicts. Bush's declaration after the September 11 attacks gave the executive branch significant latitude in its counterterrorism efforts, including the use of military force and the implementation of surveillance programs. Obama, too, used national emergencies to justify actions like imposing sanctions on Russia for its annexation of Crimea. These cases show that while emergencies can address immediate crises, they also serve as a precedent for future administrations to justify unilateral actions that may have long-term consequences.

Recess Appointments: Sidestepping Senate Approval

Another method presidents use to expand their power is through recess appointments. The U.S. Constitution allows the president to fill vacancies without Senate approval when the Senate is in recess. This was designed as a practical solution to keep the government functioning during lengthy congressional breaks. However, modern presidents have used this authority to bypass Senate opposition, appointing officials who would likely face confirmation difficulties.

George W. Bush, for example, made 171 recess appointments during his two terms, including the controversial appointment of John Bolton as ambassador to the United Nations. Bolton, a polarizing figure, was unlikely to secure the necessary votes in the Senate. By appointing him during a recess, Bush circumvented the legislative process and ensured that Bolton could take office temporarily. Obama similarly faced Senate resistance and used recess appointments to fill key posts, including members of the National Labor Relations Board. However, his use of this power while the Senate was technically holding "pro forma" sessions led to a Supreme Court ruling that his actions were unconstitutional. This illustrates the delicate balance presidents must navigate when attempting to expand executive authority through appointments.

Recess appointments highlight the tension between the executive and legislative branches and demonstrate how presidents often push the boundaries of constitutional provisions. By strategically using these appointments, presidents bypass the traditional confirmation process, temporarily extending their influence over government agencies and international relations. However, such actions also provoke legal battles and set precedents that complicate the separation of powers, reinforcing the notion that the executive branch can act unilaterally when legislative opposition arises.

Veto Power: Controlling the Legislative Agenda

The presidential veto is one of the most direct tools for asserting executive power over Congress. While the veto is constitutionally provided as a check on legislative overreach, presidents have often used it as a political weapon to shape legislative outcomes and control the national agenda. Andrew Jackson's extensive use of the veto power in the 19th century set a precedent for this approach. Jackson vetoed bills not just because he believed them to be unconstitutional but also because they conflicted with his policy priorities, as seen in his famous veto of the reauthorization of the Second Bank of the United States.

By threatening or using vetoes, presidents can force Congress to align legislation with executive preferences. Modern presidents continue this practice, with veto threats serving as a bargaining chip in negotiations. This ability to control the legislative agenda through veto power extends the reach of the executive branch beyond its traditional role, enabling presidents to influence policy outcomes even when they lack full legislative support. The veto, while constitutionally legitimate, has thus become a strategic tool for presidents to enforce their authority and maintain political leverage.

Signing Statements and Legislative Control: Reinterpreting Laws

Presidents also expand their influence through the use of signing statements, which allow them to express their interpretation of legislation as they sign it into law. George W. Bush notably used signing statements to assert that his administration would interpret laws in a manner consistent with his understanding of executive authority. This practice allows presidents to reshape the enforcement of laws according to their policy agendas, effectively rewriting legislative intent.

For example, Bush used signing statements to indicate his interpretation of laws related to interrogation techniques, despite Congressional intent to limit such practices. By issuing these statements, he asserted executive autonomy over matters of national security and counterterrorism. While not legally binding, signing statements can serve as a powerful executive tool, demonstrating how presidents reinterpret laws to expand their authority while appearing to comply with Congressional mandates. This approach raises significant questions about the separation of powers, as it blurs the line between legislative and executive authority.

Federalism Tensions: Federal Overreach and State Autonomy

The expansion of presidential power also manifests in tensions between federal and state authority, highlighting the struggle between centralized control and state autonomy. One historical example is President Dwight D. Eisenhower's decision to send federal troops to Little Rock, Arkansas, in 1957 to enforce desegregation following the Supreme Court's *Brown v. Board of Education* decision. While this action was necessary to uphold civil rights, it also illustrated the power of the executive branch to override state decisions, challenging the principles of federalism.

In more recent years, presidents have used federal power to enforce national policies that conflict with state interests. Obama's administration, for example, enforced environmental regulations that several states viewed as overreach, sparking legal battles over states' rights. Similarly, Trump's administration sought to override state policies related to immigration and environmental protections, using federal authority to impose uniformity across the country. These actions demonstrate how presidents assert executive power in ways that often strain the balance between federal and state authority, provoking debates over the limits of executive influence.

These examples underscore how the expansion of presidential power is not limited to bypassing Congress; it also involves encroaching on state autonomy, reinforcing the centralization of power in the executive branch. While some actions are justified in the name of national unity or security, they set precedents that future presidents can use to justify further federal interventions, challenging the traditional separation of powers between the federal and state governments.

Military Power and the Commander-in-Chief's Reach

The power of the U.S. presidency has long been intertwined with its military might. In the American constitutional framework, the president is designated as the commander-in-chief, a role that grants broad authority over military operations. However, the scope and execution of this authority have often gone beyond the intentions of the Founding Fathers, as presidents have increasingly used military power to bypass Congressional approval, influence domestic and international policies, and assert their dominance in global affairs. This chapter delves into the evolution of presidential military power, highlighting key examples where commanders-in-chief acted unilaterally, sometimes in ways that blurred or even crossed constitutional boundaries. By examining the War Powers Resolution, domestic surveillance, the use of executive orders, and the influence of the military-industrial complex, we uncover how military power has become both a tool and a weapon for American presidents.

The Evolution of Unilateral Military Action: The War Powers Resolution

The War Powers Resolution, passed by Congress in 1973 in the aftermath of the Vietnam War, was intended to check presidential power and restore some balance between the executive and legislative branches. It mandated that presidents must notify Congress within 48 hours of committing armed forces to military action and that such operations must end within 60 days unless Congress grants an extension or declares war. On paper, this resolution appeared to be a safeguard against unchecked military action, a mechanism to ensure that Congress remained an active participant in decisions of war and peace. However, in practice, it has often been used as a justification for presidents to engage in military interventions without Congressional approval.

Take, for example, President Barack Obama's intervention in Libya in 2011.

Obama authorized airstrikes against Muammar Gaddafi's regime without seeking Congressional approval, relying instead on the War Powers Resolution's 60-day provision. He justified the intervention on humanitarian grounds and argued that it was in the national interest to prevent a humanitarian disaster. However, critics argued that the intervention stretched the legal framework beyond its intended scope. Congress was left sidelined, with the administration claiming that the operation did not constitute "hostilities" as defined under the War Powers Resolution. This reinterpretation highlighted the flexible nature of the law and underscored the expanding reach of presidential authority in military matters.

This example illustrates a broader trend: while the War Powers Resolution was designed to curtail unilateral action, it has, paradoxically, enabled presidents to act first and seek approval later, or sometimes not at all. In the modern era, military engagements have become shorter, more technologically advanced, and often covert, making it easier for presidents to justify their actions as limited operations that fall within the scope of their commander-in-chief role. The result is an executive branch with unprecedented military freedom, setting significant precedents that are difficult to reverse.

The Commander-in-Chief Role: Engaging in Military Conflicts Without Declarations of War

Since World War II, the U.S. has engaged in numerous military conflicts without formal declarations of war from Congress. The Korean War, initiated by President Harry Truman in 1950, marked a pivotal moment in the expansion of presidential military power. Truman described the conflict as a "police action," arguing that it did not require Congressional approval because it fell under the mandate of the United Nations. This precedent set the stage for future presidents to engage in military operations under the guise of international cooperation or defensive action, often circumventing the need for Congressional approval altogether.

The trend continued with the Vietnam War, where successive presidents escalated military involvement without Congressional declarations. In recent decades, U.S. involvement in conflicts like Afghanistan and Iraq further highlighted the growing reach of the commander-in-chief. Although the 2001 Authorization for Use of Military Force (AUMF) granted the president broad authority to combat terrorism after the 9/11 attacks, it has since been used as a catch-all justification for military operations across the globe, many of which are far removed from the original intent of combating al-Qaeda.

This overreach became particularly evident during Obama's presidency. While Obama campaigned on ending "endless wars," his administration expanded drone warfare and special operations missions in countries like Yemen, Pakistan, and Somalia. These operations, often conducted under the umbrella of the AUMF, demonstrated how flexible and far-reaching the legal interpretations of presidential military authority had become. Critics argue that this flexibility undermines the Constitution, reducing Congress to a secondary role in matters of war and peace, while empowering the president to act as a unilateral force on the global stage.

Military Operations as Political Tools: The Strategic Use of Military Presence

Presidents have long used military operations and presence as political tools, leveraging them to shape public opinion, gain support, or project strength. This tactic is not new; it has roots stretching back to the 19th century when presidents like James K. Polk used military action to further their political and territorial ambitions, as seen during the Mexican-American War. However, in the modern era, the strategic use of military power has taken on new dimensions, especially with the rise of media coverage and the immediacy of information.

One illustrative example is the 1983 invasion of Grenada under President Ronald Reagan. The operation, aimed at overthrowing a Marxist government and rescuing American medical students, was widely criticized as unnecessary. Yet, for Reagan, it was an opportunity to project strength and assert America's anti-communist stance during the Cold War. The invasion was timed to coincide with growing concerns about American strength following the Beirut barracks bombing, and it successfully diverted public attention while showcasing decisive presidential action.

Similarly, military strikes or shows of force are often used as rallying points during periods of low approval ratings or political scandal. The 1998 missile strikes ordered by President Bill Clinton in response to al-Qaeda attacks in Africa came at a time when his administration faced intense scrutiny over the Monica Lewinsky scandal. Critics accused Clinton of using the strikes to divert attention and regain public support, a tactic that demonstrates how military power can be wielded not only as a tool of foreign policy but also as a domestic political instrument.

The use of military action for political purposes raises questions about the integrity of executive decisions and the potential for conflicts of interest. When military power is wielded to serve short-term political goals, it not only undermines democratic processes but also sets dangerous precedents, encouraging future presidents to act unilaterally in pursuit of political gain rather than national security or strategic interests.

Executive Orders and Military Decisions: Shaping Policy Beyond Congressional Reach

Executive orders have become a powerful tool for presidents seeking to bypass Congressional approval, particularly in military and national security matters. These orders allow presidents to act swiftly, but they often push the boundaries of constitutional authority, sometimes with long-lasting consequences. One of the most controversial examples is President Franklin D. Roosevelt's Executive Order 9066, which authorized the internment of Japanese Americans during World War II. Framed as a wartime necessity, this order led to the relocation and internment of over 120,000 individuals, raising profound questions about civil liberties and presidential power.

The use of executive orders for military purposes has continued into the modern era. In 2018, President Trump issued an executive order authorizing the deployment of thousands of troops to the U.S.-Mexico border in response to migrant caravans. Critics argued that this action was politically motivated, aimed at galvanizing his base ahead of the midterm elections. The executive order highlighted how presidential military authority could be leveraged for domestic political advantage, raising concerns about the appropriate limits of executive power.

These examples illustrate how executive orders, particularly those related to military and security matters, allow presidents to act quickly but also bypass established legal and constitutional frameworks. While executive orders are often justified on the grounds of urgency or national interest, their frequent use for military purposes underscores the expanding reach of presidential power and the diminished role of Congressional oversight.

The Military-Industrial Complex: Influence and Alignment with Presidential Policies

The intersection of presidential power and the military-industrial complex further complicates the dynamics of American military policy. Presidents often align their military strategies with the interests of defence contractors and lobbyists, which influences policy decisions and perpetuates America's involvement in prolonged conflicts. President Dwight D. Eisenhower famously warned of the military-industrial complex in his 1961 farewell address, cautioning that the unchecked influence of defence contractors could shape policy in ways that prioritize profits over national security.

The alignment between presidential military decisions and defence contractors raises critical questions about accountability and the true motivations behind military actions. The influence of the military-industrial complex blurs the line between national interest and corporate gain, complicating the perception of presidential authority. When presidents are aligned with powerful defence interests, it reinforces the illusion of decisive and necessary leadership, even as these actions serve a complex web of political and economic motivations.

Judicial and Legislative Manipulation: The Long Arm of Executive Influence

The judiciary and legislative branches were designed as crucial checks on executive power, however presidents throughout history have found ways to navigate, influence, and even manipulate these branches to expand their authority and push their agendas. The evolution of presidential power reveals a pattern of executive strategies, ranging from judicial appointments and executive orders to treaty-making and the selective enforcement of laws.

Judicial Appointments and Court Packing: Shaping the Judiciary

The power to appoint federal judges, including Supreme Court justices, is one of the most significant tools a president has to influence American politics long beyond their tenure. By shaping the judiciary, presidents can leave a legacy that aligns with their ideological and policy preferences, as judicial rulings on constitutional matters can alter the legal landscape for generations.

Franklin D. Roosevelt's (FDR) 1937 court-packing attempt remains one of the most prominent examples of a president trying to reshape the judiciary. At the time, the Supreme Court repeatedly struck down key elements of FDR's New Deal, threatening his ambitious agenda aimed at pulling the country out of the Great Depression. Frustrated, Roosevelt proposed adding up to six new justices to the Supreme Court, one for every justice over the age of 70 who refused to retire. Although the plan faced significant backlash and was ultimately defeated, it was a clear demonstration of how far a president might go to influence judicial outcomes. The controversy surrounding the proposal underscored the tension between executive ambition and the judiciary's supposed independence. Even without success, the threat itself pressured the Court to become more favourable to New Deal legislation.

In more recent history, the power of judicial appointments has continued to be a potent tool. President Donald Trump, with the support of a Republican-controlled Senate, appointed three Supreme Court justices, reshaping the ideological balance of the Court for years to come. These appointments were strategically made to ensure a conservative tilt that aligned with Republican priorities, from abortion rights to corporate regulations and voting laws. Trump's ability to fill these vacancies was not simply a matter of timing but also of political manoeuvring, as seen when Senate Majority Leader Mitch McConnell blocked the confirmation of Merrick Garland, Barack Obama's nominee, in 2016, citing the upcoming election. This delay allowed Trump to appoint Gorsuch after assuming office, demonstrating how judicial appointments are as much about political strategy as they are about filling vacancies.

Beyond the Supreme Court, presidents also appoint judges to federal appellate and district courts, which decide the vast majority of federal cases. By appointing judges with particular ideological leanings, presidents can influence decisions on a wide range of issues, including immigration, healthcare, and environmental regulation. These lower court appointments, while less visible, are equally significant in shaping the judiciary's long-term trajectory. The judicial appointment process thus serves as a powerful mechanism for presidents to extend their influence beyond their immediate term, embedding their political and legal philosophies within the fabric of American law.

Federal Regulations and Rulemaking: Reinterpreting Laws
Another way presidents extend their influence is through federal regulations and rulemaking. While Congress passes laws, the executive branch, through its various agencies, interprets and enforces these laws.

250

This gives presidents considerable power to direct how laws are implemented, often reinterpreting existing statutes to align with their policy objectives. This process, while technically within executive authority, can sometimes circumvent Congressional intent, raising questions about the balance of power.

A prime example of this is the Trump administration's approach to environmental regulations. Trump's team, led by then-Environmental Protection Agency (EPA) Administrator, systematically rolled back numerous environmental protections put in place by previous administrations. This included reinterpreting the Clean Water Act to reduce the number of waterways under federal protection, effectively weakening pollution controls. Despite Congress's intention to strengthen environmental safeguards, the administration's regulatory changes highlighted how presidents can use the rulemaking process to shift policy without the need for new legislation.

Similarly, Barack Obama's administration leveraged executive agencies to implement significant policy changes, particularly around climate and labour regulations. Unable to pass comprehensive climate legislation through a divided Congress, Obama directed the EPA to classify carbon dioxide as a pollutant under the Clean Air Act, allowing the agency to regulate greenhouse gas emissions. This move bypassed Congress but faced significant legal challenges, illustrating both the power and the precariousness of using federal regulations as a tool of executive influence.

Rulemaking also provides presidents with the ability to dismantle or build on policies from previous administrations. This process has become increasingly politicized, as seen with Biden's efforts to reverse many of Trump's regulatory rollbacks. The constant tug-of-war over regulations underscores the long-term impact of executive power on policy and governance, and how it can be used to either reinforce or dismantle Congressional intent.

Executive Orders: The Broad Reach of Presidential Decrees

Executive orders have long been a powerful instrument for presidents to enact policies swiftly and unilaterally, bypassing the legislative process. While the Constitution does not explicitly grant presidents the authority to issue executive orders, they have become an accepted, and sometimes controversial, mechanism for exerting executive power. By issuing these orders, presidents can direct federal agencies, set policy priorities, and respond to crises, all without requiring Congressional approval.

Historically, executive orders have been used to achieve both monumental and controversial changes. President Franklin D. Roosevelt's Executive Order 9066, which authorized the internment of Japanese Americans during World War II, remains a dark chapter in American history. Although justified at the time as a national security measure, it later faced legal and moral challenges, revealing the risks of unchecked executive power. On the other hand, executive orders have also led to positive social change, such as Harry Truman's order to desegregate the military in 1948, demonstrating the dual nature of this tool.

In contemporary politics, executive orders continue to be a central strategy for presidents seeking to implement their agendas quickly. Barack Obama used executive orders to advance progressive policies, including protecting undocumented immigrants brought to the U.S. as children under the Deferred Action for Childhood Arrivals (DACA) program. This decision bypassed a gridlocked Congress but faced legal challenges that highlighted the limits and risks of executive actions taken without legislative backing.

Similarly, Donald Trump used executive orders to enact key campaign promises, from travel bans targeting certain predominantly Muslim countries to revoking regulations on businesses. These actions, while effective in signalling presidential priorities, often sparked legal battles and public controversy, demonstrating the contentious nature of executive power when used to bypass traditional legislative channels. The frequent use of executive orders in recent decades reflects not only the expanding reach of presidential authority but also the limitations of a polarized Congress unable to pass comprehensive legislation.

Treaty-Making Power: Circumventing Senate Approval

The Constitution grants the president the power to negotiate treaties with other nations, but these treaties must be ratified by a two-thirds majority in the Senate. When the Senate refuses to cooperate or when time constraints loom, presidents have turned to executive agreements as an alternative. These agreements, while not requiring Senate approval, allow presidents to bypass legislative hurdles and engage in international diplomacy on their own terms.

One prominent example is Barack Obama's Iran Nuclear Deal (Joint Comprehensive Plan of Action, or JCPOA). Rather than seeking a treaty that required Senate approval, Obama entered into an executive agreement with Iran and other world powers to limit Iran's nuclear capabilities in exchange for lifting economic sanctions. While this allowed Obama to quickly enact a critical foreign policy initiative, it also meant that the agreement lacked the permanence and bipartisan support of a Senate-ratified treaty. When Donald Trump assumed the presidency, he unilaterally withdrew from the agreement, highlighting the vulnerability and temporary nature of executive agreements that bypass legislative approval.

Another example is the Paris Climate Accord, which Obama entered through executive agreement rather than treaty ratification. This decision was politically expedient, given the resistance from a Republican-controlled Senate. However, the subsequent withdrawal by the Trump administration demonstrated the fragility of such agreements when they are not backed by a broader legislative consensus. These examples underscore how the use of executive agreements, while providing flexibility in foreign policy, often undermines the stability and continuity of U.S. international commitments.

Impeachment and Legislative Manoeuvres: Navigating Political Landmines

Impeachment serves as a constitutional check on presidential power, yet its effectiveness depends on the political landscape and the ability of a president to navigate partisan divides. Presidents have historically relied on political allies and strategies to mitigate or influence impeachment proceedings, underscoring how they can manipulate legislative processes for their advantage.

Bill Clinton's impeachment in 1998 serves as a classic example. Despite being impeached by the House of Representatives for perjury and obstruction of justice, Clinton's ability to maintain Democratic support in the Senate ensured that he was acquitted. By effectively using his political influence and rallying his party, Clinton demonstrated that impeachment, while theoretically a tool for holding presidents accountable, can also become a partisan battle where outcomes are determined by loyalty rather than legal principles.

Donald Trump's two impeachment trials further illustrate this dynamic. In both cases, Trump leveraged Republican loyalty in the Senate to secure acquittal, despite significant evidence presented against him. The highly polarized nature of modern American politics means that impeachment, instead of being a straightforward constitutional process, has become a strategic manoeuvre where presidents can exploit partisan alliances to avoid removal.

Civil Rights and Selective Enforcement: Presidential Discretion in Action

The enforcement, or lack thereof, of civil rights laws highlights another dimension of presidential influence. Throughout history, presidents have selectively enforced or ignored laws based on their political priorities, using discretion to shape social policy and reinforce their authority.

Woodrow Wilson's administration, for instance, selectively enforced civil rights laws, particularly against African Americans, while promoting policies that supported segregation. This selective enforcement was driven by political motives, as Wilson sought to maintain support from Southern Democrats. Similarly, during the Civil Rights Movement of the 1960s, presidents like John F. Kennedy and Lyndon B. Johnson used executive orders and federal intervention to enforce desegregation and voting rights laws. While these actions were morally justifiable and politically necessary, they also illustrated how executive power can selectively shape the enforcement of laws based on the administration's priorities.

In more recent history, the Obama administration's selective approach to immigration enforcement, particularly with programs like DACA, demonstrated how presidents use executive discretion to achieve policy goals when legislative avenues are blocked. While DACA provided protections for millions of undocumented immigrants, it also faced criticism and legal challenges, highlighting the precariousness of policies enacted without legislative backing.

Pardoning Power: Shaping Perception and Controlling Fallout
The presidential power to pardon is another tool often wielded to manage public perception and minimize political damage. While the pardon power is constitutionally granted and can be used for compassionate or justifiable reasons, it has frequently been employed to control fallout from political scandals or to influence how history remembers certain administrations.

One of the most famous examples of the strategic use of the pardon power occurred in 1974 when President Gerald Ford pardoned Richard Nixon following the Watergate scandal. The pardon was framed as a necessary act to heal the nation and move past a turbulent period, but it also effectively shielded Nixon from further investigation or prosecution. Ford's decision was widely criticized as an abuse of power, seen by many as a means to protect a fellow Republican and a former president from legal accountability. It highlighted how the presidential power to pardon could be used to reshape narratives and minimize long-term political damage, maintaining an illusion of benevolence while serving partisan or personal interests.

More recently, President Donald Trump used his pardon power to benefit political allies and associates, issuing controversial pardons to individuals like Michael Flynn, Roger Stone, and Paul Manafort—figures who were implicated in the investigation led by Special Counsel Robert Mueller into Russian interference in the 2016 election. By granting these pardons, Trump signalled loyalty to his base and positioned himself as a defender against what he termed a "witch hunt." In this way, the pardon power served not just as a legal mechanism but as a tool for narrative control and political strategy, reinforcing loyalty among his supporters while shaping public perception around his presidency.

Final Thoughts
The conclusion of this chapter highlights a fundamental truth about the American presidency: while the Constitution envisions a system of checks and balances, the reality is far more complex. Presidential influence over both the judicial and legislative branches demonstrates a continuous and often strategic expansion of executive power. Presidents have long found ways to extend their authority beyond traditional limits, through judicial appointments, executive orders, selective enforcement, and treaty-making. Each of these tools, while constitutionally grounded, has been pushed to its limits to serve specific political and policy goals.

These strategies allow for flexibility and swift action, particularly in times of crisis, but they also blur the lines of constitutional governance. The balance of power, a cornerstone of American democracy, is repeatedly tested as the executive branch manoeuvres to increase its influence.

The illusion of a fully balanced system is apparent when examining how presidents manage and, at times, override legislative and judicial checks. This tug-of-war between the branches underscores that the system's checks and balances, while present in theory, are frequently negotiated and challenged in practice. Whether it's through the manipulation of budget authority, emergency declarations, or the employment of recess appointments and signing statements, the presidency has become a flexible, evolving entity. This adaptation often extends beyond what the framers of the Constitution originally intended, revealing both the resilience and vulnerabilities of the American political structure.

Nowhere is this expansion more evident than in the realm of military power. As commander-in-chief, the president has evolved the role far beyond its initial constraints, leveraging tactics like the War Powers Resolution, executive orders, and the support of the military-industrial complex to bypass Congress and act unilaterally in military matters. These moves, while often justified under the guise of national security, reveal the deepening complexity of presidential power. The ongoing debate over the role of Congress in war-making decisions and the influence of political motivations on military actions highlights the risks associated with an increasingly powerful executive.

The consistent stretching of constitutional boundaries by the executive branch reveals a pattern: the presidency is continually evolving into an office with authority that exceeds its original design. This shift has profound implications for the separation of powers and the overall health of American democracy. As presidents test and expand these boundaries, the risk of executive overreach becomes an ever-present concern, one that challenges the foundational principles upon which the nation was built. If unchecked, this expansion may not only alter the balance between branches but also reshape the very nature of American governance. Understanding and addressing this evolution is essential for preserving the constitutional integrity and democratic ideals that have long defined the United States.

CHAPTER 13

I'LL BE WHOEVER YOU WANT ME TO BE

"I'll be whoever you want me to be." The words could belong to any number of political figures throughout history, but they're especially fitting for the modern American president. In an age where charisma often outweighs policy, the art of crafting a compelling narrative has become an essential tool for political survival. Today, the president is as much a performer as a leader, and speeches have evolved into performances designed to captivate, persuade, and mobilize. This chapter delves into the intricacies of political rhetoric and the power it wields, examining the speeches of figures like Bill Clinton, Donald Trump, Kamala Harris, and Joe Biden to unravel the underlying strategies that shape public perception and, ultimately, the course of American politics.

The concept of political speechmaking isn't new, but the way it's executed today is a finely tuned operation. Behind every major address is a team of speechwriters, communications experts, and image consultants, all working to craft the perfect message, one that projects authority, yet feels relatable; one that inspires hope, yet also stirs a sense of urgency. The speeches themselves are carefully calibrated to connect with audiences on an emotional level, strategically invoking fear, hope, unity, or division, depending on the moment and the political need. In this way, the modern president becomes a chameleon, shifting personas to match the expectations and desires of the public, a performance choreographed down to the smallest detail.

Take Bill Clinton, for instance. Known for his charm and folksy demeanour, Clinton mastered the art of appearing empathetic and relatable while still projecting a sense of authority. His speeches were crafted to establish a connection with the everyday American, each story he shared, each pause he took, was designed to make his audience feel seen and heard. Clinton's speeches were not just about policy; they were about creating a sense of trust, a sense that he understood the struggles of his fellow citizens. His ability to fuse storytelling with policy details gave him an edge, making him not just a president, but a leader people felt they could rely on.

Donald Trump's speeches, on the other hand, reveal a different kind of mastery. Trump doesn't just aim to connect; he seeks to dominate. His rhetoric often employs hyperbole and fear, painting a world full of dangers that only he can resolve. It's a tactic that shifts the focus from substantive policy to a battle of personalities, where Trump positions himself as the protector against looming threats. By using charged language and vivid imagery, he amplifies anxiety and reinforces a loyalty-based dynamic among his supporters. His speechwriters know the power of urgency, each phrase and slogan is designed to energize his base and shift the narrative in his favour. Trump's approach highlights how political rhetoric can be wielded not just to inspire, but to divide and polarize.

Kamala Harris represents yet another style of rhetorical influence, one focused on vision and inclusivity. Harris and her speechwriters have crafted a message of hope, one that aims to unify a diverse electorate under a common mission.

Her speeches often use inclusive language, inviting audiences of various backgrounds to see themselves as part of a collective movement for progress. It's a strategy that seeks to expand the reach of her influence, building coalitions that transcend typical demographic divides. Her rhetoric, while optimistic, is also strategic; it aims to create a sense of shared purpose that can translate into electoral momentum.

Joe Biden's rhetorical approach, meanwhile, leans heavily on contrast. Biden's speeches frequently set him up as the antidote to division, subtly highlighting the flaws of his opposition without resorting to direct attacks. This technique allows him to project an image of unity and stability, even as he positions himself against the backdrop of chaos or uncertainty. It's a tactic that blends subtlety with strength, suggesting that Biden's steady hand is what the nation needs to navigate through turbulent times.

This chapter explores these different speechmaking strategies, illustrating how modern presidents and their teams craft their messages to maintain control of the narrative and influence public perception. Through careful dissection of key speeches, the chapter uncovers how the language of American politics has shifted, how leaders tailor their personas, and how each word is chosen to maximize impact. We'll see how political speech has become less about the content of policy and more about the performance of leadership, an artful exercise in shaping an image that aligns with the public's hopes, fears, and expectations.

In the end, "I'll be whoever you want me to be" encapsulates the essence of the modern American presidency: a role that adapts, shifts, and evolves based on the political moment and the demands of an electorate that, in turn, craves reassurance, excitement, and a hero to champion their cause. Look beyond the words themselves, see the hands that craft them, and understand the motivations behind every line, every gesture, and every carefully chosen phrase. This is a journey into the heart of political performance, one that reveals the intricate balance between power, persuasion, and the illusion of leadership.

The Blueprint of Leadership
The art of speechmaking has become a central tool in shaping presidential identity. The projection of authority and leadership, the creation of empathy, and the delicate balance between relatability and power are all elements carefully crafted behind the scenes. In this first

section, "The Blueprint of Leadership," we delve into how speechwriters engineer these messages, focusing on Bill Clinton's presidency as a case study. Clinton's speeches provide a fascinating glimpse into how language can be wielded to convey both strength and empathy, and how a president, with the help of a dedicated team, crafts an image that aligns with the public's needs and desires.

Bill Clinton was a master communicator, and it's no coincidence that he was dubbed the "Great Communicator" of his generation, following in the footsteps of Ronald Reagan. But Clinton's style was distinct, less about grand gestures and sweeping rhetoric, and more about weaving personal stories and common experiences into the fabric of his political message. His speeches weren't just performances; they were conversations. Clinton had a unique ability to make his listeners feel like he was speaking directly to them, even in a room of thousands or through the screen of a television set. This approach was not accidental; it was the result of meticulous planning by his team of speechwriters and advisors who understood the power of blending relatability with authority.

Consider Clinton's speech at the 1992 Democratic National Convention in New York. Facing an audience hungry for change after twelve years of Republican leadership, Clinton needed to present himself as both a figure of hope and a man who understood the struggles of everyday Americans. His speech opened with a powerful line: "I have news for the forces of greed and the defenders of the status quo: your time has come and gone. It's time for a change in America." This line was strategic, it created a sense of urgency while painting Clinton as a champion of the people. But what followed was even more telling. Clinton pivoted to a personal story about his upbringing in Hope, Arkansas, explaining how his mother, a nurse, struggled to make ends meet. This wasn't just rhetoric; it was a calculated move to humanize himself, to show that he was not a distant political elite but someone who had lived the American experience.

Clinton's speechwriters knew the power of narrative. They wove stories like this into his speeches, not merely as a backdrop but as a central theme. This storytelling approach allowed Clinton to project empathy, a quality that would become a cornerstone of his political brand.

By sharing these personal anecdotes, he created a sense of intimacy, making audiences believe that he truly understood their struggles. It was a tactic designed to foster trust, to paint him as someone who could not only relate to the average American but who could also be trusted to lead with their best interests at heart.

Take, for instance, his famous 1995 State of the Union Address, delivered after the Republicans had taken control of Congress. Clinton was in a vulnerable position; his leadership was under scrutiny, and the nation was divided. His speech had to accomplish two things: reassert his authority as president and show that he was still in touch with the needs of the American people. The speechwriters crafted a message that balanced these two objectives. Clinton spoke about welfare reform, promising to "end welfare as we know it" while stressing that he would not abandon those in need. The language was carefully chosen to communicate both strength and empathy. By presenting himself as a reformer willing to make tough decisions but also as a protector of the vulnerable, Clinton walked a tightrope that kept his base engaged while reaching out to the centre.

His team's strategy was evident in the way they structured his speeches. They often began with broad, policy-driven language to establish authority and expertise before narrowing down to personal stories or examples that made these policies feel tangible and immediate. This structure was designed to build credibility first and then connect emotionally, ensuring that the audience felt both informed and personally involved. In the 1996 re-election campaign, Clinton's team frequently used this blueprint. In a speech in New Hampshire, a state critical for his campaign, Clinton spoke directly to workers affected by globalization and economic change. He began with a detailed outline of his administration's economic policies but quickly shifted to anecdotes about meeting factory workers and single parents struggling to make ends meet. By blending the macro and the micro, Clinton could make broad policies feel personal, connecting them directly to the lives of his listeners.

Another hallmark of Clinton's speeches was his use of inclusive language. His speechwriters were adept at crafting phrases that made every American feel seen, regardless of their background.

Phrases like "We're all in this together" and "No one should be left behind" became staples of his addresses, creating a sense of shared purpose and unity. This inclusive rhetoric was particularly visible during moments of national crisis. After the Oklahoma City bombing in 1995, Clinton addressed the nation with a speech that combined mourning with resilience. He spoke directly to the families of victims, saying, "You have lost too much, but you have not lost everything." The speech was a powerful display of empathy and strength, designed to reassure a grieving nation while also positioning Clinton as a compassionate leader. His choice of words, tone, and the emotional cadence of his delivery all contributed to building the image of a president who was both protector and consoler-in-chief.

Clinton's use of body language also played a significant role in how his speeches were received. Unlike other politicians who could appear stiff or detached, Clinton had a natural warmth that his team amplified through careful coaching. In televised appearances, he would often lean into the podium, making his engagement with the audience feel direct and personal. His hand gestures were open and expressive, inviting rather than commanding. Even his fashion choices were intentional, his team opted for crisp, yet approachable suits that communicated professionalism without the aloofness often associated with more formal political attire.

The effort that went into making Clinton appear relatable and authoritative was not just about style but about constructing a presidential identity that could weather the political storms of the 1990s. The language he used, the stories he shared, and the persona he projected were all meticulously planned elements in his political arsenal. His team's strategy relied on the belief that Americans were more likely to support a leader who felt like one of them, even if that meant occasionally blurring the lines between authenticity and performance.

It's important to recognize that while Clinton's speeches often seemed spontaneous or off-the-cuff, they were anything but. Each word, each pause, was crafted with a purpose. For example, in his second inaugural address in 1997, Clinton spoke of building a "bridge to the 21st century." The metaphor was deliberate, bridges symbolize progress, connection, and support, all themes his administration wanted to highlight as they prepared for the challenges ahead.

His speechwriters knew the power of metaphor, and this particular one was used repeatedly throughout his speeches to reinforce the idea that Clinton was leading America towards a hopeful, united future. It was a rhetorical device meant to reassure voters that they were on a collective journey, one that only he could guide them through.

This emphasis on relatability and connection was not without its critics. Some argued that Clinton's emotional appeals were manipulative, designed to distract from policy flaws or political scandals. Indeed, the balance between authenticity and performance is always precarious in politics, and Clinton's ability to walk that line was a skill honed by years of practice and a dedicated team of experts. But regardless of the criticisms, the effectiveness of his approach cannot be denied. Clinton's ability to shape public perception through his speeches was a key factor in his electoral success and his enduring popularity even amid controversy.

In understanding Clinton's approach to speechmaking, we gain insight into the broader mechanics of American presidential rhetoric. It is not simply about communicating policies or responding to crises; it is about constructing an image, projecting authority, and, most importantly, creating an emotional bond with the electorate. Clinton's presidency offers a blueprint for how modern presidents, with the help of their speechwriters and communications teams, blend leadership and relatability, showing how rhetoric can be the most powerful tool in a president's arsenal.

Fear

Mobilizing support through fear has long been a tactic used in politics, but few modern leaders have wielded it as effectively, or as controversially, as Donald Trump. Trump's approach was not just about stirring the pot; it was about shaking the foundation, about creating a sense of impending doom unless his supporters rallied behind him. This strategy, which was central to his campaign and presidency, was meticulously crafted to harness fear as both a motivator and a unifier, drawing people closer to him and reinforcing the image of a leader standing against chaos.

From the very beginning of his presidential campaign, Trump set the tone.

During his campaign announcement speech in 2015, he famously declared, *"When Mexico sends its people, they're not sending their best. They're bringing drugs. They're bringing crime. They're rapists."* This was more than just a controversial soundbite; it was a strategic framing of immigration as an existential threat to America's safety and values. By framing immigrants, particularly those from Mexico, as dangerous invaders, Trump was not only appealing to a base concerned with border security but also tapping into deeper, long-standing anxieties about cultural and economic change. The message was clear: there is a threat at our doorstep, and only he could fix it.

Throughout his campaign and presidency, Trump's rhetoric repeatedly amplified these themes, and his speechwriters expertly crafted language that reinforced the image of an America under siege. At rallies, his tone would shift to match the urgency of his words. In front of his most devoted supporters, he painted vivid pictures of a nation in decline, beset by enemies both within and beyond its borders. *"Our country is in serious trouble. We don't win anymore,"* he said at a 2016 rally in Pensacola, Florida. Here, the image was not just one of political or economic strife but of a country losing its very identity, its greatness slipping away unless something radical changed. The fear he invoked wasn't subtle; it was meant to shock, to energize, and to galvanize his supporters into action.

The genius of Trump's strategy lay in its simplicity and repetition. In his rhetoric, everything became a battle of good versus evil, a classic framing technique that psychologists have noted is effective in uniting groups against a common foe. Trump's speeches frequently emphasized an "us versus them" dynamic, an approach that has roots in authoritarian playbooks but also finds resonance in democratic societies facing rapid social changes. Whether speaking of immigrants, Democrats, the media, or foreign nations like China, Trump used language that not only cast these groups as threats but positioned them as fundamentally opposed to American interests and values. In this way, his supporters weren't just political allies; they became soldiers in a cultural and ideological war, their loyalty tied not just to a candidate but to a cause.

At the Republican National Convention in 2016, Trump's acceptance speech was a masterclass in fearmongering.

He painted a dystopian vision of America, describing an almost apocalyptic scenario: *"The attacks on our police, and the terrorism in our cities, threaten our very way of life. Any politician who does not grasp this danger is not fit to lead our country."* By depicting the country as teetering on the edge of chaos, Trump effectively framed himself as the last bastion of hope, the only leader capable of restoring order and protecting the American people. The use of stark, dire language, *"threaten our very way of life"*, was not accidental. It was a calculated choice meant to elicit an emotional, rather than rational, response from the audience.

Trump's speeches also frequently employed hyperbole as a tool to amplify the stakes and exaggerate both threats and his own achievements. When he spoke about his administration's accomplishments or the dangers posed by his opponents, his language was often inflated to the point of distortion. For instance, during the 2018 State of the Union address, Trump claimed, *"The coalition to defeat ISIS has liberated very close to 100 percent of the territory just recently held by these killers in Iraq and Syria."* While the defeat of ISIS was a significant achievement, the way Trump framed it made it seem as though his administration had single-handedly orchestrated this victory, ignoring the complexities and contributions of international allies and previous administrations. The hyperbole served a dual purpose: it not only inflated his accomplishments but also reinforced the narrative that he was the decisive and singular force behind America's success.

Similarly, when addressing the issue of crime, Trump often employed inflated statistics to amplify fear and urgency. In his speeches, American cities, particularly those governed by Democrats, became symbols of lawlessness and chaos. *"Look at Chicago, look at what's going on in Chicago. People are being shot left and right,"* he said at a rally in 2019. Trump's speechwriters knew that by focusing on specific locations and using vivid, alarming language, they could turn isolated incidents or localized crime rates into a nationwide crisis, framing it as a consequence of his opponents' policies. This tactic not only mobilized his base but also justified the need for his hardline approach to law and order, suggesting that without him, the entire nation would descend into chaos.

Similarly when playing an audience he needed to win over he would also use European examples. His remarks about knife crime in London became a prominent part of his broader political strategy to critique liberal governance both domestically and abroad.

He first brought up knife crime in London during his address to the National Rifle Association (NRA) Annual Meeting in Dallas, Texas, in May 2018. Standing before a crowd of gun rights supporters, Trump used the issue as a way to underscore his defence of the Second Amendment and criticize what he viewed as ineffective policies in countries with stricter gun control laws.

In his speech, Trump claimed that a "one very prestigious hospital" in London had become overwhelmed with knife crime, comparing it to a "war zone." He painted a vivid picture for his audience, describing the hospital as filled with blood, and doctors reportedly showing the aftermath of the violence. "They don't have guns. They have knives. And instead, there's blood all over the floors of this hospital," Trump said, emphasizing the dangers that he believed liberal policies could create. The implication was clear: without firearms, people resort to other weapons, and cities that impose gun control are not immune to violence. By presenting this imagery, he aimed to instil a sense of fear and urgency among his audience, reinforcing his stance that gun rights were essential to personal and national security.

The comments drew an immediate and sharp response from Sadiq Khan, the Mayor of London, who had previously clashed with Trump on several occasions. Khan, a vocal critic of Trump's rhetoric and policies, dismissed Trump's comments as an attempt to politicize an issue and spread misinformation. He pointed out that while knife crime was indeed a serious problem in London, Trump's portrayal was an exaggeration designed to serve his own political agenda. Khan highlighted the differences in gun violence between the United States and the United Kingdom, arguing that the scale and severity of the problem were incomparable.

Khan's office released statements emphasizing that while tackling knife crime was a priority for London, it was crucial to remember the context: the UK had one of the lowest gun-related death rates in the world, and incidents involving knives, while serious, were far less frequent than gun violence in the U.S. Khan also reiterated that London, like many other cities, was working hard to address and reduce knife crime through community programs, law enforcement efforts, and new policies focused on prevention.

Khan's response went beyond refuting Trump's claims; it was a broader defence of London's reputation and governance. He framed Trump's remarks as an attack not just on him personally, but on the city's progressive leadership and its policies. By standing firm against Trump's criticism, Khan aimed to demonstrate that London was resilient and capable of handling its own challenges without outside interference or commentary.

The media in both the UK and the U.S. seized on the exchange, amplifying the clash between Trump and Khan. In the UK, many publications criticized Trump's comments as an opportunistic move that failed to grasp the complexities of knife crime and urban safety. In the U.S., Trump's supporters used the incident as evidence that strict gun control laws were ineffective, pointing to London as a cautionary tale.

For Trump, the narrative was clear: London's issues served as a warning of what could happen in American cities under liberal governance. By continuing to highlight and exaggerate these incidents, Trump not only critiqued Sadiq Khan but also reinforced his own image as a defender of American safety and gun rights, positioning himself as the leader who would prevent similar situations in the United States. His rhetoric aimed to connect with his base, stoking fears about urban violence and the potential consequences of stricter gun control measures.

In subsequent interviews and social media posts, Trump doubled down on his claims, continuing to use London as an example whenever the topic of gun control or urban safety arose. Despite being called out for inaccuracies, Trump's remarks had already served their purpose: they had mobilized his supporters and reinforced his narrative of strength and security against what he painted as liberal mismanagement. The controversy also fit neatly into his pattern of clashing with progressive leaders, both in the U.S. and abroad, allowing him to cast himself as the lone voice of reason against a backdrop of what he framed as misguided policies.

During ABC's presidential debate, Donald Trump employed a vivid and shocking claim that became a focal point of his rhetoric: *"In Springfield, they are eating the dogs. The people that came in, they are eating the cats. They're eating, they are eating the pets of the people that live there."*

This statement, delivered with his characteristic certainty and conviction, was designed to stir emotion, evoke fear, and ultimately mobilize his base. Yet, as often happened with Trump's assertions, the claim was entirely baseless. Springfield city officials, as reported by BBC Verify, stated that there were "no credible reports" of such incidents. Nevertheless, Trump's rhetoric had already achieved its desired effect, anxiety, outrage, and an energized response from his supporters.

The nature of Trump's statement reveals a deliberate strategy: using emotionally charged, often shocking imagery to create a narrative that plays directly into his audience's fears and biases. The image of people resorting to eating pets, especially in a town like Springfield, an archetypal American city, is carefully chosen. It taps into a deep sense of moral and social collapse, suggesting that the presence of outsiders or economic mismanagement has pushed a typical American community to a point of desperation. Even as local officials denied the claim, the damage was done. The idea had been planted, amplified through social media and right-wing news outlets, and for many in Trump's audience, the denial only reinforced the belief that the "mainstream media" and "officials" were part of a larger cover-up.

This is a textbook example of how Trump's rhetoric often works: by presenting an alarming situation that is unverifiable yet emotionally resonant, he creates a scenario where denial from official sources doesn't negate the effect. Instead, it serves to deepen the sense of distrust among his supporters. This is the power of *false proximity*, where the closer a fabricated story feels to everyday life, like the notion of losing pets to some horrific circumstance, the more potent its emotional impact.

The spread of this narrative also highlights the role of Trump's allies in amplifying his claims. Republican vice-presidential candidate JD Vance, for example, echoed the statement on social media platform X, garnering over 11 million views. The virality of such posts is part of the broader strategy, social media becomes a multiplier, where misinformation or unverified claims quickly gain traction and influence public perception before any factual rebuttal can take hold. Vance's repetition of Trump's baseless assertion further solidified the narrative within Trump's base, turning a single comment into a widespread belief among millions.

Critics like US National Security Council spokesman John Kirby called out these tactics, labelling Vance's remarks as *"dangerous"* and a *"conspiracy theory...."* Kirby's response underscores the damaging impact of such rhetoric, it goes beyond mere misinformation. By invoking a sense of racial or cultural "otherness," Trump's statement wasn't just about creating fear; it was about reinforcing a worldview where "outsiders" are the cause of societal decay, and his leadership is positioned as the only solution to prevent this supposed downfall.

Even when confronted with the facts, such as the official denials from Springfield's city officials, the Trump camp has often embraced a posture of defiance, suggesting that these sources cannot be trusted. This tactic, often referred to as *"flooding the zone"* with misinformation, creates a climate where the truth is constantly questioned, and any attempt to debunk falsehoods is met with suspicion. It's a strategy that relies on overwhelming the audience with so much conflicting information that they either cling more strongly to their preconceived notions or become so disoriented that they are open to whatever narrative Trump offers as clarity.

The focus on hyper-local, relatable stories like the one about Springfield also serves another purpose: it distracts from larger policy discussions or critiques that might be harder for Trump to navigate. By shifting the conversation to visceral, emotional topics, he moves the debate away from more substantive issues like economic policy or healthcare reform, where his positions might not hold up under scrutiny. It's a sleight of hand that pulls the audience's focus to a fabricated crisis rather than the complexities of governance.

Moreover, this strategy is not limited to Trump. It reflects a broader trend within modern populism, where emotional, fear-based rhetoric replaces nuanced debate. The success of this tactic underscores how political messaging has evolved in the digital age, facts often take a backseat to emotionally charged narratives that can be amplified quickly and widely. In Trump's case, the effectiveness of this approach has not only mobilized a loyal base but has also reshaped American political discourse, making fear a central tool in the arsenal of modern campaign strategies.

In dissecting Trump's rhetoric, it's crucial to note the strategic use of imagery and metaphors that make his speeches resonate on an emotional level. His language is rarely neutral; instead, it is charged with words meant to evoke fear and urgency. For instance, his repeated use of terms like "invasion" when describing immigration wasn't just rhetoric; it was a deliberate strategy to create a sense of imminent danger. The imagery of an "invasion" suggests a militaristic threat, one that demands immediate and forceful action. It also aligns his supporters as defenders of their homeland, reinforcing loyalty and galvanizing their support.

Furthermore, Trump's speeches often blur the line between reality and fiction, creating a narrative that suits his agenda. His assertion at a 2020 campaign rally that *"If Joe Biden is elected, your American dream will be dead"* is a clear example of how he escalates rhetoric to create a stark, black-and-white scenario. The implication is that without him, the country will not just suffer but will be utterly destroyed. This kind of messaging taps into an existential fear, pushing his supporters to see the election as a matter of life and death for the nation itself.

Another critical aspect of Trump's rhetoric is his consistent framing of the media as an enemy. By branding journalists as the "enemy of the people," Trump not only discredited unfavourable coverage but also built a fortress around his narrative, making his supporters question any information that didn't come directly from him or his trusted allies. This tactic ensured that fear remained his exclusive domain, he controlled the narrative, and anything that challenged it was dismissed as fake or hostile. This strategy wasn't just about delegitimizing criticism; it was about monopolizing the emotional landscape of his base, keeping them locked into his worldview and suspicious of anything outside it.

It's important to recognize that Trump's use of fear is not an isolated phenomenon but part of a broader pattern within populist politics. Fear is an effective tool because it unifies; it creates a sense of shared danger and, by extension, a shared identity among those who perceive themselves as being under threat. Trump's speeches often included phrases like, *"They are coming for you,"* or *"They want to take away your freedom,"* which blur the identity of the enemy, making it vast and all-encompassing. By leaving "they" vague, he allowed his supporters to project their own fears onto this nebulous enemy, deepening their emotional investment in the fight he was leading.

Moreover, Trump's hyperbolic style was not merely an accident of his personality; it was a deliberate communication strategy designed to keep his supporters energized and engaged. By painting every issue as a crisis, whether it was immigration, crime, the economy, or political opposition, he ensured that his base remained in a constant state of vigilance and readiness, loyal to him as the protector against these ever-present threats. The effectiveness of this approach lay in its ability to foster a deep emotional bond between Trump and his supporters, one that went beyond traditional political allegiance and became almost personal, akin to a shared struggle against a common enemy.

In this analysis, it becomes clear that Trump's use of fear was a calculated strategy, not a mere byproduct of his unfiltered speaking style. His speechwriters, communications team, and campaign strategists understood the power of fear as a motivator and wielded it with precision. They crafted speeches designed to tap into existing anxieties and magnify them, ensuring that Trump's base remained loyal, energized, and ready to act. The imagery, the hyperbole, and the constant invocation of threats were all tools used to build a narrative where Trump stood as the singular saviour against a world filled with enemies.

Hope or A Sales Tactic?

Kamala Harris has emerged as a central figure in contemporary American political rhetoric, leveraging her platform as Vice President to champion a vision of unity and hope while carefully navigating the complex landscape of identity politics. Her speeches, often laden with inclusive language and emotional storytelling, aim to create an image of progress and optimism. However, as with all political figures, there are moments where the veneer of hope reveals a more strategic side, where messages are tailored to manipulate perception and mobilize support. By dissecting her rhetoric, we see both the inspiring and calculated aspects of Harris's public addresses.

Harris's rhetorical style is deeply rooted in her identity and personal history. She frequently invokes stories of her upbringing, her mother's immigration journey from India, and the values of hard work and perseverance instilled in her from a young age. In her acceptance speech at the 2020 Democratic National Convention, Harris shared her mother's story, describing her as a woman who "raised us to be proud, strong Black women." By intertwining her personal narrative with broader themes of the American experience, Harris seeks to create a sense of relatability and authenticity. The message is clear: her story is America's story, a tale of overcoming obstacles, pursuing equality, and embracing diversity.

One of Harris's most significant moments came on November 7, 2020, when she delivered her victory speech after the election results confirmed Joe Biden's win. Standing before a divided nation, she opened with, "While I may be the first woman in this office, I will not be the last." The speech was designed not just to celebrate her achievement but to inspire a broader movement of women and minorities, suggesting that her victory was a collective one, a win for all those who have been marginalized. Harris's words were aimed at reinforcing the idea that American progress is possible, but only if everyone feels included and empowered to participate.

Her speechwriters masterfully crafted the moment to emphasize inclusivity, using phrases like "we, the people" and "we are in this together," very Clinton-esq, which create an atmosphere of unity and solidarity. By doing so, she offered a message that transcended political divides, suggesting that regardless of someone's background or political affiliation, there was a shared stake in the future. This was an attempt to rebuild trust in American institutions after years of polarization, aiming to reframe the American story as one of collective hope and shared values.

However, Harris's use of rhetoric also extends beyond mere inspiration; there are moments where her speeches also reveal a more personally strategic side, designed to mobilize support and align specific groups with her vision. For instance, when she delivered a speech to the NAACP in July 2022, Harris focused on the systemic challenges facing Black Americans, specifically highlighting issues such as voting rights suppression and racial discrimination. By framing these issues as direct threats to the progress made by civil rights leaders, she effectively painted a narrative of urgency, compelling her audience to rally behind the administration's policies.

While her message was one of empowerment, the tone was also intended to stoke a sense of crisis, an approach that is common in political speechmaking but is not without its downsides. By amplifying fear over the erosion of rights, Harris aimed to energize her base and galvanize action.

Critics argue that this tactic, while effective in mobilizing support, can also deepen divisions and polarize audiences, turning complex policy debates into emotionally charged confrontations.

Another example of this dual nature in Harris's rhetoric can be seen in her approach to immigration. Harris often speaks about the need for compassion and reform, appealing to the shared humanity of Americans. In a 2021 speech delivered in Guatemala, she emphasized the importance of addressing "the root causes of migration" and framed her administration's approach as one of compassion and collaboration. By portraying America as a country of opportunity and welcoming to those who seek a better life, Harris used her platform to foster a sense of moral responsibility and empathy. Her language was carefully chosen to resonate with immigrants and those sympathetic to their plight, portraying the United States as a beacon of hope.

However, this empathetic narrative contrasts sharply with her statement during the same visit, when she told potential migrants, "Do not come." This moment revealed a strategic pivot designed to appeal to both domestic and international audiences. While in America, her language emphasizes empathy and reform; abroad, she adopts a firmer stance, aligning with the administration's desire to stem migration at its source. This shift demonstrates the dual-edged nature of her messaging, which balances compassion with deterrence, depending on who is listening. Critics of this speech argued that Harris's approach was inconsistent and painted her as a politician more interested in managing optics than delivering on the administration's promise of comprehensive immigration reform.

In another speech at George Mason University in 2021, Harris addressed the issue of climate change. Framing it as "the existential crisis of our time," she called on students and young Americans to take action, invoking the need for immediate and decisive change. Her speech highlighted the generational divide and positioned the administration as an ally to the youth, working to secure their future. This messaging was clearly intended to align the Biden-Harris administration with the younger, more progressive voter base, an essential demographic for maintaining political support.

Yet, despite the hopeful tone, there was also a strategic manipulation of the urgency surrounding climate change. By painting the issue in stark, immediate terms, Harris and her speechwriters aimed to create a narrative that positioned the administration as the only viable solution to a looming catastrophe. This tactic, while galvanizing support, can also create a perception that opposition or alternative approaches are not just misguided but dangerous. It reduces complex debates on climate policy to a binary choice, sidelining nuanced discussions in favour of rallying cries.

Harris's rhetoric of hope and unity is not limited to domestic issues; it extends into her international addresses, where she seeks to position America as a global leader committed to democracy and cooperation. In her 2021 speech to the United Nations, Harris focused on the global struggle for democratic values, emphasizing the need for unity among nations to combat authoritarianism and human rights abuses. Her speechwriters crafted a vision of America as a stabilizing force, a nation that upholds international norms and leads by example.

Yet, as with her domestic speeches, this message also carries a layer of strategic influence. By framing America's role in such unequivocally positive terms, Harris reinforced the idea that the United States remains a benevolent force for good in the world, a message aimed at shoring up international alliances and presenting a counter-narrative to America's detractors. However, critics argue that such rhetoric often ignores America's own struggles with democracy and transparency, creating a narrative that serves to mask the complexities and contradictions of American foreign policy.

Furthermore, in her address at Selma in 2023, marking the anniversary of the historic civil rights marches, Harris emphasized the unfinished work of achieving racial equality in the United States. She highlighted recent voter suppression efforts, linking them directly to the ongoing legacy of systemic racism. This speech was a powerful appeal to mobilize African American communities and rally support for the administration's voting rights agenda. By drawing on the symbolism of the Civil Rights Movement, Harris positioned herself as a torchbearer for progress, aligning her image with iconic figures like John Lewis and Dr. Martin Luther King Jr.

However, there's a subtle strategic element at play. While Harris champions these civil rights issues, the emphasis on the historic struggle also allows her to frame the current political landscape as a battleground for America's soul, a fight that requires unity and loyalty to her administration's policies. In doing so, she uses the rhetoric of urgency and legacy to solidify her base while casting political opponents as regressive forces intent on undoing decades of progress. This tactic, while effective, runs the risk of framing complex political debates as black-and-white moral choices, potentially polarizing audiences and oversimplifying the underlying issues.

In examining Kamala Harris's speeches, one sees a dual narrative: a leader who champions hope and unity while simultaneously using rhetoric to mobilize and control public perception. Her emphasis on inclusivity and optimism paints a vision of America that is forward-looking and filled with promise, but it is also a carefully constructed image designed to secure support and navigate the complex dynamics of contemporary American politics. This balance, between authentic connection and strategic manipulation, highlights the skill of Harris and her team in crafting a message that resonates across diverse audiences, even as it raises questions about the authenticity and consistency of her political vision.

The politics of hope that Harris espouses are undeniably powerful, offering a sense of possibility and progress at a time when the nation is deeply divided. Yet, like all political narratives, it is also a tool, a means of managing perception and building a coalition of support. Her speeches reveal both the inspirational and strategic sides of modern American leadership, where the lines between authenticity and calculation blur in the pursuit of influence and power.

The Use of Contrast
Joe Biden's approach to political rhetoric, especially when compared to the bombastic styles of his immediate predecessors, is a study in subtlety and contrast. While others have wielded language like a sledgehammer, Biden's technique is more akin to a scalpel, precise, careful, calculated and meant to frame the opposition in a way that appears balanced and reasonable, yet clearly focussed on his own objectives. In a political landscape polarized by extremism and fiery speeches, Biden's rhetorical style offers an alternative, one where he positions himself as the calm in the storm, the unifier amid division.

But there's more to this method than meets the eye. It is a calculated approach designed to both elevate his own image and undercut his opponents without seeming confrontational. Biden distinguishes himself from his political rivals not through direct attacks, but through carefully crafted distinctions that paint him as a figure of reason and stability.

The power of this technique lies in its subtlety. Biden rarely goes on the offensive with overt hostility. Instead, he draws a quiet line between himself and his opponents, suggesting that while he represents the voice of reason, moderation, and unity, others represent chaos, extremism, and division. It's a tactic that allows him to appeal to a broad audience, those who are weary of the endless political vitriol that has come to define American politics, and who crave a return to stability and normalcy.

Take, for instance, his acceptance speech at the Democratic National Convention in 2020. Here, Biden framed the election as a "battle for the soul of the nation," but he didn't attack his opponent, Donald Trump, directly. Instead, he painted a picture of America as it could be: a country of decency, hope, and unity. He spoke of light versus darkness, making the choice seem less about individual candidates and more about two competing visions for the future of America. "We can choose a path of becoming angrier, less hopeful, more divided," he said, "a path of shadow and suspicion. Or we can choose a different path and together take this chance to heal, to reform, to unite." Biden's words carried a deliberate ambiguity; while he never explicitly named Trump, the contrast was clear. He set himself up as the alternative to the darkness he described, leaving it to the audience to fill in the blanks about who represented that darkness.

This method is not just about words; it's about image. Biden's speechwriters craft a persona for him that embodies empathy and patience, subtly creating a contrast with his opponents who are often characterized as brash or divisive. It's a tactic rooted in his decades of public service, and he uses it to build an image of experience and maturity. His campaign often highlighted his role as "Uncle Joe," a man who understands the struggles of everyday Americans, who has faced personal loss, and who, therefore, can empathize with a grieving nation. This stands in stark contrast to the image of a detached or self-serving leader that he implies his opponents represent.

In a speech given in Warm Springs, Georgia, in October 2020, Biden invoked Franklin D. Roosevelt, seeking to draw a parallel between FDR's leadership during a time of national crisis and his own candidacy during the pandemic and economic downturn. He didn't criticize Trump directly, but instead spoke of a country needing healing and unity, implying that the current leadership was incapable of providing either. He used phrases like "coming together as one America" and "building back better," which were meant to reassure the public of his intentions without descending into the kind of antagonistic rhetoric that could alienate moderate voters. This approach allowed him to reach across party lines, appealing to those who may have been disillusioned by the aggressive, hyper-partisan atmosphere of recent years.

But Biden's approach isn't without its pitfalls. The subtlety that allows him to seem above the fray can sometimes come off as evasive or weak. In avoiding direct confrontation, he risks appearing disconnected from the urgency and passion that drives a significant portion of the electorate. Critics argue that his refusal to engage more directly with his opponents can make him seem complacent or unwilling to take a definitive stand on critical issues. For instance, during the 2020 campaign, while Biden was often praised for his moderate and unifying rhetoric, some progressive factions felt he was too vague or unwilling to call out Trump's most controversial actions in clear, unambiguous terms. This perceived lack of clarity led some to question his commitment to the progressive causes he promised to champion.

Another aspect of Biden's contrastive rhetoric is his portrayal of himself as a champion of unity and bipartisanship. In his inauguration speech in January 2021, he emphasized the need to "end this uncivil war that pits red against blue" and spoke of "the forces that divide us" versus "the common objects we love that unite us." The imagery of civil war was a potent choice, suggesting a nation torn apart, not by a single figure, but by deep, systemic issues. In positioning himself as the healer, Biden implicitly distanced himself from those who might be seen as contributing to the division. The strength of this rhetoric lies in its appeal to a collective identity, a "we" that is larger than any single political party or movement. But this technique also has its drawbacks. By positioning himself as the unifier, Biden sets an almost impossible standard for his administration. Any partisan conflict that arises can then be interpreted as a failure of his own making, as evidence that his promise of unity was, in fact, unattainable.

The contrastive method that Biden employs goes beyond merely casting himself as the calm, steady hand. It also involves highlighting what he portrays as the recklessness or extremism of his opponents, without directly naming names. In his speech commemorating the anniversary of the January 6 Capitol riot, Biden spoke of the need to "stand for the rule of law, to preserve our democracy, and to remember who we are." The implication was clear: those who incited or participated in the riot were not only opposing him, but they were also betraying the very principles America was built upon. Again, he refrained from explicitly targeting his predecessors or political rivals. Instead, he framed the issue in broader, almost moral terms, making it seem as though the choice wasn't about individuals but about the soul of the nation itself.

This nuanced, almost indirect approach works well to maintain Biden's image as a statesman above the fray, but it's not always effective in the fast-paced, hyper-partisan world of modern American politics. For some, his reluctance to engage in the combative style that has become the norm makes him seem out of touch or hesitant. In an era where political messaging often thrives on conflict and clear distinctions between "us" and "them," Biden's preference for ambiguity can be a double-edged sword. It offers him the advantage of appearing presidential, above the nastiness of modern politics, but it also leaves room for his opponents to define the narrative in his place.

Biden's speeches, then, are exercises in strategic ambiguity. By employing contrast without confrontation, he navigates a fine line between appearing reasonable and risking irrelevance. His speechwriters are careful to craft a tone that suggests strength through restraint, a choice that reflects his campaign's broader message of restoring normalcy. But this approach also relies heavily on the audience's willingness to read between the lines, to interpret his words as critiques without the bluntness that usually accompanies political attacks. It's a gamble, and while it may appeal to those seeking a break from the vitriol of recent years, it also risks alienating those who crave clarity and bold action.

At its core, Biden's technique reveals an understanding of one section of the American public's fatigue with partisan warfare. His rhetoric aims to appeal to a collective desire for stability, unity, and a return to pre-partisan normalcy.

But this contrastive approach is also emblematic of the broader challenges he faces. In attempting to unify a deeply divided nation, Biden's preference for subtlety and moderation may be as much a reflection of his political constraints as it is a choice of style. It's a strategy that works best when the public is ready for compromise and healing, but in moments of heightened polarization, it risks being overshadowed by the louder, more direct voices that have come to dominate the American political landscape.

In the end, Biden's subtle use of contrast illustrates both the power and the limitations of modern political speech. It highlights the delicate balancing act required to maintain authority while appealing to a divided electorate. For a country so wedded to winners and losers, whether this approach will prove successful in the long term remains to be seen. But for now, it serves as a reminder of the shifting dynamics of American political rhetoric, one where perception, contrast, and subtlety are as much tools of power as the policies they aim to promote.

CHAPTER 14

HOW AMERICA'S FOCUS ON LEADERSHIP IS
UNDERMINING ITS EMPIRE

So how do we conclude this exploration into *The Illusion of Presidential Power and How America's focus on leadership is Undermining it's Empire?*

Throughout the book, we have traced how the U.S. presidency has morphed from a position of institutional balance into a stage for spectacle, where short-term wins and public-facing charisma overshadow enduring policy goals and strong leadership has transitioned to showmanship. In an age where tweets replace diplomacy, and charisma outweighs substance, the foundations of America's global empire face a quiet but potent erosion. Once a steady force in global affairs, the U.S. increasingly struggles to maintain the very influence that defined its post-WWII leadership. Indeed, when did the people of America shift from being citizens to become the audience?

Short-termism has become the Achilles' heel of American foreign and domestic policy, a tendency that sees every administration scrambling for immediate wins, even at the expense of long-term stability. This is not a phenomenon unique to the United States, but it is one that is uniquely amplified by the intense focus on the presidency. It's a paradox: the world's most powerful nation, wielding immense resources and influence, yet often finds itself unable to craft and sustain policies that endure beyond the tenure of a single leader. As an external observer, it is impossible to overlook how this focus on short-termism is undermining America's role as a global power. What was once a beacon of consistency is now viewed as increasingly unreliable and unpredictable, a pattern that has become all too familiar in the shifting dynamics of empires.

The American political system, with its fixed four-year electoral cycle, is perfectly designed to incentivize short-term thinking. Presidential administrations are under constant pressure to deliver immediate, visible results that will boost approval ratings and appease the electorate. This cycle of approval and re-election drives the kinds of policies that focus on quick, tangible achievements, lowering taxes, imposing tariffs, or making high-profile diplomatic overtures, rather than those that require time, patience, and bipartisan cooperation to implement effectively. For the president, the timeline is simple: deliver something that makes headlines within the first two years, use the remaining two years to campaign on that success, and hope it's enough to either secure a second term or leave a lasting legacy.

This dynamic has led to a governance approach that prioritizes spectacle over substance. Take, for example, the recent pattern of trade negotiations. Each administration comes in promising a new era of economic agreements or tariffs that supposedly put "America First," as seen during the Trump presidency. Tariffs were slapped on China, the EU, and even traditional allies like Canada, all under the guise of rebalancing trade and protecting American workers. The problem, however, is that these measures often offer short-term gains—appealing to industries or demographics key to re-election campaigns—but create long-term consequences that outlast the administration and complicate international relationships.

The Biden administration, too, has had to reckon with the consequences of this short-termism. In its attempts to undo or reverse Trump-era policies, it often finds itself navigating a web of international scepticism. Allies and adversaries alike wonder how long any new agreement will last before it's discarded by the next occupant of the White House. The Iran Nuclear Deal (JCPOA) is a stark example: initially brokered during the Obama administration, it was unilaterally abandoned by Trump, only for Biden to express interest in reviving it. Such policy reversals create a kind of diplomatic whiplash that undermines U.S. credibility. For other nations, negotiating with the United States has become a gamble, as they weigh the costs of engaging with a partner whose commitments may not outlive a single presidential term.

The parallels to past empires, particularly the British Empire, are striking. The British, at the height of their global power, maintained influence through a network of consistent colonial policies, implemented and sustained by civil servants, viceroys, and governors who often outlasted prime ministers. While not without flaws, this system created a sense of stability and predictability, London's decisions, for better or worse, set the course for decades. The American system, by contrast, is shaped by a singular fixation on the president, leading to erratic shifts that weaken its perceived reliability. Where Britain centralized its imperial vision, the U.S. has increasingly fragmented it, leaving its allies guessing and its rivals emboldened.

Consider climate policy as another example of America's short-termism. The United States, as the world's largest economy and one of the biggest carbon emitters, plays a critical role in international climate agreements. The Obama administration made significant strides by joining the Paris Agreement, signalling a commitment to global climate cooperation. But when Trump pulled out of the accord, he upended not only Obama's legacy but also the trust of America's international partners. The short-term political gain of appealing to Trump's base came at the cost of long-term global trust and cooperation. Fast forward to the Biden administration, and we see yet another reversal, with efforts to rejoin and reaffirm America's commitment to the climate fight. While these efforts are well-intentioned, they are met with scepticism. Allies now question the durability of any U.S. pledge, wondering whether the next administration will again reverse course.

The impact of these policy reversals is not limited to environmental agreements or trade deals; it extends to military alliances and foreign interventions. Under Trump, the abrupt withdrawal of U.S. troops from Syria, followed by the equally sudden decision to broker a peace agreement with the Taliban, left allies and adversaries alike scrambling to adapt. These decisions, made swiftly and with an eye towards creating the appearance of decisive leadership, often disregarded the complexities of on-the-ground realities and the long-term strategic interests of the United States. The Biden administration's chaotic withdrawal from Afghanistan in 2021 underscored the broader consequences of such decisions. The swift exit, while fulfilling a long-promised objective, appeared hasty and poorly coordinated, leading to images that damaged U.S. credibility and emboldened adversaries. It's a pattern that reveals how America's fixation on the optics of presidential action often leads to decisions that prioritize appearance over substance.

Another aspect of this short-termism is the tendency of administrations to focus on symbolic gestures rather than substantial change. When a new president takes office, the pressure is on to distance themselves from their predecessor, particularly when the transition involves a shift in party control. The rhetoric around "undoing the damage" of the previous administration becomes a rallying cry, leading to a flurry of executive orders and policy reversals. But while these actions generate headlines and give the impression of decisive leadership, they often lack the legislative and institutional support needed for long-term impact. The reliance on executive orders, while providing short-term political wins, further entrenches the cycle of inconsistency, as each new administration is likely to reverse these orders, perpetuating a cycle of instability.

This instability isn't lost on the world. Allies like Germany and France, once confident in the reliability of American leadership, have openly expressed concerns about the sustainability of U.S. commitments. This has led to initiatives aimed at strengthening European defence mechanisms, such as French President Emmanuel Macron's push for "strategic autonomy," an effort to reduce Europe's reliance on American military support. The ripple effect of American inconsistency extends beyond the diplomatic sphere; it affects global markets, trade partnerships, and the trust that underpins alliances formed over decades. America's adversaries, particularly China and Russia, have been quick to exploit this unpredictability, positioning themselves as more consistent and reliable alternatives.

Reflecting on the British Empire again, the United States would do well to learn from Britain's decline. As the empire expanded, British leaders eventually fell into the trap of short-term thinking, prioritizing immediate profits from colonies without investing in sustainable governance. The reliance on quick economic gains through exploitative policies, rather than building enduring alliances and infrastructure, hastened the empire's collapse. The parallels are evident in America's approach: prioritizing short-term economic gains through tariffs, trade wars, and rapid military disengagement without considering the long-term consequences of these actions.

The fixation on presidential leadership also has domestic implications. As the focus remains squarely on the figure of the president, the broader mechanisms of governance, Congress, the judiciary, and the civil service, become sidelined or, worse, politicized. The result is a weakened institutional framework that struggles to sustain policies beyond a single term. The erosion of these institutions not only affects America's international standing but also contributes to domestic polarization. The narrative becomes one of constant crisis and salvation, where each election is framed as a battle for the nation's soul, rather than a process of incremental progress and collective governance. This dynamic fuels division, making it increasingly difficult for the United States to project unity and resolve on the global stage.

In the end, the consequences of America's short-termism extend far beyond policy reversals or diplomatic confusion. They signal a deeper, more systemic issue within the American political system: the inability to commit to and sustain long-term strategies that transcend the interests of individual presidents or electoral cycles. The focus on immediate wins may deliver political victories and headline-grabbing moments, but it erodes the trust and stability that form the foundation of a true global power.

America's empire is not built on colonies or vast territories but on alliances, economic influence, and military reach. To maintain this position, it needs more than charismatic leaders and bold declarations; it requires the ability to demonstrate consistency, reliability, and long-term commitment. Without this shift, America risks following the path of other empires that once believed their power was unassailable, only to find that, in the absence of sustained strategy, their influence waned and their reach diminished.

The lessons of history are clear: empires are not maintained by spectacle but by the stability and trust that only long-term planning can provide.

The American presidency, for all its power and prestige, has increasingly become a stage where personalities overshadow policies, and charisma trumps consistency. The United States, a global superpower with an intricate web of diplomatic relations, has seen its foreign policy become a reflection of its leaders rather than its long-term interests. This trend toward personality-driven diplomacy has made American alliances and adversarial relationships increasingly unstable, undermining the very foundations of its global influence. Like the British Empire before it, America risks finding that the focus on individual leaders rather than strategic consistency may erode its standing and authority on the world stage.

When we think of American diplomacy today, it's not the State Department's seasoned diplomats or the legacy of agreements that come to mind; it's the image of presidents shaking hands, standing before monuments, and tweeting their views. We remember the sight of Donald Trump meeting Kim Jong-un at the DMZ or Barack Obama's historic handshake with Raúl Castro. These are powerful moments, laden with symbolism, but they often prioritize spectacle over substance. The result is a foreign policy that shifts as presidents change, making the United States appear unpredictable, its promises and alliances contingent on the whims and charisma of its leaders.

Take, for instance, Donald Trump's relationship with North Korean leader Kim Jong-un. Trump, unlike his predecessors, pursued a strategy of direct, personal engagement. He famously called Kim his "friend" and exchanged letters described as "love letters." In doing so, Trump bypassed traditional diplomatic channels, sidelining experts and State Department officials who had long worked to stabilize tensions on the Korean Peninsula. For a time, it seemed as though this unorthodox approach might yield results. But what it really underscored was the fragility of such personalized diplomacy. When Trump left office, the momentum he claimed to have built evaporated. The Biden administration, returning to a more conventional approach, faced the same old challenges with North Korea, but without the direct lines of communication that Trump had established. The diplomatic gains, fleeting as they were, proved to be entirely dependent on Trump's presence, his style, and his unorthodox charm.

This is a pattern that has played out time and again in American diplomacy. From Richard Nixon's personal rapport with China's Zhou Enlai, which opened up the possibility of U.S.-China relations, to George W. Bush's strained relationship with French President Jacques Chirac during the Iraq War, the success or failure of America's foreign engagements has often hinged not on long-term strategy but on the chemistry, or lack thereof, between individual leaders. Such a system is inherently unstable. When diplomatic relationships are built around personalities rather than policies, they become as volatile as the individuals who manage them.

The emphasis on charismatic leadership in diplomacy not only creates short-term solutions but also leaves the United States vulnerable to abrupt shifts when the leadership changes. For allies and adversaries alike, it becomes difficult to ascertain the United States' long-term intentions when its policies pivot every four to eight years. Imagine trying to build a sustainable, trusting relationship with a partner whose priorities and commitments shift dramatically with each new leader. That's the predicament America's allies and foes face, and it weakens the very fabric of its international influence.

The transition from one administration to another often brings a stark change in tone and policy, unsettling the global order. We need look no further than the Paris Climate Accord to see how this plays out. Barack Obama's administration negotiated the agreement in good faith, aiming to re-establish the United States as a leader in the fight against climate change. For America's allies, it was a sign of stability, commitment, and long-term planning. Yet, when Donald Trump assumed office, he swiftly withdrew from the accord, calling it unfair and economically damaging to American interests. The reversal not only damaged U.S. credibility but also signalled to the world that American commitments were not to be trusted, they were merely temporary, contingent upon the preferences of its current leader.

This pattern isn't unique to recent administrations. The British Empire, too, faced similar challenges as it transitioned from one prime minister to another during its decline. The shift from the stability and diplomatic prowess of William Gladstone to the imperial ambitions of Benjamin Disraeli created an inconsistency that confused allies and adversaries alike.

Britain's reliance on the personal diplomacy of its leaders, rather than on a consistent imperial strategy, led to miscalculations and an erosion of influence in regions like Africa and Asia. America now finds itself in a comparable position, where its global strategy is perceived not as a coherent vision but as the sum of its leaders' whims.

The Middle East offers another example of how American policy can fluctuate dramatically between administrations, leaving allies uncertain and adversaries emboldened. George W. Bush's invasion of Iraq was grounded in a vision of reshaping the Middle East through force and establishing a pro-American, democratic regime. Whether one agrees with the rationale or not, the approach was clear and consistent. Yet, Barack Obama's administration, seeking to distance itself from Bush's aggressive policies, pivoted toward disengagement and diplomacy. This shift led to the controversial withdrawal from Iraq, a decision that created a power vacuum later filled by ISIS. When Donald Trump took office, he promised a mix of disengagement from "endless wars" while simultaneously employing aggressive rhetoric and military action against Iran. Allies like Saudi Arabia and Israel struggled to adjust to the unpredictable shifts, and adversaries like Iran exploited the inconsistency.

These transitions reveal the inherent instability of a system reliant on the personality and decisions of a single leader. It makes alliances appear fragile, as foreign nations must navigate these shifts with caution, never fully committing to the United States' plans for fear that they will change in the next election cycle. The result is a weakening of trust, a critical component for maintaining a robust and enduring empire.

The Problem with Personalized Diplomacy

The risks of a personality-driven diplomatic strategy become even clearer when we consider the potential for negative outcomes. Presidents who lean heavily on their own charisma or negotiating prowess, bypassing traditional diplomatic structures, often leave their successors with a diplomatic vacuum or, worse, a series of conflicts that are difficult to untangle. The image of Ronald Reagan and Mikhail Gorbachev shaking hands in Reykjavik is iconic, a moment when two personalities seemed to steer the course of history. But for every Reykjavik, there is a fallout when that fragile rapport is disrupted by a shift in administration or a change in leadership on the other side.

When leaders rely on their charisma, they also take on the risk that their successors won't be able to sustain the same level of engagement. This approach creates diplomatic relationships that hinge on personal rapport rather than institutional trust. For instance, while Barack Obama's pivot to Asia was grounded in strategic policy, much of the diplomacy with leaders like China's Xi Jinping also relied on personal negotiations and summits. When Donald Trump took office, the shift in tone, moving from cooperative engagement to adversarial brinksmanship, left allies like Japan and South Korea uncertain and worried. It also left adversaries like China sceptical about the longevity of American commitments.

Similarly, Trump's personal diplomacy with Middle Eastern leaders, including Saudi Arabia's Mohammed bin Salman, showcased the risks of such an approach. While Trump's personal rapport allowed for a semblance of stability, it also meant that alliances became entangled in the controversies surrounding the individual leader. The murder of journalist Jamal Khashoggi put the U.S.-Saudi relationship under intense scrutiny. Trump's decision to continue supporting bin Salman, despite international outrage, demonstrated how personal connections can sometimes compromise national principles and create ethical dilemmas. The next administration, faced with these entanglements, must either undo the connections or be forced to navigate within them, even if they conflict with broader strategic goals.

The British Empire, in its twilight years, provides a poignant parallel. British prime ministers increasingly found themselves navigating an empire reliant on personal relationships rather than cohesive policies. The reliance on individual "men on the spot", like Lord Kitchener in Sudan or Lord Curzon in India, meant that British influence was subject to the abilities, biases, and priorities of these individuals. As the political will of the British government shifted back home, the empire's strategy became inconsistent, relying too heavily on the personal influence and charisma of its leaders to maintain control. When these leaders retired or lost favour, the stability of Britain's hold on its colonies often wavered.

America's reliance on presidential charisma and personalized diplomacy is reminiscent of this pattern. The risk is that, like the British Empire, America's influence will be seen as unreliable and inconsistent, causing other nations to hedge their bets, seeking new alliances or strengthening old ones independent of U.S. influence.

NATO allies, for instance, have increasingly sought to strengthen European defence initiatives, wary that American commitments to their security could be subject to change with the next administration.

The United States, by emphasizing the personalities of its leaders rather than building sustainable, institution-driven policies, risks undermining its empire. The diplomacy that once underpinned its global influence becomes a patchwork of personal relationships, subject to the volatility of electoral cycles and individual leaders. As allies and adversaries alike struggle to navigate the inconsistencies of American foreign policy, the U.S. finds its influence waning, much like empires of the past that relied too heavily on the power of charismatic individuals. The path forward requires a shift from personality-driven politics to a renewed focus on strategic consistency, rooted in institutions and long-term national interests. Only then can America reclaim the trust, stability, and reliability that are essential for sustaining its global influence.

The United States was designed with an inherent scepticism of centralized power. The Founding Fathers, with their deep aversion to monarchies, built a government of checks and balances, one where the president would be but a cog in the larger machine of governance. The goal was to ensure that no single figure could wield excessive influence, and that power would be distributed among Congress, the judiciary, and the president to maintain a balanced and functioning republic. But today, the illusion of balance is waning. America's obsession with its presidents, from their personalities to their decisions, has not only centralized power in a way that the framers of the Constitution would find alarming, but it has also weakened the very institutions meant to safeguard against such concentration. This, in turn, is undermining the foundations of the American empire, eroding institutional trust, and diminishing the country's governance capacity.

When examining the rise of presidential authority, one must start with the marginalization of Congress. Once seen as the most vital branch of the American government, Congress was intended to be the epicenter of lawmaking, oversight, and the representative will of the people. Today, however, the legislative body increasingly finds itself sidelined. The narrative of American power has become so entrenched in the figure of the president that the role of Congress appears more reactive than proactive, its authority undercut by the growing influence of executive orders and presidential proclamations. From immigration policies to military actions, presidents have taken matters into their own hands, often bypassing Congress altogether. This shift isn't merely the result of power-hungry leaders; it's also a consequence of a political culture and media landscape that exalt quick action and visible leadership, demanding presidents act decisively, even if it means circumventing the legislative process.

Consider the recent trend of using executive orders as a primary tool of governance. The reliance on executive actions to implement policy, rather than working through the slower and more deliberative legislative process, reveals how the focus on presidential power distorts the intended function of American democracy. President Obama's Deferred Action for Childhood Arrivals (DACA) program, Trump's ban on travel from several Muslim-majority countries, and Biden's efforts to cancel student loan debt all illustrate this trend. Each of these policies, monumental in their impact, bypassed Congress. Whether these actions were motivated by the urgency of the moment or the intractability of a divided legislature, the result was the same: Congress, the body constitutionally responsible for crafting and debating policy, was left sidelined.

The erosion of trust in Congress is evident both domestically and internationally. Within the U.S., public faith in Congress has reached historic lows. Americans, seeing the body's inability to pass comprehensive legislation or respond quickly to crises, increasingly look to the president as the figure who should "get things done." But this shift only feeds a vicious cycle: the more Americans depend on the executive branch for decisive action, the less effective Congress appears, and the more the president is expected to wield outsized influence. Internationally, allies and adversaries alike have learned that the key to understanding and dealing with American policy is not through Congress but through the White House. Whether negotiating trade agreements or discussing military alliances, foreign leaders often bypass traditional diplomatic channels and focus directly on the president. This approach further erodes the role of career diplomats and the State Department, another casualty of America's leadership-centric culture.

The State Department, once the hub of American foreign policy expertise, is increasingly overshadowed by presidential envoys, special advisors, and the president's inner circle. The focus on building personal relationships between presidents and foreign leaders has diminished the role of career diplomats, who are often left out of critical negotiations or major policy decisions. This was perhaps most evident during the Trump administration, when high-profile foreign policy initiatives, such as negotiations with North Korea or attempts to broker peace deals in the Middle East, were spearheaded not by seasoned diplomats but by close allies and family members. While Trump's approach was particularly unorthodox, it highlights a broader trend of presidents seeking to centralize diplomatic efforts under their direct control, sidelining the expertise and continuity that institutions like the State Department provide.

This shift undermines America's ability to maintain a consistent and reliable foreign policy. When diplomatic efforts are tied to the personality of a single leader, as they increasingly are, they become vulnerable to the whims of that leader and the inevitable shifts that come with changes in administration. A country that once prided itself on its steady hand in international affairs now appears erratic, its policies subject to abrupt reversals every four to eight years. Allies who once saw America as a dependable partner must now navigate an uncertain landscape, recalibrating their alliances and strategic priorities with every new president. Adversaries, in turn, exploit this inconsistency, taking advantage of the knowledge that American commitments may not outlast the next electoral cycle.

This erosion of institutional trust, both at home and abroad, represents a deep and growing vulnerability. When the United States acts as though its presidency is the only source of power that matters, it effectively undercuts the foundations of its own empire. The credibility of American governance depends not just on the president but on the entire system, the collective strength of its institutions. But as Congress and the State Department continue to be marginalized, the system loses its resilience. Decisions made without the backing of robust institutions are inherently fragile; they lack the continuity and stability necessary to maintain long-term influence.

The long-term consequences of this centralization of power are significant. With each administration, as the focus narrows further onto the individual occupying the Oval Office, America's capacity for consistent governance diminishes. Multi-administration strategies become nearly impossible to sustain, as each new president feels the need to overturn or dramatically reshape the policies of their predecessor to assert their own authority. Consider the U.S. approach to climate change: from Obama's involvement in the Paris Climate Agreement, to Trump's withdrawal, to Biden's re-entry. These constant shifts do not project strength; they project inconsistency and indecision. The rest of the world sees these reversals not as the product of a functioning democracy but as the byproduct of a system increasingly dominated by short-term political gains and personality politics.

At home, the overemphasis on the president as the singular figure of authority has further fuelled political polarization. The image of the president as a near-monarchical figure, a savior or a villain, depending on one's political alignment, creates a deeply divided electorate. Each side invests enormous emotional and political energy in the presidency, either to elevate their champion or vilify their opponent. This dynamic distracts from the broader systemic challenges that require collective, institutional solutions. Issues like healthcare reform, immigration, and economic inequality demand long-term strategies and cooperation across multiple branches of government. Yet, the focus on presidential power, with its emphasis on quick fixes and bold proclamations, obscures the need for systemic reform.

In essence, the erosion of institutional trust and the centralization of power not only weakens America's governance capacity but also its democratic principles. The emphasis on the president above all else transforms governance into spectacle. Presidents become symbols rather than leaders of policy, their administrations more concerned with optics than substance. The result is a political landscape where the illusion of power is maintained through media narratives, dramatic gestures, and crisis management, but the underlying structures that should support and sustain American power remain fragile and neglected.

As the world becomes increasingly complex and interconnected, America's ability to respond effectively is hampered by its own fixation on leadership. The focus on a single figure of authority, rather than the collective strength of its institutions, leaves the country vulnerable to both internal division and external manipulation. It is a paradox: in seeking strength through centralized leadership, the United States may be weakening the very structures that made it a global power in the first place.

If America is to reclaim its capacity for consistent and effective governance, it must begin by rediscovering the value of its institutions, reinforcing the checks and balances that were designed to maintain stability, and recognizing that true power does not lie solely in the hands of one, but in the collective strength of many.

In the annals of American history, the United States has long been regarded as a beacon of stability, a nation that not only projected its military might but also exported its ideals, culture, and sense of democracy across the globe. The idea of "soft power," as political scientist Joseph Nye coined it, was more than just a theoretical construct; it was a lived reality. The world watched American movies, listened to American music, and adopted American technological innovations. More importantly, many nations saw the U.S. as a reliable ally and a model of freedom and opportunity. But in recent years, the veneer of this carefully crafted image has begun to fade, and the global perception of America is no longer one of unwavering leadership and principled governance. The United States, once a symbol of democratic steadiness, now finds itself viewed through a lens of unpredictability, inconsistency, and self-interest. The impact of this shift is profound, and it threatens to undermine America's empire from within and diminish its influence abroad.

The core issue is one of unpredictability, a quality that, while intriguing in a theatrical context, becomes a liability in international politics. The fluctuations in U.S. foreign policy, largely driven by the focus on the individual style and priorities of each administration, have created a sense of instability. Allies and adversaries alike are left guessing, forced to recalibrate their strategies with each new occupant of the Oval Office. Consider, for instance, the shifts in policy toward NATO, the Paris Climate Agreement, and the Iran Nuclear Deal. Under one administration, NATO is hailed as a critical alliance; under another, its relevance is questioned, and member nations are chided for failing to meet defence spending targets. The Paris Climate Agreement saw a similar vacillation, entered into with much fanfare under Obama, only to be exited by Trump, and then re-entered under Biden. The Iran Nuclear Deal, an emblematic piece of diplomacy, was brokered with careful negotiation, only to be dismantled and left in limbo when the presidency changed hands. The consequence of these policy zigzags is a growing perception that the United States cannot be counted on to maintain long-term commitments, making it increasingly unreliable as an ally.

This unpredictability stems, in large part, from America's fixation on the personality and style of its leaders rather than a consistent national strategy. When the image of the president becomes the focal point of policy rather than the institutions and principles that once defined American governance, diplomacy becomes a performance rather than a strategy. Each administration feels the need to not only establish its own identity but to undo the legacy of the previous one, leading to a cycle of short-term policies and, at times, contradictory actions. For nations that have traditionally relied on the stability of U.S. leadership, this inconsistency poses a significant challenge. European leaders, for example, have found themselves grappling with sudden and dramatic shifts in policy that upend long-standing diplomatic arrangements. In this climate, it's not surprising that some nations have begun to hedge their bets, seeking other alliances and avenues to secure their interests as they question the reliability of America's word.

The decline of America's soft power is another casualty of this leadership inconsistency. The U.S. was once seen not just as a military superpower but as a cultural and ideological beacon. Hollywood, the tech giants of Silicon Valley, the rhetoric of liberty and justice, these were not mere exports; they were symbols of the American ideal. But when the focus shifts to the spectacle of leadership—when the president becomes the central figure of both governance and entertainment, the ideals that once inspired admiration and emulation start to blur. The emphasis on populism and charisma has, at times, led to a kind of performative leadership, where policies are announced in tweets and alliances are negotiated or dismantled in soundbites. This style of leadership might captivate an audience at home, but it sends mixed messages abroad.

Take the example of Donald Trump's presidency, where the allure of populism and a focus on personal charisma overtook the usual decorum of diplomatic engagement. Trump's approach, often brash and confrontational, appealed to a significant segment of the American electorate but left many international allies bewildered. His willingness to meet with adversarial leaders like North Korea's Kim Jong-un while disparaging long-standing allies created a sense of confusion about America's intentions. Traditional allies, from Europe to Asia, began to question the reliability of U.S. commitments. While the spectacle of summits and photo ops captured headlines, the substance of diplomacy, rooted in trust, consistency, and mutual interest, was undermined.

Nations that once saw America as a dependable partner started exploring other options, reducing their reliance on a country that had become, at least in their eyes, unpredictable.

This erosion of soft power has far-reaching consequences. Soft power is not just about diplomacy; it's also about the ability to influence and persuade through cultural and ideological appeal. When America is viewed as erratic and unreliable, the narrative of American exceptionalism loses its persuasive force. Countries that once looked to the U.S. as a model of democracy and stability begin to turn elsewhere, seeking alternatives that seem more consistent or, at the very least, more predictable. China, for example, has seized on this opportunity, promoting its model of economic development and state-driven capitalism as a viable alternative to the "unpredictable" and "unstable" American democracy. As America's soft power wanes, other nations and entities are quick to fill the vacuum, reshaping the global order in ways that reduce America's influence.

The impact on alliances is palpable. In Europe, the Trump administration's unpredictability led to a wave of scepticism about American commitments. The rhetoric questioning NATO's value left European allies scrambling to reassess their defence strategies. French President Emmanuel Macron's call for a "European army" was not just a reaction to Trump's comments but a signal that Europe could no longer rely solely on American security guarantees. This sentiment persists even beyond Trump's tenure, as nations recognize that future U.S. administrations could once again pivot unpredictably. Similarly, in the Indo-Pacific, where nations like Japan and South Korea have long relied on U.S. support to counterbalance China's influence, the inconsistency of American policy raises concerns about the long-term reliability of such alliances. When the policies of an administration can be so easily reversed with each electoral cycle, the sense of continuity and stability that underpins alliances becomes fragile.

Domestically, the emphasis on leadership has also fuelled polarization, which further weakens America's standing abroad. As the focus remains on the president as the central figure of power, the country's internal divisions become more pronounced. Presidents are either idolized or vilified based on party lines, turning the executive office into a battleground for ideological supremacy.

This deepening polarization distracts from the broader systemic challenges facing the nation and, in turn, affects America's ability to project unified strength. When foreign nations observe such stark internal divisions, the message they receive is one of a fragmented empire struggling to maintain its cohesion. The spectacle of political gridlock and division diminishes America's appeal as a model of stable democracy and erodes its authority as a global leader.

The weakening of America's soft power and global influence is not just about the loss of appeal; it's also about the erosion of trust. Soft power depends on the perception that a nation not only embodies certain values but also adheres to them. When the focus shifts to the personality and unpredictability of the president, the principles of democracy, liberty, and cooperation that America once championed take a backseat. The spectacle of leadership, whether it's in the form of high-stakes summits or domestic political theatre, may attract attention, but it rarely builds the long-term trust necessary for sustainable alliances and influence.

Furthermore, as America's focus remains on its internal political drama, other nations are emboldened to expand their influence. Russia and China, both of which have long viewed the U.S. as a strategic competitor, are quick to capitalize on America's unpredictability. Russian disinformation campaigns, for instance, exploit the divisions within American society, amplifying polarization and sowing distrust in American institutions. China, meanwhile, continues to build its economic and political influence, presenting itself as a stable and reliable partner, particularly in regions where American influence has waned. The Belt and Road Initiative, a massive infrastructure project spanning multiple continents, offers countries an alternative to U.S. economic influence, one that seems less contingent on the political whims of a single leader.

The consequence of these developments is a slow but steady erosion of America's global standing. The U.S., once viewed as the keystone of international order, now appears increasingly insular and inconsistent. The emphasis on leadership over long-term strategy has left America vulnerable to challenges that undermine its influence and credibility. Allies are less willing to take American commitments at face value, while adversaries are more emboldened to test the limits of American resolve.

The focus on leadership as a spectacle rather than governance as a strategy has created a paradox where the world's most powerful nation finds its influence diminished not by external threats but by its own internal contradictions.

If America is to reclaim its place as a stable and reliable leader on the global stage, it must shift its focus away from the spectacle of leadership and towards the principles and institutions that once defined its strength. Until then, the illusion of presidential power will continue to undermine the very empire it seeks to preserve.

READING LIST

Understanding the dynamics of presidential power and influence requires a deep dive into the strategies, rhetoric, and historical contexts that have shaped the American presidency. For those intrigued by the themes explored in *The Illusion of Presidential Power*, this curated reading list offers insightful perspectives and analyses. From political strategy to the subtle art of rhetoric, these books provide a comprehensive look at how presidents and their administrations wield power. Below are eight recommended books, each accompanied by a brief synopsis to guide your reading journey.

1. The Audacity of Hope by Barack Obama
In this reflective memoir, Obama offers an inside look at his vision for America's future, while revealing the intricacies of political decision-making. He discusses the power of rhetoric in shaping public opinion and the balancing act required to maintain authenticity as a politician.

2. Team of Rivals: The Political Genius of Abraham Lincoln by Doris Kearns Goodwin
This detailed biography delves into Abraham Lincoln's leadership style and his skilful management of opposing viewpoints within his cabinet. It highlights how he used rhetoric and strategic alliances to consolidate power and navigate the complexities of the Civil War.

3. What It Takes: The Way to the White House by Richard Ben Cramer
Cramer provides a comprehensive look into the presidential campaigns of 1988, exploring the personal and political strategies candidates used to persuade voters. The book offers an in-depth analysis of how power and image are crafted during campaigns, providing a fascinating look at the pursuit of presidential authority.

4. The Power Broker: Robert Moses and the Fall of New York by Robert A. Caro
Although not directly about the presidency, this book is a powerful study of influence, manipulation, and the subtle ways power is wielded behind the scenes. Caro chronicles how Robert Moses dominated New York politics for decades, offering lessons on the power dynamics and strategies that echo in presidential politics.

5. The Art of Political Warfare by John J. Pitney Jr.

This book explores the strategies politicians use to gain power, comparing them to military tactics. Pitney examines how rhetoric, alliances, and conflict are instrumental in framing opponents and shaping public perception, providing insight into the art of political manoeuvring.

6. The Concise Princeton Encyclopaedia of American Political History edited by Michael Kazin

This comprehensive guide offers essential background knowledge on the key political events, figures, and concepts that have shaped the American presidency. It's a valuable resource for understanding the broader context and complexities of presidential power and influence.

7. Presidential Power and the Modern Presidents: The Politics of Leadership from Roosevelt to Reagan by Richard E. Neustadt

Neustadt's classic work provides an in-depth analysis of presidential power, focusing on how modern presidents have influenced, and been influenced by, political structures. It offers essential insights into the limitations and capabilities of the office, making it a must-read for those exploring the dynamics of presidential authority.

8. The Gatekeepers: How the White House Chiefs of Staff Define Every Presidency by Chris Whipple

Whipple provides a behind-the-scenes look at the White House Chiefs of Staff and their critical role in managing presidential power. The book reveals how these individuals shape policy, influence decisions, and manage crises, offering an eye-opening perspective on the unseen power structures within the White House.